The Peterloo
Massacre

The Peterloo Massacre

JOYCE MARLOW

EBURY
PRESS

1 3 5 7 9 10 8 6 4 2

Ebury Press, an imprint of Ebury Publishing
20 Vauxhall Bridge Road
London SW1V 2SA

Ebury Press is part of the Penguin Random House group
of companies whose addresses can be found at
global.penguinrandomhouse.com

Penguin
Random House
UK

This edition published by Ebury Press in 2018
First published by Rapp and Whiting in 1970

www.penguin.co.uk

A CIP catalogue record for this book is available from the British Library

ISBN 9781785038648

Typeset in India by Integra Software Services Pvt. Ltd, Pondicherry

Printed and bound in Great Britain by Clays Ltd, St Ives PLC

Penguin Random House is committed to a sustainable
future for our business, our readers and our planet.
This book is made from Forest Stewardship Council®
certified paper.

To the memory of my mother
Mary Thorpe Lees

About the Author

Joyce Marlow was born and raised in Manchester in the 1930s. Soon after the Second World War she became an actress and later a full-time writer. A life-long Labour supporter and feminist, she edited anthologies such as *The Virago Book of Women and the Great War*, as well as *Suffragettes: The Right to Vote for Women*. She was also the winner of the Romantic Novelists' Best Historical Novel Award. Married with two sons, she lived in the High Peak District in Derbyshire.

PETER LOO MASSACRE!!!

Just published No. 1 price twopence of PETER LOO
MASSACRE Containing a full, true and faithful account of the
inhuman murders, woundings and other monstrous Cruelties
exercised by a set of INFERNALS (miscalled Soldiers) upon
unarmed and distressed People.

Manchester Observer, August 28th, 1819.

As the 'Peterloo Massacre' cannot be otherwise than grossly
libellous you will probably deem it right to proceed by arresting
the publishers.

Letter from Home Office to Magistrate
Norris, August 25th, 1819.

CONTENTS

ACKNOWLEDGEMENTS

I should like to express the customary, but nonetheless genuinely meant, thanks to the many people who have helped me in the preparation of this book:

To all the staff of the Public Records Office, Ashridge, Herts, for their unfailing courtesy and assistance, with particular thanks for bringing to my attention the Treasury Solicitor files on Peterloo which I was, I believe, the first member of the public to see.

To the Librarian and staff of the Local History Section of the Central Library, Manchester.

To the Librarian, Keeper of the Manuscripts and staff of the John Rylands Library, Manchester, with added thanks for placing at my disposal the most splendid room in which I have ever typed, lined from floor to ceiling with the illuminated ecclesiastical books for which the Rylands Library is world famous.

To the Librarian of Middleton, Lancashire, for showing me the Peterloo relics and for the prompt manner with which he dealt with several queries.

To the Librarian and Staff of Hemel Hempstead, Herts, public library.

To the Town Clerk of Oldham for his assistance on population figures.

To the Secretary of the Reform Club, Manchester, for facilitating my access to that male *sanctum sanctorum,* the club library, and its Peterloo material.

To Miss Margaret Smith of Middleton, Lancashire, for her assistance on Bamford queries.

To Vivien Pilton, my ex-history teacher and present friend, for her Devonshire hospitality and for all her help and advice.

To Doctor Aline Sullivan of Fleetwood, Lancashire, for reasons which she will understand.

Map showing principal towns mentioned in the text.

1

AGRICULTURE COULD NOT HAVE MADE SUCH A PLACE AS MANCHESTER

Among the thousands of British troops who fought at Waterloo was an eighteen-year-old named John Lees. He came from Oldham in Lancashire. Had he died at Waterloo we should never have heard of him, for the blood of such ordinary young men stained the Belgian cornfields red. But he survived the three days of bitter fighting that culminated on June 18th, 1815, in the final defeat of Napoleon and the end of twenty-odd years of war. He was discharged and returned home to follow his trade as a cotton spinner. Four years later he was dead as the result of injuries received on another field.

The ground on which John Lees sustained his mortal wounds was an area of open land near the centre of Manchester known as Saint Peter's Field. The date was August 16th, 1819, and the occasion was a mass meeting in support of Parliamentary reform. The injuries were inflicted by fellow Lancastrians, who were members of the Manchester and Salford Yeomanry Cavalry, and by the 15th Hussars, ex-comrades in arms from Waterloo. Before he died John Lees said he was never in such danger at Waterloo as he was at the meeting, for at Waterloo it was man to man but at Manchester it was downright murder. He was not alone in this assessment. Other people seized upon the presence of Waterloo veterans such as himself in the unarmed crowds, and upon the actions of the 15th Hussars on the June and August days.

On the August day the savage sobriquet 'Peterloo' was bestowed.

John Lees lingered in agony for three weeks after Peterloo. His inquest was used as a test case to try and prove that what happened on Saint Peter's Field had been 'downright murder'. Thus in death his name rang round England. But if in life he was unsung he was also, by being such an ordinary young man, typical of thousands of Lancastrians. The reasons that made him attend the meeting also drove half the 60,000 present, the army of John Leeses who do not move until a situation has reached desperation point or the way has been so clearly sign-posted they cannot fail to follow. Of these reasons a few were understood by him at the time, others he was not sufficiently clever or educated to grasp, while others need a retrospective eye.

The stuff of which Peterloo was made has as many threads as a length of woven cotton, but the main ones were contained in John Lees's brief life span. For he was a child not only of the Industrial Revolution* but of the world cradle of that revolution (or evolution). A small-time cotton manufacture had existed in south-east Lancashire since the beginning of the seventeenth century, with Manchester as its weak heart and the villages such as Oldham, Middleton, Rochdale and Royton as the anaemic arteries. In the

---

* The term 'Industrial Revolution' was used in John Lees's lifetime though he certainly never heard it. A French economist named Blanqui saw that the implications of the industrial upheaval in England were as vast as the more immediately obvious ones of the recent French Revolution, and he thus coined the phrase. It has since been decried. The process was evolutionary rather than revolutionary, but Monsieur Blanqui deserves full marks for his percipient and apposite use of the term.

old days a cosy structure had existed which memory made cosier as it disappeared. The merchants bought the raw cotton from the Liverpool dealers, sold it to small-time masters who in turn sold it to spinners working in their cottages. When the yarn was spun it was sold back to the masters or directly to the aristocrats of the trade, the hand-loom weavers, who duly wove the cloth and sold it to other masters. Within this structure everybody, so they imagined, was independent. That they were subject to recessions, and could be thrown out of work, either escaped them or they later forgot. What everybody did have, and certainly remembered, was the freedom to impose their own tempo on life.

In the 1770s everything changed. A burst of mechanical inventions meant that high quality cotton could be produced in hitherto unimaginable quantities. It was because the initial inventions were connected with the cotton trade that Lancashire became the world cradle of the Industrial Revolution, suffering from the incalculable pressures of being first in the field. At the start there was an insatiable market, both at home and abroad, for this splendid, cheap material. Capital poured into Manchester. Shillings turned overnight into massive fortunes. Small-time masters became manufacturers and in the process grew further and further away from the men with whom they had hitherto worked amicably. Chasing their pot of gold, or at least better wages than they could earn as joiners, hatters and locksmiths, butchers, bakers and candlestick makers, the people poured in too. The stampede turned Manchester from a fair sized town to the second largest city in England. Manchester and Salford's joint population of 40,000 in 1750 had risen to 95,000 by 1800. It turned the sleepy villages into cotton towns. Oldham with less than 4,000 inhabitants in 1750 had grown to 12,000 by 1800. The whole area resembled a new-found colony, called Eldorado.

However, by the time John Lees was born the cotton bandwagon was running off the rails. England was at war with France, and the longer the wars dragged on, the more erratic its course became. The boom days when spinning families were earning between 30s and 40s a week, and those involved in weaving averaging between 40s and 60s, became memories told by father. And grandfather started to recall the good old days before mechanization. For if wages were plunging downwards and unemployment, with the new concentration of people dependent on a single manufacture, was becoming mass, other forces could not be checked either. Industrialization had changed the structure and tempo of life irrevocably.

The two main changes were the growth of the industrial slums and the Factory System. When the hordes first poured into the area they needed housing. So a builder and a carpenter joined forces (not everybody climbed on to the cotton bandwagon but practically everybody lived off it). They bought a stretch of land as near as possible to the centre of the places where the manufacturing activity was concentrated—Manchester, Oldham, Rochdale, Stockport and the rest. If the land already contained ditches, that was fine as it saved digging foundations. In the ditches cellars were constructed, forming a damp working area for the weavers. For yarn needed to be kept supple while being woven, and the only way to keep it thus was in a damp atmosphere. The houses from which the people had come had not been palatial but neither had they been built on top of sewage ditches, hundreds of rows, without gardens, without sight of a tree, without the smell of the fresh air (or freshish, remembering the sewage ditches found in every town and village). The only amenity the new houses possessed was running water, not from a tap, but rising from the rotten foundations and pouring down the walls.

While wages remained high most people accepted the conditions. Money, if not producing happiness, took the edge off unhappiness. It provided the wherewithal to buy luxuries such as best beef and butter, or to drown your sorrows in drink. While the money was coming in many people, albeit sullenly and considerably fewer in number, also accepted the Factory System. This arose initially for simple, practical reasons. The first inventions occurred in the spinning branch of the industry and soon the whole processing of cotton had become infinitely more complicated. The waste of time spent plodding between individual cottages became ridiculous, and in any case the weight of the new machines was too great for a single cottage. So they, and all the spinning processes, became concentrated in a mill. The Factory System itself, therefore, made sense. Unfortunately, the manner in which it was conducted in most mills from the very beginning was dreadful. The major impulse was profit for the master, so conditions were harsh, brutal and degrading, not only to increase profits but also to keep the workers submissive.

John Lees's father, Robert, was among the spinners who accepted the new fact of economic life—that hand-spun yarn could not compete with machine-produced. When John was in his early teens his father opened a small mill in Oldham where John, his mother, brother and sisters and a dozen or so others worked. Most of the mills were small, though a few employed workers in their thousands. Robert Lees's was not among the worst, but even so conditions there were of economic necessity harsh. On the whole it was in the small factories, where the masters were scrambling their way upwards or fighting to make a living, that the most brutal conditions prevailed. Spinners worked a fourteen-hour day in steaming temperatures up to 90°Fahrenheit. They were heavily fined for sending out for a drink of water, or opening a window, or whistling, or slipping with a gas lighter, or falling asleep at their machines. Spinners included men, women and children from the age of five. For most of the factory jobs were menial and tedious and could easily, and more cheaply, be performed by the women and children. The female of the spinning species was from the age of puberty regarded as anybody's meat. Male visitors to many factories were invited to take their pick for a lusty roll.

By 1815 there were sixty factories in the Manchester area, employing some 24,000 workers. Over 90 per cent were spinning mills. However, there were still as many spinners operating from their cottages. But in and out of the factories wages had dropped to an average of 24s a week, prices had risen and the Corn Bill had been passed. The shadow of the Corn Laws hung over the whole period like a carrion crow. The Bill was passed in the phoney peace between Napoleon's incarceration on Elba and Waterloo. As soon as its terms were made known, that foreign corn could not be imported until the price of home-grown wheat had reached 80s a quarter, there were riots and protest meetings throughout the country. It was finally passed in a House of Commons ringed by troops with bayonets fixed, for it protected the interests of an élite alone. True, the farmers it protected needed help, but passing a law which adversely affected everybody else in the country was not the best way to go about it. For the Corn Bill meant that come the next bad harvest the price of corn would rocket. It did not require a weather prophet to foretell that in England it would be sooner rather than later. Nor an economist to tell the thousands of spinners and weavers what a rise in the price of bread, their 'staff of life', would mean. As an added thorn for the manufacturing districts, of which Lancashire from its industrial cradling position was always in the van for good or ill, the Corn Bill also meant that their goods could not be exchanged for foreign corn as they had been in the past.

John Lees, therefore, returned home from the wars to find that both the conditions and wages of spinners had fast detenorated.* The plight of the weavers, the former aristocrats of the trade, was infinitely worse. Although the first inventions had occurred in

---

* John Lees may have enlisted in the army because of economic distress but his enlistment was more or less voluntary. Not every soldier in Wellington's army was the scum of the earth. Some were decent, semi-literate young men such as he.

the spinning branch, the power loom had been invented in 1785, thirty years before. In that period, following the normal head-long pattern of industrialization, the power loom should have mechanized and transformed weaving. The weavers should have been in the factories in their thousands. But they weren't. There was a bare handful of weaving mills, and over 40,000 hand-loom weavers were living and working outside the Factory System.

Why weaving remained outside the system for so many years is a point that has been argued for as many subsequent ones. Nobody has found a crystal-clear answer. Was it because the hand-loom weavers had been the aristocrats that they clung to their 'independence'? But the people who flocked into hand-loom weaving in the early boom days had never been craftsmen. Did the immigrants assume the mantle of superiority due to the excellent early wages, and become loath to abandon it? Was it the ease with which you could acquire a hand-loom and set it up in your cellar and seem to be your own master? But you could acquire a spinning wheel, or even a small mechanized Spinning Jenny, just as easily. Remembering the conditions in the factories one does not blame the weavers for clinging to their indepen-dence, however illusory. But why did the spinners not cling as a mass to theirs so tenaciously? Was there something in the differ-ent branches that made the spinners accept the industrial facts while weavers did not. Or could the weavers not see why indus-trialization was inevitable? Could they not initially believe that the boom days had gone for ever, and later absolutely disbelieve that they could be left in such appalling conditions, to endure such extreme suffering?

For with dreadful irony, by rejecting industrialization, the weavers created for themselves conditions worse than those in the factories. Already by 1815 there were far too many of them chas-ing far too little work. In their struggle to earn a living they were undercutting themselves to the extent that *hand-woven cloth was cheaper than machine produced.* Their wages had plummeted from

40s–60s a week to an average of 12s. Over the years they had tried to redress their economic grievances by economic means, petitioning Parliament for a minimum wage, but without success. They were not well organized. The temperament which made the more educated cling so desperately to their independence was not conducive to the co-operation demanded by an effective pressure group. The illiterate swarm of migrants had either something of the same temperament or were too sunk in misery to care. Against them anyway was the power of the masters who were getting what they wanted, cheap cloth, and did not feel it was their business to inquire in what conditions the cheap cloth was being produced. If the weavers wanted to be self-employed and independent that was their privilege, as long as they did not make a fuss in the process. In 1815, vast and potentially disturbing force as the 40,000 hand-loom weavers were, they had not protested greatly. So the majority of masters were content to let the sleeping dogs lie in their damp, rotten, rat-infested, cholera-prone cellars.

Physically the area was, by today's standards, rural. The boundaries of Manchester were narrow. Hulme, Ardwick, Cheetham, Charlton Row—the essential dreary ring of the late nineteenth-century industrial city with which the twentieth century is belatedly trying to cope—were outlying districts. There were toll gates barring the entry to Manchester proper. In the heart of the town around Mosley Street the rich manufacturers and merchants lived in their large houses. The outward drift, away from the smells, the dirt and *hoi polloi* had not started. There were many remnants of the medieval village Manchester had been, timber houses and early eighteenth-century brick and plaster ones. Main thoroughfares such as Market Street were twisting and narrow, with pavements only eighteen inches wide. The tearing down of old Manchester to make way for the mills and warehouses and counting houses, the ugly palaces of King Cotton, had not yet begun. The concentration in rotten housing had started, but it was confined to comparatively small areas around New Cross and Newtown in Manchester, and in the centres of the old cotton villages. The River Irwell, which flows through Manchester and even in the heart of the town had not so long ago been clear and unpolluted, was already dirty and muddy, 'the most overworked river in the world'. Of the sixty mills in the area, a considerable proportion were darkening the skyline along the Irwell's banks. But in 1815 the first industrial city in the world was rising on hitherto derelict or open spaces, and its messy sprawl was limited.

Once out of Manchester you were in open country. The eight miles between the town and Oldham, for example, were unspoiled. After his discharge from the army John Lees walked home on rutted turnpikes, across bridle paths, down through deep wooded valleys, scrambling up mossy banks where honey-suckle and wild roses grew, stopping to slake his thirst at a clear rindle (the local word for a stream), until he hit the foothills of the Pennines, tufty, gorse-strewn moorland.

If the physical scars were minimal, the economic stresses were already heavy. The spinners on the one hand herded into the factories, the weavers on the other in their wretched cellars, all suffering from a sharp drop in wages, an equally sharp rise in prices with the black shadow of the Corn Bill looming over them. The spiritual and moral pressures emerging from the rapid change both in tempo and mode of life, and from the harsh new industrial beat, had also bitten deeply. The predominant emotion in 1815 was sullen acquiesence. The major cause for concern was economic. They wanted sufficient money to live decently, or indecently as the case might be. They were not over-interested in why they were unable to earn a living. But if wages and conditions did not improve they knew something would have to be done, either for or by them. What that something should be neither John Lees nor the anonymous thousands had any clear idea.

2

THE MOST WICKED AND SEDITIOUS PART OF THE COUNTRY

There were people who had definite views on what was necessary to combat the existing conditions and prevent their further deterioration. They were a small section of the community in comparison to that represented by John Lees, but by 1815 their efforts had already helped to earn Manchester and the surrounding area the reputation of being the most turbulent and seditious in the country. Reforming activity had gone hand-in-hand with the Industrial Revolution. Its first major outbreak was in the 1790s, inspired by the French Revolution and the works of Tom Paine.

The practical platform in those early days was the repeal of the religiously discriminating Test and Corporation Acts* and a

---

* These Acts prevented any non-Anglican from holding public office. In practice loopholes had been made for certain Dissenters. but large sections of the population, Nonconformist, Catholic and Jewish, were disbarred from public life.

moderate reform of Parliament. But the masses in 1790 were earning high wages and were caught up in the patriotic fever of the onset of the French wars. They showed their disapproval of reform by stoning the houses of the Jacobins. The authorities, with the people behind them, acted swiftly and harshly and reforming zeal lost its impetus. The violence that erupted between 1810 and 1812, the period of the Luddite Riots, was not instigated by the reformers, and the riots in this instance did not originate in Lancashire, though they soon spread there, but in Nottingham. The mill burning, machine breaking and food rioting that occurred in these years was wholly economically inspired. However, the experience of mass unemployment and starvation swung the people away from their previous wholesale loyalty to King and Country and the established order. In 1812 it had not swung them *towards* anything specific, but it was in this year that political agitation reared its head again.

The doyen of the working-class reform movement in the area was John Knight. Born in 1763 he was a Yorkshireman who spent most of his life on the Lancashire side of the Pennines. Originally he was a weaver, a small-time but successful master. In early manhood he became convinced that the ills of his adopted county and the country at large stemmed from the corruption of an unrepresentative Parliament. Over the years he spent the greater part of his money in furthering the cause of Parliamentary reform. Knight had conviction and a full measure of Yorkshire determination, with an equal measure of Tyke caution. The authorities considered him wild, as they did anybody with similar ideas, but he was not by nature rash. Being convinced that he was right and holding a minority view, he had to stick his neck out sometimes but on the whole he proceeded with cautious, dogged perseverance.

In 1812 he considered the time ripe for further action. In June of that year he organized a meeting at a public house in Manchester attended by thirty-eight weavers. In a small room they hammered out a petition to the House of Commons and an address to the Prince Regent, urging the necessity of Parliamentary reform. As they were finishing they were arrested and charged with holding an unlawful meeting for a seditious purpose. At their subsequent trial the case against them was not proven. But the arrests put a further temporary stop to reforming zeal. On the release of the thirty-nine men, only the convinced, dogged Knight remained politically active. However, there was one difference between these arrests and those of the 1790s. This time the people neither stoned the houses of Knight or the other weavers, nor showed their approbation of the authorities' actions in any way. It was a difference appreciated, literally and metaphorically, by Knight and one which encouraged him to carry on. The times were maturing with him.

Between 1812 and 1815 there was a political lull, partly because the economy picked up as the French wars entered their last phase and markets re-opened, partly from the feeling that the titanic struggle was coming to an end and the hope that peace would bring prosperity. The passing of the Corn Bill re-opened the field for the reformers. The anti-Corn Bill meetings were again economically inspired. But the emotions aroused made more converts to the theme that *they* would always be against *us* until *we* had a voice in the governing of *our* country.

That the people had no say in the election of their representatives, that England bore no relationship to the democracy she was supposed to be, was incontestable. No borough had been enfranchised since Newark in the time of Charles II. The franchise had never been arranged with equity and justice—the Tudors had been great ones for creating new boroughs wherever it suited their patronage. Since the time of Charles II the centres of population and activity had changed beyond measure. But in 1815 of 489 English seats in the House of Commons, 293 were returned by the southern and south-western counties including London. As a specific example, Cornwall with a diminishing population returned 44 members, while Lancashire whose population had leapt over the 1,000,000 mark had only 14 for the entire county. Manchester, the second largest city in England, had no member of Parliament. The same pattern existed throughout the country: long established rural areas returned umpteen members while Birmingham, Leeds and the fast rising industrial cities were unrepresented.

Manchester had been represented in Cromwell's time as a reward for stalwart support in the Civil War. But when the sitting member died during the Restoration, Charles II declined to renew the representation as a punishment for opposition. In 1774 efforts had been made to buy a seat in Parliament so that Manchester should have a member to represent her problems. These attempts, which came to nothing, were not organized by reformers of the John Knight ilk. They were the work of the more forward looking of the reactionary élite that governed the town. Thus the people who became known first as radicals, then Radicals with a capital, were neither original nor alone in considering that not all was for the best in the best of all possible parliaments.

The younger Pitt had entered Parliament as a reformer (though he could not count upon the Manchester loyalists as his supporters; they merely wanted their city represented in the system as it stood). However, Pitt's reforming aims had been limited to the lessening of the rottenness of the most rotten boroughs, of which the most famous was Pitt's father's constituency of Old Sarum which had not a single voter within its boundaries; to the curtailing of the vagaries of election date and place, which had led to the classic eighteenth-century example of two candidates postponing and removing the poll from Winchester to the Isle of Wight when they found the campaign not going to their liking; and to the curbing of the most outrageous forms of bribery and patronage—election 'expenses', i.e., bribing of voters, in some cases had reached £40,000.

Where the radicals differed, and why from the start they roused such Establishment opposition, not to say terror, was in the extent and scope of their aims. The earliest and most consistent of the radicals was Major John Cartwright, born in Nottinghamshire of an old-established family in 1740. Cartwright possessed the ideal temperament for the missionary or reformer: limited intelligence, no sens of humour, extreme obstinacy and great courage. It was Cartwright who first expounded the idea of the need for a completely new system based on democratic representation, rather than moderate reform of the existing one. By 1815 he was the national doyen of the radical movement, 'the old heart in London from which the veins of sedition in this country are supplied'.

In 1812 Cartwright founded the Hampden Club in London. Qualifications for membership were the same as for the House of Commons, one had either to be the owner of or heir to £33 per annum from landed property, and the subscription was two guineas. The declared aim was to gather together rich and influential reformers to discuss future plans and to provide leadership for the rest of the country. By 1815 his dream of rich and influential leadership had come to nothing. He was, sadly, the only member to turn up at a meeting. Undeterred, he decided to establish provincial Hampden Clubs. Their object was to channel and provide with leadership the disorganized working-class unrest. There were no qualifications for membership and the subscription was reduced to one penny a week. Cartwright travelled hundreds of miles up and down the country, by coach and on horseback. He was already seventy-five years old but like John Knight, who incidentally was known as the Cartwright of the North, he had conviction and determination. The county in which he had the greatest success in establishing the clubs was Lancashire.

The first provincial Hampden Club was founded in August 1816, in Royton, a small cotton town nine miles from Manchester. Its leading figure was William Fitton, a surgeon of great physical and mental energy, a devotee of Tom Paine, with a biting line in sarcasm and an ardent belief in the rights of man. He was one of the many local figures who helped shape Peterloo. Other clubs soon mushroomed in the cotton belt, in Oldham, Rochdale, Ashton-under-Lyne, Middleton and Stockport—the latter, lying just over the Cheshire border, had a reputation second only to Manchester as a sink of seditious iniquity.

The secretary of the Middleton club was Samuel Bamford, the most *human* character directly connected with Peterloo if only for the reason that we know most about him. For he grew up to be a bad poet and a good prose writer who left behind several autobiographical books, notably *Passages in the Life of a Radical.* Bamford was born in Middleton in 1788. He came from a family of weavers who represented another thread in the working-class Lancastrian weft, literate and articulate by tradition. The young Samuel was educated at the local Methodist school and the Free Grammar School of Manchester. Free that was to children of reasonable standing (his father at the time being governor of the workhouse—he later lost the job because of his radical views) and intelligence. Bamford's schooling was not of course full time. As all working-class children of the period, even those fortunate enough to receive schooling, he learned the family trade from babyhood, and spent half his youth weaving and half in the class-room.

Temperamentally Bamford was headstrong, romantic, idealistic, touchy and intelligent. Physically he was 5 ft. 10 in., lithe and well-proportioned. His features were irregular, he had what he called 'a snubby nose', but the whole made a most pleasing impression, particularly on the ladies. His early manhood was stormy. Before he was twenty Bamford had an illegitimate child by a Yorkshire lass but fortunately she did not ask him to marry her, being content with an allowance. His lusty sexual instincts, coupled with an eagerness to sample life, made him well known in the shady haunts of Manchester. With thousands of spinners escaping from the steaming oppression of the factories, and thousands of weavers emerging from their damp cellars, the shades were luridly coloured. In one short alley, alone, there were forty-seven brothels. But at the ripe old age of twenty-three, having worked on a collier in the meantime, Bamford decided it was time for him to settle down. Accordingly he married his local Middleton sweetheart Jemima, known to everybody as Mima. At the wedding feast 'a being which was dearest to me of any in the world save my wife' had a place of honour, his baby daughter by Mima. However, he did settle down, and even if the lusty, roaming instincts remained he enjoyed a long, happy married life.

In the Years before and after his marriage Bamford read voraciously, his reading matter including the poems of Robert Burns and Cobbett's *Political Register*, both of which influenced him. Cobbett planted him firmly on the road to which his family background had guided him, by teaching him to question the causes of the current distress and to try and seek the answers. Following in Burns's footsteps he began to write the poems in the local vernacular which were to make him Lancashire's 'Weaver Boy'. By 1816 he had left the security of a warehouse in Manchester and started up as a cottage weaver. Mima, in fact, seems to have done most of the weaving, and not *all* hand-loom weavers were destitute.

A stalwart supporter of the Hampden Club established in Oldham was Bamford's friend, 'Doctor' Healey. Born at Bent in 1780, Healey was a quack doctor in the eighteenth-century sense of one who practised medicine, often very well, without being qualified. He was virtually illiterate but he possessed a great sense of justice and injustice. A diminutive fighting cock of a man, he had the strongest of Lancashire accents and the true simplicity that does not change, for better or worse, whatever the circumstances. He behaved in exactly the same, cocky, friendly manner whether he was urging workers to strike in Oldham, being questioned by Privy Councillors in Whitehall, addressing an open-air meeting, or offering snuff to a distinguished prosecution barrister at the post-Peterloo trials.

The Mancheter Hampden Club was founded, after the rapid growth of those in the cotton towns and villages, in October 1816. In the year up to Peterloo this pattern was repeated, the cotton towns remaining in the van, but Manchester gaining the plaudits or disasters by virtue of being the centre of the area. John Knight was closely associated with the foundation of the Manchester club. Among those who assisted him, or became prominent in its affairs, were John Thacker Saxton and his wife Susanna, and Joseph Johnson. Saxton, born 1776, had been connected with the cotton trade but by 1816 had found an outlet for his writing talent. He was to play an important part on the *Manchester Observer*, the Radical paper founded in 1818. He was a vigorous, consistent, determined Radical with the supposed journalistic weakness for the bottle. His wife Susanna shared his views and determination and later became secretary of the Manchester Female Reformers. Joseph Johnson, born 1791 and therefore the youngest of the prominent local radicals, was a brush maker. He was a vain, indecisive, romantic character who cherished a dream of building Jerusalem in Lancashire's still green and pleasant land, with himself as a leading prophet. After Peterloo, when the dream turned to nightmare, he came down from his euphoric cloud and disintegrated. But between 1816 and 1819, and particularly from 1818 onwards when he put money into the *Manchester Observer* and became its part owner, he was a leading and influential figure.

The proceedings of the Hampden Clubs were similar throughout the area. Originally meetings were held in a house or cottage, say Bamford's in Middleton, where the tougher, more idealistic, enthusiastic and lively minds would gather. 1816 produced a dreadful harvest. As predicted, the Corn Bill caused the price of bread to rocket and with it everything else, except wages. This added distress made more people turn towards the Hampden Clubs as an organization offering solutions. With increased membership chapels were rented for the meetings. These were usually held twice a week after work. When everybody was gathered the best reader would impart the news and views (mostly views) from Cobbett's *Political Register* which were then discussed. A travelling delegate might appear to tell of the other Lancashire clubs or those over the border in Yorkshrre. At some point in the earnest discussions, which often lasted into the small hours, refreshment would be provided in the shape of beer and muffins.

During the endless discussions another concept was rekindled —that of universal suffrage, the right of every adult of sound mind to participate in the government of that society of which he was a member. The idea had been voiced as early as 1792 by a London shoemaker named Thomas Hardy, had flourished briefly and then been trampled on by Pitt's 'Gagging Acts' as having obvious affiliations with the French Revolution, and had lain dormant ever since. But in 1816, in Hampden Clubs up and down south-east Lancashire, it was given the kiss of life. The importance of this resurgence cannot be over-emphasized. For Cartwright himself, the doyen of radicalism, did not envisage the mob, the labouring classes, or the common people as they were variously called, sharing in the election of his reformed Parliament. The mob would continue to be guided by their betters, though their betters would include a much larger and more balanced section of the community than before. In fact, although Cartwright's demands outraged (or in some cases amused) the existing power structure, they were basically as paternalistic as that structure. But Cartwright had helped to rouse the sleeping tiger and he should not have been surprised when its brain started to tick. His conception of limited household franchise was not sufficient for the members of the Hampden Clubs *for they were not householders in franchise terms*. Consequently, 'Equal Representation' became one of their battle cries. When Bamford attended a Radical meeting in London in early 1817, it was his faction that swung the vote to acceptance of universal, not household, franchise. It was not only the first time the Northern influence made itself felt, but the first time the voice of the mob for whom the reforms were intended was clearly heard.

Every adult of sound mind did not include women, although from the start they were active in the clubs' affairs. In 1816 and early 1817 they had not yet founded their own clubs and their efforts were devoted to furthering the aims of their menfolk. They spread the good word, cleaned the chapels and prepared refreshments. They were also frequent attenders at the open-air meetings that became another method of spreading the radical gospel. Here it must be stressed that, even at the height of their success, membership of the Hampden Clubs was limited. John Lees, for example, was not a member and probably knew only vaguely of their existence. The hard, convinced core knew they had to spread their message by wider methods. Open-air meetings were one of these.

Some of the meetings were held on the moors. People walked from the surrounding villages and towns, up the cart tracks that wind through the lumpy grey-green hills with their short stumpy trees, across the boggy springy turf where the rivers and springs flow, to the rolling high moors around Saddleworth where the black rocks jut and the wind always blows. The moorland meetings were not graced by the military's attendance, but at those held in the towns troops were often present. On one rain-drenched occasion near Rochdale a weaver observed sardonically of the watching soldiers: 'as the water was already running over at the muzzles of their guns, they might squirt us, but they could not shoot us'. With or without the military's presence the crowds at these alfresco meetings increased. Some people attended because they were interested in what the Radicals had to say. They warmed to the interesting new theme that men are born free, equal and independent; that the source of all legitimate power was the people; that only through the support of the people themselves—would equality and independence be achieved; that the first step on the road lay in the reform of the corrupt Houses of Parliament. Some people attended because an outdoor meeting was an event in the dreary, oppressive round of life. Some went simply to hear the speakers. And the movement was throwing up some thumping good orators who larded in the boring facts of economic grievance and the unrepresentative state of Parliament with spice and drama, and indulged in vitriolic attacks on the Establishment, national and local.

John Lees may have attended an alfresco meeting in the early days of 1817. 'Doctor' Healey was operating in the Oldham area and was a big draw. If he did attend John came away no more a confirmed or convinced radical than on arrival. Neither economic distress nor Radical organization had mounted sufficiently for mass adherence to the movement, although the ripples were fast spreading.

There was another force, another 'spirit' at work in south-east Lancashire. This was the embryonic trade union movement. Its roots were more deeply embedded in the Industrial Revolution than the Radical movement's. (Again it was Lancashire's industrial cradling position, not chance, that put the county in the union vanguard and later led the first Trades Union Council to be held in Manchester in 1868.) The reasons and aims that motivated both trade union and radical movements to a great extent overlapped, but in 1817 they were pursuing different courses.

The hard core of trade unionists lay in the factories among the spinners. The majority of spinning tasks might be menial, the majority of spinners leading degrading lives, but the Industrial Revolution had created a small number of highly skilled jobs. It was the new spinning élite that led the demand for improved conditions and higher wages. Against them were the Combination Acts whose repeal the Radicals also favoured. These Acts, passed in 1799 and 1800, made illegal any combination of working men for any purpose.* They were unleashed by the fear of French Revolutionary echoes in England, but the fear of working men combining had long been felt. By the end of the eighteenth century there were already forty Acts of Parliament forbidding combinations in various forms. There was, however, as always in England, a loophole in that the Benefit Societies, into which the working man could pay a subscription to cover him in times of sickness, remained legal. They thus became the cover for trade union activities.

1818 was a year of union-motivated activity and will be examined later as it was very much part of the Peterloo story. Let it suffice to say here that there were two working-class impulses. The Radical movement was convinced that all solutions lay in Parliamentary reform. The trade unionists were certain that the redress to economic grievance lay in economic weapons, and that the combined power of the masters could only be countered by the combined power of the working man. Neither group was helping the other.

Both groups would have encountered far less enthusiasm, indeed might not have come into being at all but for the influence of a third force—Methodism. The Methodists were the first to utilize the talents of the ordinary man, and the first to emphasize a respect for individual worth rather than inherited wealth. They brought Enthusiasm into the Age of Reason and, most important, they started the first Sunday Schools.

Significantly, the Lancashire radicals and reformers all came from Methodist or Nonconformist backgrounds. It was also Methodism that had made John Lees semi-literate while his father Robert could neither read nor write. As a small boy John went to a dingy little Sunday School in Oldham, a garret at the top of somebody's house. Hundreds of little boys and girls in

---

* Theoretically they also made illegal the combination of masters but in practice it was the workers who were penalized.

Manchester attended in other garrets and cellars. They were laboriously taught to read and write, albeit the word of God. But having devoured the Bible the brighter among them could, and did, pass on to other reading matter. The material most of them passed on to was radical in context. Because Methodism had imparted the revolutionary idea that Jack was as good as his master. As Bamford wrote, 'The Sunday schools of the preceding thirty years had produced sufficient working men of sufficient talent to become readers, writers and speakers in the village meetings for parliamentary reform.' It was on the lines established by Methodism that Major Cartwright based the structure of the Hampden Clubs.

In the Manchester area Nonconformists outnumbered Anglicans by two to one. The sect that had a particularly strong influence were the Unitarians. They were the most radical in outlook. This was partly because of their precepts, partly because they had not won their freedom of worship until 1813, and having fought this battle for so long were in good trim to take up another cause. Dissenters in general had been granted freedom of worship in 1689 as a reward for stalwart support in the 'Glorious Revolution' that established the Protestant supremacy in England. The Dissenting tradition took the edge off the extremities of all reformers *(a)* because such sweeping revolutions Methodism were able to occur legally and *(b)* because the Establishment, however much it disliked reform, accepted the legal right to Dissent and consequently, if subconsciously, the concept of dissent.

However, over the years, and particularly in the Radical upsurge between 1816 and 1820, Dissent to the Government and loyalists equalled sedition. Dissent equalling sedition equalled Methodism.

3

THE CONSTITUTION OF ENGLAND IS THE BUSINESS OF EVERY ENGLISHMAN

To William Cobbett, unlike the Government, 'the bitterest foes of freedom in England have been, and are, the Methodists'. It was one of his more dogmatic statements but it contained an element of truth. On the one hand Methodism had fostered the revolutionary spirit which the loyalists rightly saw as one of the root causes of the discontent in the manufacturing districts, Lancashire in particular. On the other hand, Methodism's belief that the state is ordained of God counterbalanced the spirit it had fostered. So while Dissent equals sedition was one cry, it was also said throughout the period 1816–1820 that *even* in Manchester the Methodists remained loyal.

William Cobbett was not present at Peterloo. He was not even in England in 1819 but as much as any single man, as opposed to any single creed (i.e., Methodism which he so much disliked) he helped shape the August day. Cobbett was born of humble stock in Farnham, Surrey, in 1763. He grew up with a deep respect for, love of and pride in the old rural ways, the traditions of sturdy English independence, and native intelligence. But he also possessed an aggressive, curious, seeking mind and at the age of twenty he ran away from the countryside he loved so much and later enshrined in all his writings. He was successively London clerk and regular soldier. By 1792 he had clashed with army authority—though he obtained a legal discharge—and emigrated to the United States. In the land of the free he found his *métier*—journalism. However, by 1800 he was back in England, having clashed with American authority.

At this period he was still a staunch upholder of the *status quo* and in 1802 he founded the *Political Register*, a weekly paper supporting the current Tory Government of Henry Addington. Even as an ally Cobbett was not an unreserved joy. There was his natural aggressiveness. As he himself said, 'I never was of an accommodating disposition in my life'. There was his genuine hatred of injustice. It was these two qualities that had thus far led to his defiance of authority. Slowly over the years they led him along the road to radicalism, though to the end of his days he remained the most conservative radical of all time.

He first fell foul of the Government in 1810 when he attacked the brutal flogging of British troops in East Anglia by German mercenaries. The Government reacted with its usual weapon, a trial for seditious libel. Cobbett was found guilty, fined £1,000 and sent to Newgate for two years. While he was there the Luddite Riots erupted. It was they that first turned his attention northwards, and roused Cobbett's most vital quality, a feel for the pulse of England, an almost mystical identification with the soul of his native land. Once his attention was drawn to the North, Cobbett appreciated that the 'spirit' in the manufacturing districts, about which the Government wailed so constantly, was a new force that would repay sympathetic, rather than aggressive attention. He was one of the first major figures to do so.

Throughout the Luddite period Cobbett hammered away in the *Political Register*, which he continued to edit from Newgate, about the *causes* of the rioting. 'Measures ought to be adopted, not so much for putting an end to riots, as to prevent the misery out of which they arise.' He continually urged the people to stop smashing the machines and seek those causes. His weekly utterances had considerable effect in turning them from violent methods to more peaceful solutions. When he was released from prison in 1812 Cobbett had not himself arrived at Parliamentary reform as the initial and major solution, but by 1815 he had become an advocate. Having seen the light he blasted forth with the enthusiasm and conviction of the convert.

It was in 1816 that Cobbett took the decision that put him into the position of mass influencer. In that year he launched a twopenny weekly *Register* known to its detractors as Cobbett's 'Twopenny Trash'. He continued to write in, and exert his influence through the shilling *Register* but its price had been beyond the purse of the working classes, although they had it read to them in public houses and Hampden Clubs. The new twopenny *Register*, issued as a sheet to avoid stamp duty, was aimed directly at the working classes at a price they could afford. Now thousands more people could read, and have read to them, the highly personal prose that inaugurated a new era of popular journalism. From his American experience Cobbett spoke directly to his readers in a simple, uncluttered, muscular language that contrasted sharply with the verbosity and rhetoric of the day. He employed his dislike of the 'antalluct' and 'feelosofers', as opposed to native English wit and intelligence, to make his readers feel he was as much a common man as they. The effect of the 'Twopenny Trash' in Lancashire can be gauged from the words of a Government spy: 'Cobbett hath done more with his Twopenny papers than any Thousand beside him, as anyone can get them, the price being so low and they contain so much matter as the Children can purchase and read them.' The matter contained was Cobbett's common man view of what was wrong with England and how Parliamentary reform would put it right.

Much as he cultivated the Radical climate, by 1819 Cobbett had once more fled his native land. The major Radical leader, the key figure at Peterloo, was Henry Hunt. An extraordinary character he was too. Hunt was born at Upavon in Wiltshire in 1773 of yeoman stock. He himself preferred the term 'gentleman farmer', with the emphasis on *gentleman*. His early life was typical of his class, grammar school at Andover, then managing his father's farm which left him ample time to hunt, shoot and fish and have wild parties at night. He spent the dawn of the nineteenth century in the King's Bench prison, though not for political reasons. He had a violent quarrel with Lord Bruce, refused to apologize and was consequently imprisoned. It was through his imprisonment that he first met the then leading radicals, Sir Francis Burdett, Thomas Hardy, Horne Tooke and Major Cartwright but the meetings did not constitute a dramatic turning point in his life.

On his release from prison Hunt presided over his first public meeting, for the purpose of considering how the men of Wiltshire could best assist the Government in repelling the threatened French invasion. The date of this first public meeting according to Hunt, *the least* reliable of witnesses, was August 16th, 1801, and the conclusion to be drawn, how coincidental an omen, for eighteen years on. However, self-dramatization, another besetting sin, could have had more connection with the date than accuracy. But in 1802 he became infatuated with Mrs Vince, the wife of a friend. They went to Brighton together, Hunt's excuse for Brighton being that the Prince Regent and Mrs Fitzherbert were living there openly in sin. But then he did something which though typical of him was *not* typical of the period. He separated legally from his own wife and lived with Mrs Vince to whom he remained faithful. This act was to follow him for the rest of his life, and was to be of great disservice to the Radical cause. Cobbett before he met Hunt said, 'Beware of him! he rides the country with a whore, the wife of another man, having deserted his wife.' Cobbett was later to regret these words but, as always, they expressed most people's feelings. That Hunt surmounted his adultery is a tribute to the force of his personality.

In 1803 Hunt was still a loyalist, raising a troop of militia. But two years later he was immersed in politics on the radical side. It was in 1805 that he first met Cobbett whom he did not then like. 'He was very brief and blunt; a tall robust man with a florid face, his hair cut close to his head and himself dressed in a blue coat and scarlet waistcoat.' As a gentleman Hunt objected to the close cut hair, and took exception to the clothing because it was a boiling hot day. Hunt himself was always something of a dandy. He had a fine figure, standing well over six foot, with 'the neatest and firmest' of legs. In the days when men, not women, showed their legs off Hunt took great care to display his wellformed calves and ankles to the best advantage. He was not particularly good looking, having rather thin lips and heavy eyes, but his figure and proud bearing lifted him out of the crowd. The voice that made him the most famous mob orator of his day was clear and bell-like. In 1806 he had his *Address to the Independent Freeholders of Wiltshire* printed by Cobbett in the *Political Register*. In 1810 he was again sent to prison, for assaulting a gamekeeper, and for part of the time he shared a room with Cobbett in Newgate. In 1812 he stood as a radical candidate for Bristol (he lost).

What turned this vain, restless, arrogant, bellicose gentleman farmer into a radical?

It is a difficult question to answer. Hunt wrote his memoirs, three stunningly boring volumes, while in prison after Peterloo. In them there is no clear statement of belief, no overt reasons for his conversion. The picture that emerges is the one we already have of a selfish, self-centred, boastful, bombastic creature with the additive that post-Peterloo he considered himself exceedingly ill-used. It is a picture that his enemies, and he made many, would have certified as genuine. And one erstwhile friend, Bamford, later made the damaging statement that Hunt 'would sell his soul for the cheers of the mob'. So was he an opportunist who discovered he had oratorical ability to sway masses and climbed on to the radical bandwagon believing it would lead him to power and glory? The answer to that question *seems* clearer—with Hunt one always has to qualify—but no. When he became converted to radicalism it was not much of a bandwagon. To the end of his life, when hopes of power and glory had long faded, he remained a consistent radical, *consistent* being his own favourite adjective. He became a demagogue. He loved the mass adulation, the excitement and the power. But as a demagogue he was always legally aware of the power he wielded and he did not appeal to the *prejudices* of the masses. He appealed to a genuine distress with the genuine remedy of Parliamentary reform. In sum, however much he adored himself and the limelight, his feelings for the rights and liberties of the people seem to have been sincere. The comparison that has been made by one modern writer, Laurence Webley in *Across the Atlantic*, between Hunt and Hitler appears ridiculous. Hunt never achieved real power, neither had he Hitler's sense of the possible nor his genius for the impossible. The specious similarities are that both were great mob orators and both wrote boring memoirs in prison, even then Hitler's are revealing of motive and intent whereas Hunt's are not.

It was the partnership of the self-opinionated personification of the common man known as William Cobbett and the equally self-opinionated, but sincere, Hunt that led the front that started to gain strength. Theirs was the first working-class movement for the simple reason that they were the first people to appreciate that a working class, i.e., the new industrial masses, had arisen. They responded to the spirit induced by economic grievance, Methodism, the spread of education and the impact of the Industrial Revolution. The spirit responded to them. The movement was not intellectual. It had no brow higher than middle among its leaders, national or local, and it suffered from this lack. But it offered the most coherent political programme of the day. What were the main points? With characteristic clarity and gusto Cobbett asked and answered the question: What would a Reformed Parliament do? It would:

1. Do away with bribery and corruption at elections.
2. Do away with Parliamentary interest. People would succeed by merit.
3. Do away with sinecures.
4. It would enquire into and cut down salaries.
5. It would reduce the army and sift the navy.
6. It would employ no secret service. 'There would be none of this disgraceful spy work'.
7. It would reform the Bar and make it independent of ministers.
8. It would give real freedom to the press.
9. It would cut down the Civil List and reform administration of Crown Lands.
10. It would stop paying interest on the National Debt and reduce taxes. Thus by saving the nation from pauperism it would prevent revolution and bring back stability.

In addition, the Radicals proposed annual Parliaments and voting by ballot. They favoured the repeal of the Corn Laws, not only to help the industrial masses but also the agricultural labourers and small tenant farmers. They stressed their agricultural reforms feeling, rightly, that their support lay in the industrial areas and they needed to win over the agricultural workers. Their industrial programme was in fact vague. They proposed higher wages and shorter hours but how this was to be economically effected remained unclear. They borrowed heavily from Cobbett on the question of the National Debt which loomed large throughout the period. They urged that the boroughmongers, i.e., those who had profited by the Debt, should pay off the principal and the interest. Leading on from this, as the Debt existed and needed heavy taxes to support it, came their cry 'No Taxation Without Representation!' On the general currency question they also borrowed heavily from Cobbett, particularly from his pamphlet *Paper Against Gold*, arguing not always too clearly for a clamp-down on the spiralling value, or lack of value, of paper money and the necessity for a gold standard. The Radicals were not anti-Royalist in wanting a republic but they attacked the Crown as the lynch pin of the present corrupt system. They attacked the vast sums of public money lavished on the Prince Regent and the royal dukes. The Prince Regent, spending his time 'acquiring old masters and new mistresses', they simply attacked.

Another leading figure in the working-class Radical movement was Sir Charles Wolseley. Born in 1769, he came from an old Staffordshire family. He had witnessed the storming of the Bastille, a turning point in his life, and tended to talk as if he had personally stormed it single-handed. In the years up to Peterloo he was a stalwart Radical supporter, and post-Peterloo his generous purse was to be of invaluable help to those arrested.

Then, there were two fringes to the mainstream of the Radical movement. Incidentally, the capital 'R' came into being in 1817 as the Hunt/Cobbett front gained strength. The first group would not have cared to be referred to as a fringe, as it was led by Sir Francis Burdett. He regarded himself as the doyen of radicalism, with perhaps a backward pat to Major Cartwright who had started the whole idea. Burdett was extremely rich and eccentric, and was a disciple of Jeremy Bentham and Utilitarianism. He advocated rational reorganization of national and local government at a rational pace, with the organized education of the working classes, but with an even stronger emphasis than Cartwright's on their being guided by their betters. In the period prior to Peterloo Burdett sat sulkily on the fence, not openly opposing the new front in case it won through, but indulging in considerable back-biting and shoulder-stabbing (returned in full measure by Hunt and Cobbett) to establish his position as a moderate in case it did not. Burdett had the advantage of being one of the few radicals actually to sit in Parliament.

The second fringe group was the extremist element, the Spenceans. They were the disciples of the Yorkshire schoolmaster, Spence, who propounded a doctrine of agricultural communism and advocated the use of force. Chief among them were Arthur Thistlewood and Doctor Watson. They were important not so much for what they achieved but for the wildness of their views which alienated many people who might have been sympathetic towards the Radical movement.

Finally there was an emergent species concentrated in Manchester—the middle-class Radicals. They were taking a long, cool, careful look at the current problems and producing detailed, earnest, sober, though still radical, solutions. In 1819 they were only 'a small but determined band', a hive of similar minds with similar purpose. They had the common factor of being Unitarian by religion and Utilitarian by principle. Prominent among them were John Edward Taylor, John Shuttleworth, Archibald Prentice and the Potter family. Taylor was born in Somerset in 1791, coming to Manchester with his schoolmaster father in 1805. He had an excellent clear brain and although officially a cotton merchant he was finding a talent as a journalist, writing for the middle-of-the-road *Manchester Gazette*. Shuttleworth, known—to Cobbett anyway—as 'Cackling Shuttleworth', was born in 1786 and was a cotton dealer. Archibald Prentice was a Scot from Lanarkshire who did not settle in Manchester until 1815, but once there he quickly joined the hive. (In fact, by religion Prentice was Presbyterian, not a Unitarian.) The Potter family, father John, sons Thomas and Richard, hailed from Yorkshire, but father had started a drapery business in Manchester and Dick and Thomas were cotton merchants. It was Dick, 'Radical Dick', who emerged as the leader of the group when it became a movement rather than a gathering of like minds. Much of the early discussions took place in the big back room of the drapery house which became known as 'Potter's Planning Parlour'.

The discussions in the Planning Parlour were as earnest as those in the Hampden Clubs and much more high-minded, both in the intellectual and moral sense. The hive believed in the Benthamite view of society as a collection of individuals existing in isolation, united solely by deliberate acts of choice, and therefore saw the art of education as the instruction of the child to associate personal and corporate happiness. Part of their task, thrashed out in the Planning Parlour and their high-minded societies, lay in trying to find this balance. They believed in the rational re-organization of local government so as to be both cheap and efficient, cheapness and efficiency being synonymous in their programme. Up to 1819 their effect was confined to questions of education and local government. Taylor and Shuttleworth were prominent supporters and defenders of the Nonconformist Lancasterian Schools, while the group as a whole attacked 'the strange anomalous' system, or lack of system, provided by the High Tory oligarchy. They managed to unearth three major scandals connected with the provision of bran for the town's horses, a very high tender for the gasworks and for cement used in its construction. In each case friends and relations of the oligarchy were found to be concerned with irregular payments. In such instances they were working in concert with the working-class Radicals who were also hot on the trail of corruption and inefficiency.

Indeed up to 1819 the middle-class Radicals were in a dilemma. Fundamentally they believed in the principles and objectives of the working-class Radical movement. They too wanted Parliamentary reform, though less than the universal suffrage demanded by Hunt and their master, Bentham. They, too, strongly favoured the repeal of the Corn Laws, though their emphasis was on the Free Trade aspect which the laws negated. What they did not approve of was the methods by which the working-class Radicals hoped to achieve their objectives. Neither did they approve of the leaders themselves. Hunt, Cobbett, Cartwright, Knight and Johnson 'were not men by whom the intellect of the country will submit to be led'. They were 'lacking in that high tone of moral feeling which can alone dignify human nature'.

In high moral tone the middle-class Radicals abounded. From their lofty perch they saw themselves as the middle force. They were the people who could bridge the gap between masters and men whose future in the long run was bound together. They recognized both sides of the question with intellectual clarity, whereas the Hunt brigade saw only and appealed only to the working classes and could thus but widen the gap. They were on a much higher intellectual plane than any of the working-class Radicals, and their earnest, serious intelligence was to be the force that shaped Manchester (and England) in the years after Peter-loo. But if one were asked what their effect was on the actual day the immediate answer would be, none. However, on reflection, the very fact that they did not support the working-class Radical movement had an indirect effect on the day's events. It has been said that had they been its leaders Peterloo would never have occurred. This is so obviously true, their characters and beliefs being so contrary to the emotional approach of mass meetings, as to be hardly in need of stating. It is more interesting to spec-ulate what would have happened if they had decided it was in the general interest, the greatest good for the greatest number in which they so firmly believed, to reach a compromise with the working-class Radicals. But their cool, disapproving with-drawal from the Hunt front in one way held back people who might have been tempted to join, in another pushed the people into the arms of the working-class Radicals. It was one of the great popular movements of British history and the sober, earnest pre-Victorians might have considered adding their restraint and intelligence to the emotions aroused.

4

BRITAIN'S GUARDIAN GANDERS

Lord Grey's malicious comment on the Radicals was: 'Is there any one of them with whom you would trust yourself in the dark?' Had this question been put to the Government it would as a man have answered no, not one of them, in the dark or in the daylight. The Government of the day was Tory, as it had been for the last two decades with one brief interlude of coalition. The Prime Minister was Robert Banks Jenkinson, 2nd Earl of Liverpool.

Liverpool's administration has been called one of the most reactionary and repressive in British history. Certainly between 1812 and 1820 it did behave in a repressive and reactionary manner. Reaction had become the Tory principle, a positive adoration of things as they supposedly always had been, i.e., pre the French Revolution. Its shadow hung over the whole period far more blackly and menacingly than that of the Corn Bill. Give an inch to the spirit in the manufacturing districts and the same hideous pattern would follow in England. That France was not England, that the French differed in temperament, tradition and history, that the circumstances were dissimilar from those in 1789 was ignored. A false parallel was drawn and having drawn it the Government stuck to it. Their diagnosis that England was on the brink of revolution was ironically partially correct. Had Hunt possessed Hitler's dæmonic powers, had the Radicals produced a really great leader, the country could have pitched over the abyss. The classic symptoms of revolution were present: mass unemployment, deprivation and frustration. But having arrived at their diagnosis from the wrong angle, the Government had perforce to ignore these very real symptoms. That is not to say they were unaware of the economic distress. They not only appreciated its existence, they also accepted that distress is the parent of discontent. But they kept returning to their French Revolutionary diagnosis which led them to the belief that they must at all costs uphold the *status quo* to save the country from similar terror and bloodshed.

In addition to dealing with the tangible and intangible effects of the Industrial Revolution, of a country sloughing off one skin and trying to find another, the Government had other severe problems. Britain had been at war for twenty years, and the change-over from war-time to peace-time economy is one over which later British Governments have also stumbled. There was the enormous National Debt against which Cobbett and the Radicals fulminated so strongly. So it is fair to say that Liverpool's administration had to deal with one of the most difficult and complex periods in British history. To sail through the stormy, uncharted seas of post-French wars, embryonically industrialized Britain, men of great vision, imagination and toughness were required; men who knew how far to bend towards the new forces, what to retain and what to throw out; above all men with a sense of change and possessing flexibility. Such men are hard to find outside the realms of romance. It is not surprising that Liverpool's Government did not contain them. But unfortunately it was composed of men whose calibre was peculiarly unsuited to the needs of the hour.

Liverpool himself was born in 1770, the son of a politician. He went to Charterhouse and Oxford, then straight into Parliament. He was always a good Tory reactionary, opposing Pitt's early Parliamentary Reform Bills, consistently in favour of the French wars, against Catholic Emancipation. On becoming Prime Minister in 1812, at the peak of the Luddite Riots, it was hardly likely that he would change his spots. He stayed in office for fifteen years, the third longest tenure in British history. He was the last Prime Minister who had the personal power to govern. Since Lord Liverpool, as the business of government has become increasingly complex, no other Prime Minister has had the same power. Conversely, over the years, as single responsibility has decreased, and the mass vote increased, somebody has had to appear to be solely responsible, and the post of Prime Minister has acquired its awful, individual weight. But in Lord Liverpool's day, although he had genuine power, nobody considered him personally responsible for the state of the country. (Partly because the concept of the Government being responsible for its people's well-being was in its infancy.) Therefore to the Radicals, Liverpool was but one among a loosely linked collection of hated ministers. He escaped with such mild comments as, 'the Jenkinsons were ever liars'. The qualities that saved him from the heaviest attacks were those that kept him in office, and enabled him to hold together a cabinet which, if mainly united in being reactionary, was not united in its degrees of reaction, nor in its love of each other. He was as unflamboyant as a field mouse, and within the confines of the cabinet he was tough, tactful and an excellent administrator. What he particularly lacked was what the hour particularly needed, the trait Cobbett possessed in full measure, the feel for the pulse of the country. A public image was not a highly prized attribute. We were in power, justly with our backgrounds and traditions, and we did not greatly care in what esteem the country held us. But a politician however autocratic, and by temperament Liverpool was not, must have an instinct for the general emotion which he may then manipulate, but whichever way he acts an image is reflected back. But Liverpool was neither a one-way nor two-way mirror. Opaquely he stuck to his diagnosis.

Even more lacking in a sense of, or flair for, public feeling were Viscounts Sidmouth and Castlereagh. Sidmouth held the office most vital to Peterloo, that of Home Secretary, but on both the opprobrium was heaped.

Sidmouth was born Henry Addington in 1757. He was the son of a country doctor who bettered himself by moving to London and becoming physician and friend, on the accepted hierarchical level, to the rich and influential. Among Doctor Addington's most grateful patients was William Pitt the Elder, and their two boys, Henry and William, grew up together. The younger Pitt was the decisive influence on Sidmouth's life. On leaving Oxford, where he obtained a moderate BA and wrote bad verse, it was through Pitt's encouragement that he entered Parliament as MP for Devizes in 1778. It was due to Pitt's patronage that he became Speaker of the House within five years. Although he was a terrible speaker in the oratorical sense* he made a good Speaker in the Parliamentary one. He was an excellent organizer within narrow limits and he was generally trusted in an age of corruption as being honest and possessing integrity.

Had he remained Speaker for the rest of his life Sidmouth might not have been so well remembered, but his memory might have been held in higher esteem. Unfortunately, with Pitt the revered mentor at his elbow in life and overshadowing him in death, with his strong sense of duty, and of the obligations of a member of the élite (albeit on a lowish rung) to guide and

---

* Lady Bessborough told the story of a friend listening to Addington (as he then was) speaking in the House. 'He woke from his sleep, and heard, "For as this is that which was said to …", was quite satisfied and turned to sleep out the rest.'

thus serve his inferiors, he accepted jobs for which his talents did not qualify him. Among these, in 1801, was the highest political job in the country. As Prime Minister he had the, in retrospect, ironic privilege of having Cobbett as an ally. After two years as Prime Minister he was dethroned and Pitt recalled, to nobody's surprise. Then, in 1806, Pitt died. It was a blow from which Viscount Sidmouth never recovered (he was ennobled in 1805 as a sop for being put out to grass). For the rest of his life time stood still at 1806. The few actions he took were shaped by his idea of what Pitt would have done, bearing little or no connection with the steps the master would actually have taken.

Sidmouth stayed in Government in minor capacities until Liverpool became Prime Minister in 1812 and made him Home Secretary. Liverpool had no great opinion of his Home Secretary's capabilities, but he needed the Parliamentary votes Sidmouth carried, those of the country gentlemen who abhorred change and only too rightly believed that Sidmouth was not the man to countenance any. According to *The Times* of the day, the Home Office was 'the sink of all imbecilities attached to every ministry for the last thirty years'. Among the imbecilities were the Home Secretary's responsibility for matters of the police, the regular army, the militia and volunteers, and all civil matters. In fairness to Sidmouth, if the Home Office as an office was inadequate to the needs of 1812 onwards, the staff was even more inadequate. But it was into the hands of the man whose background had instilled implicit belief in Church, Constitution, King and Country, whose temperament contained no qualities to question these beliefs, who would not have dreamed of altering the inadequacies, that Lord Liverpool bequeathed these supreme responsibilities in years of supreme tension.

Why Castlereagh was quite so hated is now a little difficult to appreciate. He was not Home Secretary, though he was Government spokesman for civil matters in the House of Commons. And he was a worse orator than Sidmouth, with an even greater tendency to perform the contorting act of putting his foot in it every time he opened his mouth. Some of the virulence carried over from his embroilment in Irish affairs, the personification of the Anglo-Irishman, stamping on the Irish patriots, while some of it stemmed from his being Foreign Secretary at the Congress of Vienna, a settlement unpopular in Radical circles. On the handsome head of Viscount Castlereagh—as Talleyrand exclaimed at the Congress of Vienna, 'Ma foi, c'est distingué'— the venom was truly spewed. He came second only to Sidmouth in the infamy stakes. After Peterloo he was Shelley's first target in *The Masque of Anarchy:*

> I met murder on the way,
> He had a mask like Castlereagh.

Liverpool, Sidmouth, Castlereagh and the rest of the administration believed to a lesser or greater degree that the country was on the brink of revolution. But the system with which they had to enforce law and order, to uphold their precious *status quo*, was far more outdated than their approach to the current circumstances. The pivot of the system was the magistrates. They were chosen by the Crown on the recommendation of the Lord Lieutenants of the various counties. The qualifications to be a magistrate were residence in the county, plus an income of £100 from freehold land, which narrowed the field to well established candidates. In addition to administering local justice, the magistrates possessed the vital powers of being able to call upon the regular army and local militia in 'times of unrest' and to read the Riot Act and order the dispersal of mobs in such periods. As they were also responsible for keeping the central Government informed of what was going on in their areas it was they who defined 'times of unrest'.

The way the system worked was that the magistrates kept their ears to the ground, or tried to, in the various areas. In the industrial districts they were, by virtue of their backgrounds, divorced from the populace, so they employed spies to inform them what was taking place in the factories, public houses and clubs. On the information thus supplied far too many magistrates placed far too much reliance. Having acquired this dubious information they then sat down and wrote their reports to the Home Office. At the receiving end Lord Sidmouth sat in the Home Office with his inadequate staff, reports flowing in from all over England, Scotland and Wales. If a legal question was raised, and in dealing with Radical speeches, mass meetings and strikes it frequently was, the matter had to be referred to the Solicitor or Attorney General's office. Replies then had to be written and sent hundreds of miles over rotten roads by coach and horse. Anything could, and did, happen in the interim between report and reply.

Lord Sidmouth possessed the ultimate responsibility for the maintenance of law and order, for the events such as Peterloo that happened in an interim period. It was he who counselled and advised the magistrates in their difficulties. But they possessed those vital powers of calling upon the military and reading the Riot Act in self-defined times of unrest. Once having done this they were in control. It will thus be seen that the system was dependent on how industrious, able, intelligent and liable *not* to panic the local magistrates were.

Sidmouth's greatest mistake in his relations with the magistrates, particularly those of Manchester, stemmed from his own character and beliefs. He had to over-rate, not so much their actual reports, as their general capabilities. He had to believe in their industry, intelligence and liability not to panic, for otherwise he could not have operated within the system. On their actual reports his reliance was less than implicit. Thus by the limitations of the system he was temperamentally incapable of changing he too was forced to employ spies. To gain a clearer picture, to counterbalance such reports as common sense made him regard askance, he sent men to snoop around the manufacturing districts. Hence Cobbett's pledge that in a reformed Parliament 'There would be none of this disgraceful spy work'. The disgraceful business came to a head in 1817. Here it should be noted that the English love of the amateur cropped up. The men who were sent on their snooping missions were not trained for the job. They were anybody who would volunteer and the result tended to be—no sedition, no pay. It was the imagination and acting ability of one man working along these lines that erupted in 1817.

If the system by which Liverpool's Government hoped to maintain order throughout the disturbed country belonged to another era, the means of enforcing it were pitiably weak. The Government had no large standing army on which they could call to suppress the revolution they anticipated. There was no central police force, in many places no police force at all. They could not, and would not, greatly augment these means because traditional English liberty in which they believed (never mind how they acted) would not have allowed such measures. If the Government was to survive without disaster it was imperative that it remove the causes of unrest, and bring the system into line with the needs of the expanding towns and cities. But this it was emotionally and temperamentally incapable of doing. So it reacted, instead of acting, on the principle that what had been good enough for grandfather's day would hopefully see us through today.

5

THAT ANOMALOUS
HERMAPHRODITE RACE
CALLED PARSON-JUSTICES

In Manchester it was a question not so much of what had done for grandfather as for antecedents long mouldering in their graves.

In a judicial decision of 1360 Manchester had been classified as a market town. In a charter dating from the same period her government was put in the hands of the Mosleys of Rolleston Hall in Staffordshire. According to the terms of this charter the head of the Mosley family appointed a steward who in turn appointed a jury, known as a Court Leet, from the freemen of the town, who in turn appointed a corps of officials headed by a Boroughreeve and two Constables. The steward's duty was to collect rents for the Lord of the Manor, the Court Leet's to make bye-laws for the market users, the Boroughreeve's to distribute endowed charities and to call and preside over public meetings, while the Constables' was to keep order within the market town.

Since 1360 very little had happened to the structure of Manchester's government. It had ambled along comfortably until the middle of the eighteenth century. As the effects of the Industrial Revolution began to make themselves felt, a few citizens became aware of the dangers of continuing to impose a medieval system on the fast expanding and violently changing town. In 1763 attempts were made to bring the system more up to date. The plan was to provide a corporation equally divided between high and low Anglicans and Dissenters. But the scheme came to nothing, the High Anglicans refusing to share the power they already possessed. In 1770, however, something was accomplished. By an Act of Parliament Manchester obtained a police commission which was authorized to clean the streets, supervise the lighting, provide fire engines and a night watch of constables. But the Act also preserved the rights and prerogatives of the existing medieval charter, so what began as an attempt towards incorporation, to the vesting of local amenities and authority in representative local hands, drifted back to the same old élite. Then in 1807 Sir Oswald Mosley, the head of the family, offered to sell his manorial rights for £90,000. The élite countered with an offer of £70,000 and no compromise being reached, the deal fell through. The judicial system, which was carried out by the magistrates, was a little more up to date having been instituted in Tudor times. In Manchester's case the magistrates were from Lancashire and Cheshire.

In 1815, therefore, the second largest city in England, with an overall population of just under 200,000 was still owned by the Mosley family. Its day-to-day government was in the hands of men with no qualifications but old-established background. Moreover, there were too few of them to deal with the problems, while in times of unrest the magistrates were empowered to enter the city and take absolute control.*

---

* Some towns were incorporated, as, for example, Nottingham. Although its local magistrates bombarded the Home Office with reports during the Luddite period, they had not the same power to act as had those of Manchester. This, it has been contended, helped save Nottingham from a Peterloo.

Who were the men who possessed such daunting power and responsibility? Among the magistrates, who held the most daunting power, it had become an unwritten rule in Lancashire that no manufacturer could serve on the bench. So they were landowners and clergymen. Theoretically, this ruling was to keep the bench unbiased in the many industrial disputes with which it had to deal. Practically, as critics, radical and otherwise, pointed out, it meant that the bench was composed of men entirely divorced from the problems not only of the masses but also of the respectable citizens. The magistrates were all High Anglican and High Tory. For as the establishment of the Protestant supremacy had been a bitterly fought battle, and the Anglican church was, in the words of Pitt the Younger, 'an essential part of the constitution', the two were one and the same. It was for this reason that Anglican clergymen in general, and magistrate-clergymen in particular, were regarded with such hatred an bitterness by the masses, and attacked so unmercifully by the Radicals. By propping up the Establishment so stoutly Anglican clergymen had grown further and further away from the feelings and needs of their flock, and by so doing had left the field wide open for the Nonconformists.

The three most important magistrates were the Reverend William Robert Hay, James Norris and the Reverend Charles Wicksted Ethelston. Hay was born in 1761, went to Westminster School, then up to Oxford. He qualified as a barrister on the Northern Circuit but, receiving few briefs, abandoned the law and entered the church. In 1802 he became rector of Ackworth near Pontefract, and Chairman of the Salford Quarter Sessions—posts which he still held at the time of Peterloo. He was an ambitious man who gave more attention to his job as chairman than as rector. Rightly so, for success as a magistrate was more likely to, and indeed did, bring rewards than slogging away as a country parson. On the surface he was smug, complacent and self-righteous but the papers and correspondence he left behind disturb the image. The Reverend Hay wanted not only to be righteous but to be loved and respected for his righteousness. After Peterloo he was detested, and if the righteousness was never destroyed it was dented. For his great personal weakness was that he was not complacent enough, and in his letters to the Home Office there is an explanatory self-justification of his actions not shown by the other magistrates.

James Norris, born *c.* 1774, was a local barrister who lived in Manchester. His legal knowledge, according to a contemporary radical, was co-extensive with the weakness of his judgment. According to Sir John Byng, the officer commanding the Northern area, he was an amiable man but timorous. Ethelston, born 1767, was a less amiable character. Educated at Manchester Grammar School and Cambridge, he took holy orders and became vicar of Cheetham Hill (then near, now in, Manchester), and later a fellow of Manchester's Collegiate College. He aspired to poetry, writing *A Pindaric Ode to the Genius of Great Britain* and *The Suicide with Other Poems*—an interesting contrast in subject matter. He was prominent in the foundation of the National, i.e., Anglican, Schools and a Book Repository for circulating Anglican tracts. He needed to be, as the Dissenters had earlier founded the Lancasterian Schools (named after their founder, Joseph Lancaster), and, of course, outnumbered Anglicans by two to one in the area. Ethelston's christianity did not run towards charity to his fellow men. 'Some of the reformers ought to be hanged, and some of you are sure to be hanged—the rope is already round your necks' was typical of comments. He as the type of magistrate who made Lord Sidmouth employ his own spies. For Ethelston believed every report, however wild or unsubstantiated, supplied by his numerous spies and transmitted them *ad hoc* to the Home Office.

Among other magistrates empowered to enter Manchester and take command of the town in times of unrest were William Hulton and Thomas William Tatton. Hulton was a prominent local landowner. He was chairman on the fatal day of Peterloo, but apart from acting with anything but a clear head, and apparently possessing some conscience, he leaves no strong impression. Tatton came from Wythenshawe Hall (Wythenshawe was then well outside the Manchester boundaries and is now the site of a 1930s model corporation housing estate). He emerges as a bluff, stupid man of few words. He answered most questions at the post-Peterloo trials with a 'Yes' or a 'No'. Advisedly, as he admitted in his deposition to the Treasury Solicitor, though nowhere else, to being short-sighted so hardly the most qualified witness of what occurred on Saint Peter's Field on August 16th, 1819. Individually or combined the magistrates were not calculated to fill one with enthusiasm as to their qualities of intellect or judgment. It will also be noted that only one of them, Norris, was resident within the 1819 boundaries of Manchester, another point on which contemporary critics seized as evidence of the magistrates' divorce, this time physical, from the problems of the town.

The men in control of the general administration of the city were also Tory and Anglican but much less church in their attitudes. They were drawn from the merchants and manufacturers and tended to be Pittites, in favour of limited Parliamentary and economic reform in so far as it affected Manchester and cotton. The Boroughreeve in 1815 was Hugh Hornby Birley. In the Pittite tradition he presided over the anti-Corn Bill meeting in Manchester, representing the masters' view that the Bill would cause a rise in prices and a consequent demand for higher wages. But the office of Boroughreeve, unlike that of magistrate, was for a limited period only. By 1819 the holder was Edward Clayton, a calico printer of no lasting imprint. However, Hugh Hornby Birley was to play an even more vital role at Peterloo as commander of one troop of the Manchester and Salford Yeomanry Cavalry. The two Constables by 1819 were John Moore Junior, a retired wine merchant, and Jonathan Andrew, a manufacturer. Moore was a gentle character, more interested in abstract science than flesh and blood beings. The bitterness, hostility and finally the violence that surrounded his days of office distressed him greatly. Although one sympathizes with his distress, he did nothing to lessen the bitterness and hostility that led to the violence. Temperamentally he was quite unsuited for the office. Jonathan Andrew was made of slightly sterner stuff but he had no understanding or appreciation of the spirit within the area.

The most important office in the day-to-day maintenance of law and order was that of the paid Deputy Constables. (The other posts were unpaid though the perquisites were obviously immense.) Upon the paid post of Deputy Constable more and more power had devolved, mainly due to the laziness of the various Constables over the years. If in 1819 the Boroughreeve and Constables were nice, weak men, the Deputy Constable, Joseph Nadin, was neither.

Born in 1765, Nadin began life as a spinner before finding his *métier* as a policeman, eighteenth-century version. From the start he was a renowned thief-catcher with the reputation for turning every offence into a felony. The rewards for a successful felonious charge were 40s plus a Tyburn ticket. A Tyburn ticket exempted the holder from any public office in the town of residence. Between 1816 and 1819 the selling price among the public-spirited citizens of Manchester was 350s to 400s. From his frequent sales Joseph Nadin amassed a tidy fortune. He had been appointed Deputy Constable in 1803, the oligarchy being impressed with his prowess in thief-catching. Unfortunately, the qualities required by a good eighteenth-century policeman were not the same as those required for dealing with political agitators. It was Nadin who had arrested John Knight and the thirty-eight weavers in 1812, in the same summary manner as he used towards the lowest pickpocket or murderer. As Deputy Constable with virtually unlimited powers of arrest, and holding corruptible power in a dozen other ways, he took a rake-off from all the brothels for example, Nadin was a force to be reckoned with. For twenty years he was said to be 'the real ruler of Manchester'. Retrospectively this is an inaccurate assessment, as in the final analysis, power lay with the magistrates, not Nadin.

However, to the populace Nadin represented 'power', because it was he they came into contact with. The magistrates, Boroughreeve and Constables were shadowy figures in the background, disliked but distantly, whereas Nadin was anything but shadowy. He was over six foot in height with, according to Bamford whom he twice arrested, 'an uncommon breadth and solidity of frame'. His voice was loud and coarse, his language even coarser. John Lees could not have told you who the magistrates were, but he could have named the Deputy Constable without hesitation, and sung one of the many songs that circulated.

> With Hunt, we'll go, we'll go,
> We'll bear the flag of liberty,
> In spite of Nady Joe.

The oligarchy would have done well to have sacked 'Nady Joe'. Such an action did not occur to them because he appeared to save them so much trouble, ruling the city with his iron fist. But it was an illusion. Nadin's corrupt, bullying, one-man band reaped a harvest of bitterness that helped drive more people into the Radical fold.

The final link in the shaky, obsolete maintenance of law and order was the military. The magistrates had the power to call upon regular troops in those self-defined times of unrest. The frequent presence of the military was not appreciated by the populace. Nor was the behaviour of many of the officers. The Radical newspaper, the *Manchester Observer*, was to ask early in 1819 of the 7th Hussars currently stationed in the area, 'Are these *heroes* aware they are now in England? Or does the delirium produced by the unexpected results of the battle of Waterloo still possess their faculties? Do they still suppose themselves in an occupied country?' The answers were No, Yes and Yes. Many officers strode around Manchester, arrogant, disdainful, supremely disinterested in the lives of their fellow Englishmen, regarding all Radicals as 'the enemy'. Typical of this breed was Major Dyneley of the Royal Artillery. But not all were of his ilk. There was among the 15th Hussars a young Lieutenant, nineteen-years-old at Peterloo, named William George Hylton Jolliffe, and his later account of the day shows a different attitude. And the officer commanding the Northern District, Sir John Byng, had none of Dyneley's arrogance or blinkered military vision.

Byng, born in 1772, was a veteran of the Peninsular Wars and Waterloo. He had the calmest, coolest and most liberal head of any major loyalist in the area. Throughout years 1816–20 Byng was much less in favour of the use of military force than were the Manchester magistrates. Or any magistrates in fact; those of Manchester merely happened to live in the county where the unrest was at its highest and most organized. All magistrates looked upon the military as an automatic extension of their authority, rather than as the second arm it was supposed to be, for use only in direst emergency. One cannot entirely blame them, for in the last resort what else had they to rely upon except the military? One can only say, as the Radicals said repeatedly, that the whole system needed drastically overhauling. Accepting the system as it stood, Byng's calmness and coolness, soothing the overwrought nerves and fears of the magistrates, almost certainly saved Lancashire from bloodshed in 1818. Unfortunately he was not present at Peterloo.

The loyalist side was not an entirely cohesive body, though as human beings usually find it easier to defend than attack, it had more overall coherence than the Radical side. But there was a split in outlook. On the one hand were the magistrates, clergymen and landowners, drawn from the strata least affected by the Industrial Revolution. With them almost to a man were the merchants, again drawn from the least affected because best established segment of the cotton hierarchy. On the other hand were the manufacturers, in the main as new a body as the working classes. Those actually in control of Manchester came from the longer established families, but they represented the new industrial power structure. Their lives revolved around cotton and they were well aware of what was occurring in the factories, and the implications of the Radical and trade unionist demands. In 1817 and 1818 the split widened. The magistrates, with their divorce from the practical problems of industry, showed some sympathy towards the struggles of the weavers and spinners. Although this time they were not supported by their normal allies, the merchants. They joined forces with the manufacturers in clinging to the old ways and refusing to give an inch to any demands. The manufacturers themselves were split. They might show a single obdurate face to the working-class distress, but the Nonconformist and Whig among them were less than enchanted with the actions of the High Tory, High Anglican oligarchy. And all of them were anti-Government when it hit their pockets, for example over the Corn Laws and cotton import duties. But in the years leading up to Peterloo, although divisions of viewpoint and interest existed, ranks were closed sharply in the face of the Radical upsurge.

At the bottom of the loyalist pyramid were the grass rooters who always supported the oligarchy. They were men who had either acquired or inherited a little money, received a little education and wanted these prerogatives kept within limited hands; the men who had the greatest fears of losing their small comforts, of being dragged down to starving weaver or spinner level. They included shopkeepers, publicans, watchmakers, insurance agents, tobacconists, farriers, horsebreakers and brewers. One hundred and twenty men, drawn from such occupations, played the most vital role at Peterloo as members of the Manchester and Salford Yeomanry Cavalry.

6

ALL THE GAOLS OF THE COUNTY ARE REMARKABLY CROWDED

From the melting pot of old and new, from attitudes untempered by flexibility Peterloo occurred. But the collision course merged slowly, and until the early months of 1819 it was by no means inevitable.

In the first phase, from Waterloo to the end of 1816, radical activity centred on London. Since the 'Glorious Revolution' of 1688 the people had possessed the right to petition the reigning monarch about their grievances. The best and most obvious way to air and obtain further support for grievances was the mass meeting. This was the main weapon used by the Radicals. Bills were posted announcing a meeting usually in Spa Fields, the traditional home of grievances, with Henry Hunt, Sir Francis Burdett or Arthur Thistlewood 'in the chair'. On the prescribed date thousands of people flocked to Spa Fields to hear the chairman and other speakers expound the points of the petition, for the reform of Parliament or the repeal of the Corn Laws. After the petition had been enthusiastically adopted the crowds went home, while it was carried to the Prince Regent who usually expressed a strong feeling of surprise and regret at his subjects' intransigence and stated that 'the difficulties and prevailing distresses were to be attributed to unavoidable causes'. The Prince Regent was of course acting as stand-in for the reigning monarch, George III, who had been mad for years.

It was during this period that Hunt gained his national reputation. He became known as 'Orator' Hunt, and the white hat he adopted as a symbol of the purity of the radical intentions became equally renowned. Throughout the country radicals old and young took to wearing white hats. During these months Lancashire was forming its Hampden Clubs and holding its own meetings but these were small in comparison with those in London. It was not until early 1817, when the clubs had formed a solid kernel of working-class radicalism, when Bamford and his contingent came down to London and swung the vote to universal suffrage that the emphasis began to switch to Lancashire.

Up to the end of 1816, Liverpool's administration, while hardly smiling benevolently on the radically inspired activity, did not openly interfere. Their acquiescence rose partly from a genuine distaste for imposing restrictions so soon after the long French wars, partly from their constant hope that the people would subside to a peaceful level of their own accord. The acquiescence ended with a meeting at Spa Fields in December 1816. This was organized by the Spenceans although Hunt and Burdett were involved, typically wasting time in quarrelling over the terms of the petition. When they finally arrived, Thistlewood was already addressing the crowds and there was considerable confusion to say the least. Part of the crowd, inflamed by the Spencean advocacy of violence, surged off to roam the streets. It was from this disorganized roaming that 'the plot to seize London' scare originated, and the Government took fright.

The reports of the plot were wild enough. There was to be a sudden rising in the dead of night, the Tower of London and the barracks would be stormed and the rest of the country merely waited the signal to follow suit. Whether the Government believed these reports or whether they seized upon them with heartfelt gratitude as the means of stamping out radicalism is difficult to assess. No tangible evidence of the means by which London was to be taken was produced. No caches of weapons were discovered. No detailed plans were unearthed, and by this time the spies were hard at work. Certainly the Government professed to believe the reports of imminent revolution, that such was the radical object. To this Cobbett made his famous reply, 'They sigh for a plot, oh how they sigh! ... They are absolutely pining and dying for a plot!' Whether they realized it or not, they were. The reaction was concrete and typical, a regression to the pattern set by the great mentor Pitt in the early days of the French Revolution. 'The System of Alarm' was re-introduced, whereby the Government announced it was in possession of fearful facts against which repressive measures had to be introduced for the good of the country, and when one set of fearful facts had evaporated another was produced.

The reports of the plot to seize London provided the first fearful set, and early in March 1817 Habeas Corpus was suspended. Sidmouth's reasons for the suspension were as typical as the action. A traitorous conspiracy to overthrow the Government had been discovered, occasioned by a spirit which had 'long prevailed in the country but especially since [the dread shadow] the commencement of the French Revolution'. Therefore immediate suspension was necessary 'for the security of His Majesty's peaceable subjects, the maintenance of our liberties, and the perpetuation of the blessings of the constitution.' The vital liberty of Habeas Corpus excepted, that was.

The effect of the suspension was immediate. No more mass meetings were called. Few fiery squibs or explosive articles were written. The probability of arrest and imprisonment without reason or trial made the game too dangerous to play. The

Lancashire Hampden Clubs started to disintegrate. Bamford writes of local radicals taking to the hills or the homes of 'safe' friends, visiting their wives and children at dead of night for fear of arrest. However, the subversion did not stop. Open meetings might be out of the question, but that did not prevent secret ones. In Manchester people assembled under the guise of Benefit Societies (still legal), botanical meetings, meetings for the relief of imprisoned reformers etc. In Oldham they were camouflaged as 'mowfin aetins' where hardy souls regaled themselves with muffins, cheese, beer and discussion.

One person the Government did rid themselves of, at least corporally, was Cobbett. At the end of March 1817 he fled to the United States. For this action he has been strongly criticized. Almost certainly he would have been arrested had he continued to edit the *Political Register* and the 'Twopenny Trash'. His voice would not have been heard whereas from the United States, allowing for the delay in transport, it was. But by taking himself out of the country at this vital period he lost influence. His ever-present financial difficulties—he had never recovered from the debts accrued during his two years in Newgate—probably influenced his decision. There was talk of the Government claiming back stamp duty on the 'Twopenny Trash' which would have bankrupted him. He was ever a man who believed in cutting his losses before they cut him. Bamford, who admittedly always liked Cobbett 'despite all his faults', said he fled the country to escape imprisonment. This was the general Radical view, as no toast was complete without reference to 'our absent friend Cobbett and may he soon return to carry on the good fight'. Distance did lend perspective to Cobbett's pen. His articles from the States were among the best he wrote, and they were still widely read. Nonetheless he was an absent friend and it was the Government rather than the radical movement that gained.

March 1817 burst with dramatic activity. As Habeas Corpus was being suspended, the Blanket March or March of the

Blanketeers took place in Manchester. It was organized by three characters we have not yet met, the Holy Trinity of Johnston,* Bagguley and Drummond. They were Lancashire Radicals of the wilder ilk. Their wildness did not extend to the Spencean *advocacy* of violence but they were not averse to using its *threat*. They lacked patience and any sense of the political art of the possible (in Bagguley's case the impatience was that of youth, he being only seventeen in 1817). They wanted reform *now,* not next year. They wanted power for the people *now* in the simple belief that once they had it Utopia would be achieved. All three worked devoutly and suffered greatly for the radical cause, and they were genuinely working class and had no financial backing. But their simple passionate beliefs and actions were the sort that frightened off the moderates, and gave credence to the middle-class Radical contention that the working-class Radicals did not possess the intelligence to rule the country.

The Blanket March showed both sides of their characters. It was both naïve and well-conceived. The issue was not Parliamentary reform but the distress in the area, so it was basically an economic not a political gesture. The idea was that volunteers would take the usual petition to the Prince Regent *personally* so that he would hear from the lips of the distressed themselves the true story of the terrible conditions prevailing in Lancashire. For the long march from Manchester to London the volunteers were to provide themselves with blankets to keep themselves warm at night. Hence the name. The idea had appeal and novelty, though the likelihood of many volunteers being allowed to reach London demonstrates the Holy Trinity's disregard for the stark facts of life in 1817. However, they were not as naïve as all that, and the underlying theme of the march was the threat of violence. The Holy Trinity assumed that thousands of volunteers would reach

---

* Johnston, Christian name John, is not to be confused with Joseph Johnson. Johnson is much the more important character in the Peterloo story.

London and their very number would force the Prince Regent to listen to them. A few days before the march, Johnston hinted at the need to reinforce the threat when he said: 'You will be easy prey if you have nothing but your open hands.' The men who volunteered for the march, and the main support, came from the spinners, though some weavers were involved. But the spinners were the agitators in 1817, their militancy spreading down from the factory élite.

The local Radical leaders, Knight, Johnson, Saxton and Fitton, neither approved of, nor participated in, the scheme. However, they did not condemn it as they did not wish to alienate potential or active supporters. But Bamford poured icy water on the whole idea, and noted with satisfaction that nobody from Middleton attended the Blanket Meeting. Many spinners from Oldham did, as it was already a strong trade unionist town. There is no evidence that John Lees was among them. It seems unlikely as the wholesale participation in Radical gestures, moderate or extreme, was still in its adolescence. However, on March 10th, 1817, between 10,000 and 30,000 people assembled on Saint Peter's Field, Manchester, this being the traditional home of Lancashire grievances, the nearest open space to the centre of the area's heart. Exact attendance figures are impossible to produce, as estimates vary wildly according to source. But even at the lowest level of 10,000 it was the largest meeting yet organized in the area.

In the event Bamford's scorn was justified. While Bagguley and Drummond were addressing the crowd, the magistrates who had no intention of letting thousands pour out of Manchester, sallied forth and read the Riot Act. The platform was then surrounded, the leaders arrested and the crowd dispersed. On the Riot Act being read an element of farce entered the proceedings. Between 300 and 1,000 men (again figures vary according to source) hurriedly left Saint Peter's Field and marched to Piccadilly (Manchester has one too) en route for London. A troop of cavalry followed them. The stragglers were picked up at Longsight, about a mile from the city centre. Another batch was apprehended at Stockport where it had decided to camp for the night. Less than half reached Macclesfield, a mere handful arrived at Ashbourne in Derbyshire, a distance of forty-six miles, and one solitary soul is supposed to have battled on to London. Bamford unkindly tells of the man with £50 in his purse, collected from sympathizers and the volunteers themselves, who was sent on in advance to procure food and lodgings, and who disappeared with the money, and thus 'for want of the necessaries' ended the Blanket March.

There were several repercussions, two of which had a vital bearing on Peterloo. The first was intangible in that the magistrates had their novel reading of the Riot Act and the successful dispersal *without casualties* at the backs of their minds two years later. The second was concrete. Shortly after the Blanket March, the Manchester and Salford Yeomanry Cavalry was formed. Its purpose was to assist magistrates in the future to maintain order in the unruly, seditious, Radically traduced city. The MYC, as it came to be known locally, was an amateur body, a cross between the Territorial Army and the Home Guard. From the start there was hostility between the MYC and the Radical populace because each feared the other. The Radicals feared the day when the MYC would use their actual power; the MYC feared the day when the Radicals would assume power and the roles be reversed.

The final incident of March 1817 was the 'Ardwick Conspiracy'. Following the reports of the plot to seize London, a similar conspiracy was unearthed in Manchester. Bamford, who should be explicit because he was arrested as a result of it, is vague. Deliberately perhaps, he can be as vague as a summer cloud at times, but more likely he knew little about it. Ardwick, now a part of central Manchester, was then on the fringe of the built-up area. At the end of March a secret meeting was held there. Bamford did not attend, though he professes (vaguely) to have heard about it. The plan supposedly was to 'Make a Moscow of Manchester', i.e., burn the town as the Russians had burnt Moscow in 1812, for the radical organizations to pour in, distract the military (note the Northern practicality, the military were to be distracted, not stormed as in London), release the prisoners from the New Bailey prison, and link up with the rest of the country. According to one of the many rumours circulating at the time, the Ardwick conspirators may have had the concrete idea of releasing the imprisoned Blanketeers from the New Bailey. However the Government produced nothing more definite than one spy's report of 'traces of an intention to issue proclamations, absolving the King's subjects from their allegiance and denouncing death against their opponents ... [but he] had not found any evidence of preparation of these proclamations'. The *Leeds Mercury* said categorically, 'it is altogether a paper insurrection'. Paper or not the Government again believed, or chose to believe, that insurrection was just around the corner, and used both the Blanket March and the Ardwick Conspiracy to justify further suspension of Habeas Corpus.

The Manchester magistrates were not idle either. After the Ardwick Conspiracy they arrested not only Bamford but 'Doctor' Healey and several other local leaders. That the magistrates were alarmed by the reports is unquestionable. But by their precipitate arrests they exhibited all their failings. They neither checked their facts nor sifted the evidence, such as it was. They swallowed the reports in one gulp, and by so doing put themselves in an awkward position. For later Lord Sidmouth requested, 'that in the future, when the names of persons, whose arrest is recommended by the Magistrates, are transmitted to me, they may always be accompanied by Depositions, stating as fully and precisely as possible the grounds upon which it has been deemed expedient to advise such a measure'. However displeased and annoyed Sidmouth was privately, the system remained. The magistrates continued to recommend arrests, Sidmouth to accept their recommendations and complain, if he thought fit, afterwards. Nobody thought of doing anything differently beforehand. Forewarned was always forearmed in this period but it never produced foresight.

Bamford recorded what it was like to be the under-dog at the receiving end of the magistrates' power and panic with Habeas Corpus suspended. He was summarily arrested by Nadin and lodged in the grim New Bailey prison in Salford. Together with Healey and six other men he was taken to London by coach in the custody of a King's Messenger. On the long journey they were all encased in leg irons. From Bow Street they were conducted to Coldbath prison. During this time no specific charge was made against them and their wives and children were left to fend for themselves, with no knowledge of their whereabouts or when, if ever, they were likely to be released.

Bamford's wife, Mima, a sterling character, made determined efforts to ascertain what had happened to 'our Sam', and with Sam as a husband she was accustomed to fending for herself and neither she nor the child starved. The first person she contacted was John Knight who gave her the cold shoulder. As the doyen of local Radicalism he stood an excellent chance of being arrested himself, and to be seen harbouring the wife of a man just arrested would not lessen those chances. But, for this action and one or two others, Bamford never forgave him.

Sam in fact was being interrogated in the Secretary of State's office in Whitehall. Of the interrogators he has left pen portraits. The man who first addressed him was 'a tall, square and bony figure, upwards of fifty years of age; and with thin and rather grey hair; his forehead was broad and prominent, and from their cavernous orbits looked mild and intelligent eyes. His manner was affable, and much more encouraging to freedom of speech than I had expected.' This was Lord Sidmouth. Sitting next to him was 'a good-looking person in a plum-coloured coat, with a gold ring on the small finger of his left hand, on which he some-times leaned his head as he eyed me over'. This was Viscount Castlereagh. These interrogations were Bamford's introduction to 'the upper classes'. During them he exhibited the other side of the ambitious, intelligent, working-class North-country coin, a certain envy and respect for those upper classes. It was a trait in Bamford that was to harden with success. In the same way as he found Lord Sidmouth affable and more sympathetic to freedom of speech than he had imagined, with later success he was to find other members of the aristocracy better than anticipated.

Healey enjoyed his interrogations. He was asked to spell his name. He replied, 'Haitch, hay, haa, l hay, y.' The strong Lancashire accent baffled the Privy Councillors so he was asked to write it down. Being barely able to write, he produced one of his cards which said, 'Joseph Healey, Surgeon, Middleton, Please Take Spoonsful of This Mixture Each Hours'. Somebody had inserted *200 tablespoonsful each 2 hours* in the blank spaces. The Privy Councillors enjoyed 'a great titter', and Healey roared with laughter, delighted to find them 'such a merry set of gentlemen'. Apart from underlining Healey's unswervingly simple, unabashed character the incident sheds an interesting light on the Privy Councillors themselves. Habeas Corpus was suspended. Healey had been torn from his home and taken to that very room without charge or trial at the dictates of the Councillors. Revolution was supposedly just around the corner. Yet the atmosphere was relaxed. The merry set of gentlemen could enjoy their titter.

After several interrogations Bamford and three others were released on bail at the end of April, the Privy Councillors being unable to prove High Treason or anything else against them. The rest, including Healey, were sent to prison, and with Habeas Corpus suspended the incarceration was for an unknown period. (It was after the release of Bamford that Sidmouth wrote his disapproving letter to the Manchester magistrates.)

The next incident to shake the Government was the 'Pentrich Revolution' which occurred three months later in June 1817. It was not Radically inspired, though its leader Jeremiah Brandreth was a friend of Cobbett's. It did not take place in Lancashire but on the Nottinghamshire–Derbyshire borders, and it had no direct bearing on Peterloo. But it was part of the unhappy atmosphere in England, and shaped Peterloo to the extent that it became firmly lodged in the magistrates' minds as another instance of the possibility of insurrection. In reality Pentrich was a sorry affair. Brandreth acquired only a handful of supporters and travelled but a few miles on the revolutionary road before tamely collapsing. But Pentrich helped to convince the Government that the country was on the brink of revolution and they must thus keep Habeas Corpus suspended. It also brought to a head the business of spies and *agents provocateurs*.

Brandreth and three other leaders were sentenced to death. On the scaffold one of them cried out, 'This is all Oliver and the government.' Oliver was the most famous spy of the period. He was a failed builder who drifted into the job of Government spy. His only qualifications appear to have been that he possessed a vivid imagination and that he was an actor *manqué*, ready to play whichever role suited him, composing the plot as he went along. That Sidmouth should employ such untrained, unsuitable characters has already been condemned. But once having employed them he failed to back them up efficiently. Oliver, for example, playing his role to perfection, was arrested as a genuine Radical, the magistrates not having been informed by the Home Office that he was in their area. It was this ill-timed arrest that led to his exposure, a job undertaken in the best journalistic traditions by the *Leeds Mercury*. Once the storm broke it was quickly taken up in Parliament by Whig and Radical members, Burdett included. The charges levelled at the Government were not only the disgracefully un-English one of employing spies, but the more serious one of deliberately sending out *agents provocateurs* to stir up trouble, to create Pentrich Revolutions. That Oliver acted as an *agent provocateur*, or tried to, is not in doubt. Both Bamford and Archibald Prentice have described the atmosphere in Lancashire in those oppressive months of 1817, when you could only talk to tried and trusted friends because the whole area was infested with spies. They wrote specifically of Oliver's activities, both claiming they helped save Lancashire 'from the follies perpetrated in Derbyshire'. But that Sidmouth deliberately sent Oliver out as an *agent provocateur* now seems doubtful. However, at the time belief in the Government's culpability was widespread, and this did not improve its relationship with the populace.

1817, therefore, drew to a close with the rift wider yet and widening. Habeas Corpus was still suspended. The Government no doubt felt it had acted wisely, following the only course open to it, and that by continued suspension it was nipping the Radical bloom in the bud. Its later apologists have argued that the suspension provided a breathing space, forcing all passions to simmer. But prolonged simmering can burn the pan. And Liverpool's was the last British Government that deemed it necessary or wise to suspend Habeas Corpus in time of peace.

Beneath the ill-advised repressive measures which stiffened resistance were Cobbett's favourite *causes*. The Government's attitude to the root economic cause remained rigid. That all the ills were economically induced was their unmelodic theme throughout the period. In this assessment they were not correct. The basic rights of man were in flood, too. But they would have been correct in assuming that the rights of man interest only a small section of the human race. The majority are interested in their own basic interests, and survival. So if the Government had done anything to back up their own diagnosis by removing just a few of the economic grievances they could have been home and partially dry. But they continued to fail to make an incision in the economic canker. Thus month by month they drove more people into the Radical fold. For a short while the tide of human rights merged with economic grievances, which is a formidable combination.

7

THE LOWER CLASSES ARE RADICALLY CORRUPTED

At the end of January 1818 Habeas Corpus was restored. The political prisoners were slowly released to return to their homes, mainly in the North. Why did the Government restore Habeas Corpus? 1817 had produced a good harvest, exports had risen slightly, and the distress had been minimally alleviated, but the state of the country had not basically improved or changed. Was it because there had been six months free from Blanket Marches, Ardwick Conspiracies and Pentrich Revolutions and therefore there was no further excuse for suspension? Because the Government thought the Radicals had either learned their lesson or disintegrated? Or because the ministers themselves disliked the suspension of this inviolable right for longer than they believed absolutely necessary?

As an action calculated to improve the relationship between Government and populace, the restoration was largely negated by the Indemnity Bill that followed. By the terms of this Bill nobody who had suffered as a result of the suspension could sue either the Government or any individual for wrongful imprisonment or damages. Over the next two years, references in Radical newspapers and speeches to the shameful Indemnity Bill were as frequent as those to the disgraceful Oliver.

If the Government had restored Habeas Corpus in the belief the situation in the country, particularly in south-east Lancashire, had improved, or that the Radical movement was finished, they were sadly mistaken. It was true that the movement was shaken by the suspension. The Hampden Clubs, for instance, never recovered from it, and for the first few months of 1818 the Radicals were disorganized. But they soon pulled themselves together, assisted by events on the union-orientated front.

1818 was the year of strikes in Lancashire, the largest, most solid, best organized strikes yet to have confronted Authority. The first to go on strike, in July, were the spinners. Their claims were that their average wage had slipped from the earlier level of 40s a week, to the 1815 level of 24s to a new low of 18s; that the application of the Corn Laws had in the meantime sent the price of essential food spiralling; that families could not live on such wages; finally, to quote one of the pamphlets they issued, '[Spinners] relieved their own sick, as well as subscribe to other casualties, therefore when their hours of labour, which are from 5 in the morning until 7 in the evening (and in some mills longer) of unremitting toil, in rooms heated from 70 to 90 degrees, are taken into consideration, we believe the public will say that no body of workmen receive so inadequate compensation for their labour.' But they also claimed that they were striking not so much for an increase as for a restoration of former wages. In 1816, the spinners said, the price of yarn had fallen, and wages had been reduced by mutual consent between masters and men, on the understanding that once the price of yarn rose wages would follow suit. In 1818 yarn prices had indisputably risen but the masters, so the spinners said, refused to honour the agreement. The masters repudiated the allegation and counter-claimed that the average wage was nearer 30s a week. Whatever the truth of the various claims, and the spinners' version seems by far the more accurate, the fight had deeper roots. It was for a larger working-class share of the cake, a desperate demand for treatment as human beings.

Was John Lees, spinner, involved? He worked for his father and as their relationship remained a friendly one he did not strike against him. But Robert Lees's position as a small-time employer was as difficult as that of his operatives. He was squeezed by the suppliers of yarn as much as his workers were by him. He was an independent-minded character so he may have been sympathetic to the strike. As support for it was solid, John, being a follower by nature, may have participated. In what did he participate? What did it mean to go on strike the days before unions were legal and when all tangible power lay with the other side?

To begin with there was obviously no strike pay as such. In this context, by the end of July the Home Office was urgently asking, 'By what means so large a body of mechanics has subsisted without any visible means of livelihood for so long a period?' The spinners subsisted from the accumulated subscriptions paid into the Benefit Societies, by support from other trades not on strike, and by donations from sympathizers. But it was at a very low level, a few shillings a week, sufficient only for a few pounds of potatoes, a few meat bones stewed for broth and a little bread. While their stomachs rumbled the spinners attended meetings, picketed factories and paraded through the streets of Manchester and Stockport with placards proclaiming their wages, conditions and demands. Some of the activity had been organized beforehand by their leaders, some of it was improvised and, as the weeks went by, some of it was spontaneous. For the first time the strikers also operated against blacklegs. Magistrate Norris wrote in an alarmed manner of operatives threatening 'to take the names and addresses of the individuals who work, and prevent their leaving their own houses ... the mother of a child carrying breakfast to it at Mr Houldsworth's mill was molested.' The incidental information about the child's breakfast underlines the conditions. But in this context it must be stressed that most people accepted that they and their children must toil—only for better wages.

What were the magistrates doing while meetings were held, mills lay idle, and thousands of spinners paraded daily through the streets of Manchester and Stockport? Why in the first place was the strike allowed to happen? Because to strike the operatives had perforce to combine. Many parts of the Combination Acts were, as the Government itself admitted, 'almost a dead letter'. Short of sending the military in strength there was no way of stopping the strike immediately. But the Government could, and did, urge the magistrates to repress it by means of the law. If they were not able to prove combination, and in the case of Johnston, Bagguley and Drummond the Government thought they could, surely they could prove seditious activity and unlawful intent.

The course the magistrates adopted was their usual confused one, though in the year of 1818 they acted with more restraint and sense than they showed in 1819. On the one hand they interfered so little in what was 'a matter of individual concern between masters and men' that by the end of August the Home Office was writing a tactful reprimand. 'You cannot be more fully impressed than Lord Sidmouth is, with the propriety of the magistrates forbearing to interfere in questions between masters and servant so long as the peace is unbroken, but it is impossible for the Secretary of State to contemplate with indifference the danger likely to result to the public weal from the existence in such a population as that of south-east Lancashire, of large bodies of men, exposed to the harangues of the disaffected demagogues.' On the other hand, the magistrates, too, were aware of the dangers. The hysterical Ethelston was soon convinced 'that the lower classes are radically corrupted ... their aim is revolution'. Every so often they attempted a repressive leap, yelping for Sir John Byng's military assistance (most requests being coolly turned down), or suggesting that the strikers be arrested under a

Rogues and Vagabonds Act of George III (the Home Office were not helpful on this one). But mainly they did not know what to do, and also felt very sorry for themselves. Hay expressed this sorrowful state. 'The difficulties of the situation of those who fill responsible situations here is great beyond anything I have experienced.' Faced with this solid strike the magistrates' position was a tough one. But nobody in those responsible positions took any of the actions that would have alleviated the difficulties, both for them and the workers, i.e., an improvement in wages and conditions. Part of the magistrates' difficulties was the attitude of the masters. As Hay wrote, 'The masters ... wholly decline to put the law into action. They are collectively and individually frightened ... and are ready to call upon the civil powers for responsibility while they neither take nor try any effectual means to cure or meet the evil.'

That the masters were frightened is indisputable. The slumbering giant of the working classes was awakening and the prospect terrified most of them out of their wits. They remained obdurate, refusing to placate the giant in the smallest way. It would not at this juncture have taken much to do so, but that the brute would respond to kind treatment they could not see. In the event the masters won hands down which convinced most of them that obduracy was the best, indeed the only, course of action. By the beginning of September the strike was on its last legs. Several factors contributed to the spinners' defeat, the major ones obviously being the masters' obduracy and their own starvation. The reduction to starvation level was, sadly, helped by one of their own members, the secretary of the organizing committee who absconded with £150, nearly all that was left, of the fighting fund. But a few days prior to the secretary's flight, the magistrates had finally taken a decisive step by arresting the five main committee members. This action was prompted by the spinners trying to organize a General Union of Trades, an idea which appalled the magistrates. At the beginning of September they also arrested Johnston, Bagguley and Drummond, after they had led 500 men from Stockport to Manchester and urged them to take violent action as passive means were not succeeding. Without leaders, without funds, without food, the spinners sullenly capitulated. By mid-September they were back at work, in exactly the same conditions and for the same wages as two and a half long, hungry months earlier.

As the spinners' strike was breathing its last gasp, that of the weavers started. The two strikes were unconnected. If large numbers of spinners were already politically or union-ally minded, the weavers were not, that is in the main. There were weavers engaged in reforming activity, Bamford for one. If the spinners were genuinely distressed, working long hours for decreasing wages, in stinking conditions, their distress was a minor heaven in comparison with that of the hand-loom weav-ers. If the statement that 'no body of workmen [i.e., the spinners] receive such inadequate compensation for their labour' had been considered by an observer he would have countered with—but what about the weavers? Their average wage had sunk from 11s a week maximum to the appalling sum of 6s a week minimum. Further attempts to petition Parliament for a minimum wage had achieved nothing. So finally in desperation, without any political undertones, without Radical or union organization, the weavers went on strike, for a wage increase of 7s a week.

In their case even the magistrates were sympathetic. Seven shil-lings a week would only have brought their wages up to 13s a week minimum and 21s maximum, hardly princely sums even by 1818 standards. The magistrates said the masters could well afford the increase and that to give it would relieve tension, not increase it. In this assessment, for once, how very right they were. Had the masters granted such an increase there would probably have been no Peterloo. A few of the more sympathetic or sensible masters did concede the 7s, and they were neither bankrupted nor assailed with further demands. But the majority refused to budge. It was the general failure of this strike that turned the mass of previously non-political weavers towards the Radicals as their only home for future amelioration. Once roused and committed, the weavers proved stalwart adherents. They provided the same backbone for Peterloo as the spinners had for the Blanket March.

One factor which both strikes shared was the comparative lack of violence displayed by the workers. Its significance was not lost on Sir John Byng who commented: 'The peaceable demeanour of so many thousand unemployed men is not natural; their regular meeting and again dispersing shows a system of organization of their actions which has some appearance of previous tuition.' Indeed it had, and the Radicals took note and extended the discipline and tuition greatly; it was to frighten the magistrates as much, if not more, than 'natural' violence would have done. However, to keep them comparatively happy in 1818 *some* violence occurred during both strikes. The spinners attacked a factory in Manchester, urged on by the Holy Trinity. A volley of stones was hurled at Hugh Hornby Birley's factory in Oxford Road, Manchester. The fact that he was already a prominent member of the MYC may have contributed to this action. Sir John Byng dispersed a body of weavers marching from Manchester to Ashton-under-Lyne, but he did it by 'gentle means' and everybody went home, if not happy, at least unscathed.

The failure of the direct strike action helped the Radicals. Having pulled themselves from the doldrums, they firmly set themselves to the task of convincing the masses that the repeal of the Combination Acts and the Corn Laws was inevitable once Parliamentary reform had been achieved. In fact, every known ill would disappear and Utopia would be established in England's green and pleasant land once Parliament was reformed and power lay in the hands of the People. Much of the Radical argument was as simple as that. To this all-embracing nostrum the desperate people of Lancashire began to respond in ever larger numbers. Retrospectively, it is both sad and touching how great a faith the working-class Radicals placed in Parliamentary reform. Or perhaps they were right. Had their demands been met maybe England would have been a little nearer Utopia. It is sad and touching how great a faith they placed in human nature, believing as they did, that the impetus their movement was gaining could be sustained; the cohesion, fervour and enthusiasm maintained. It was their simple nostrum (at the lowest level of the movement, that is, at a higher level it was not such a naïve programme) and their failure to assess human nature that made the middle-class Radicals so chary of them.

The impetus, the enthusiasm and the fervour did not happen by magic. It was achieved by a great deal of hard work. Open-air meetings in the cotton towns and on the moors increased. Month by month Radical orators banged the drum of Parliamentary reform. Knight and Fitton were tireless addressers of meetings, travelling miles from Blackburn to Manchester, from Oldham to Stockport, from Ashton-under-Lyne to Bolton, from Royton to Bury. Bamford was not such a tireless traveller but he was a constant supporter and organizer of meetings in the Middleton vicinity. At one held on the moors near Saddleworth, he insisted on the right of the females present to vote. 'When the resolution was put, the women held up their hands, amid much laughter; and ever from that time females voted with the men at Radical meetings.' Female attendance and, after Bamford's resolution, participation was on the increase, though the formation of their own clubs lay ahead.

It was also at this period that Bamford wrote his *Lancashire Hymn*. He said he borrowed the idea from the Methodists whose religious assemblies were much enhanced by the introduction of vocal music. Why should the Radicals not add heart-stirring songs to their meetings? So he sat down and composed the hymn 'to one of the finest trumpet strains I ever heard'. He does not state which tune, and the idea of singing it at meetings in any case fell through. John Knight cold-shouldered it, as he had

Mima in her distress in 1817, which was another action for which Bamford never entirely forgave him. But sung or unsung, the *Lancashire Hymn* became the anthem of the Northern Radicals, and Bamford's fame spread. The first and last verses—there were six in all—give the measure of Sam Bamford, poet. Handy to have around, to be able to sit down and knock out the verses, but hardly of immortal stature.

> Great God, who did of old inspire
> The patriot's ardent heart,
> And fill'd him with a warm desire,
> To die, or do his part;
> Oh! let our shouts be heard by Thee,
> Genius great of liberty.
>
> Souls of our mighty sires! Behold
> This band of brothers join.
> Oh! never, never be it told,
> That we disgrace your line;
> If England wills the glorious deed,
> We'll have another Runnimede.

8

DO UNTO OTHERS AS YOU
WOULD THEY SHOULD DO
UNTO YOU

At the end of October 1818 the first Union Society was formed in Stockport. Its founder was the Reverend Joseph Harrison. He was a local Methodist preacher and teacher who called himself 'chaplain to the poor and needy'. He was a long-standing reformer who had worked closely with Johnston, Bagguley and Drummond. It was he who felt the need for a declaration of Radical objectives that would not only provide an umbrella for the dissonant voices of discontent, but would state the means by which the common man could achieve them.

Harrison drew up the most detailed and comprehensive plans for his Union Society in Stockport, as a result of which, he hoped, a network would spread throughout the country. The heady object of the Society was to promote human happiness. Its maxim was 'do unto others as you would they should do unto you'. Its declaration stated that men are born free, that sovereignty lies with the people and that association (here the union bait) is necessary to preserve human rights. There were twenty-six very long rules which incorporated both the objects of the Society and the standards by which the members should conduct themselves to achieve them. The twenty-fifth was the most important in the Radical context. It stated that with the present corrupt Government it was impossible 'to do unto others as you would they should do unto you'. Therefore, members were expected to work for 'a radical reform of Parliament by means of suffrage of all male persons of mature age and sane minds, who have not for any crime forfeited the right of Parliament having a duration of not exceeding one year; and elections by ballot'. A strong emphasis was also placed on the training of the people for power, so that they should not abuse it once they had received it, underlining the Radical belief in the intelligence and perception of the working classes.

The system by which the people would receive their training for power was as detailed and comprehensive as the rules. Stockport was divided into twelve districts, each district subdivided into classes of twelve (presumably the biblical influence of the apostles). In the house, or room, of a class leader, duly elected by democratic vote, a meeting was held once a week. There as in the Hampden Clubs, the Radical papers were read out loud and discussion took place on how ultimate human happiness could best be achieved. All views were welcome, as were practical suggestions as to how more groups could be started and funds raised. Funds were from the start a major problem. Each member paid 1d a week, but this did not cover one half of the ambitious projects of the Society. As Harrison himself said in 1819, when the conception was spreading fast, 'As the cause of reform advances, it becomes more and more expensive, and means more and more circumscribed.' He added, 'The weavers are the best givers; but, alas, they have nothing to give now'—which shows how strong and firm the weavers' adherence to the Radical cause had become.

Apart from the intimate class meetings, central Union Rooms were rented and the money mostly went in their upkeep. Here the members gathered once a month for a general meeting at which every aspect of the Society, present and future, was discussed. For example, plans were made for libraries, funds permitting, and for electing representatives to present their petitions to the local magistrates and later, it was hoped, to London. At these general meetings the local Radical leaders appeared to give impassioned speeches. But the Union Rooms did not lie idle for the other nights of the month. Monday, Tuesday, Thursday and Friday evenings they were open for classes in reading, writing and simple arithmetic. Wednesday the members could, if not exhausted, attend for general reading out loud of important literature, both Radical and Classical.

Harrison's firm belief in education extended, as has every successful religious or political creed, to the children. On Sundays the Union Rooms were open for them. About this particular move the 'established' Methodists waxed furiously. 'The reformers ... have even opened schools to forward their detestable purpose. They have hereby infringed upon our particular territory as instructors of youth, and carried their unholy warfare into our very camp.' Officially, the Union Sunday Schools were not politically inspired. They were there to instil the rudiments of education into a few more of the thousands of children nobody else provided for. But that the atmosphere was political is undeniable. Along with the ABC the children were taught the simple rights of man, so that if the Radical cause failed in this generation it would succeed in the next.

Harrison's feeling that a detailed scheme was needed that would draw in the common man was justified in that his hopes for a network went far beyond expectation. As soon as the Stockport Society was under way, similar groups started in the nearby cotton towns. Once the official declaration of the Union Society had been published in the *Manchester Observer* early in 1819, further societies shot up like grass in a wet summer, not only in Lancashire but throughout the country. They bridged the various reforming gaps and provided the Radicals with an invaluable backbone, much stronger than the Hampden Clubs had been.

An off-shoot of the Union Societies was the formation of the all-female societies, which likewise started in 1819. The first female union was formed in Blackburn by Mrs Alice Kitchen. It was modelled on Harrison's principles, with its own indoctrination additive, 'to instil into the minds of our children, a deep and rooted hatred of our corrupt and tyrannical rulers'. Dozens of female unions followed in the wake of Blackburn. It was an interesting phenomenon. The women could have continued to assist their menfolk and to instil Radical principles into their children within the framework of the male societies. Yet they decided to go it alone. They organized and ran their own societies most efficiently. They issued their own pamphlets, some of them very high-flown in tone. One particular pamphlet written by Susanna Saxton, wife of John and secretary of the Manchester Female Reformers, was intimidatingly addressed to her 'Dear Sisters of the Earth'. Although it must be admitted that nowhere in any of the pamphlets, speeches or addresses does the claim for female suffrage appear, was it not implicit in the separate societies? Had the Radical upsurge continued surely there would soon have been a demand from these efficient ladies for *their* rights. What happened to this female spirit is not within the scope of this book. Nor why it went into Victorian decline and remained dormant for the rest of the century; to emerge again in Manchester where the Suffragette Movement was officially born in 1905, when Annie Kenney of Saddleworth and Christabel Pankhurst of Manchester interrupted a Liberal meeting at the Free Trade Hall and were subsequently imprisoned. But it is worth noting that there was this strong, active, independent female movement in the early nineteenth century, particularly for those who believe that English women have always enjoyed their role as second-class citizens.

The Union Societies, male and female, preached to the already converted, or the willing to be converted. Considerable as their numbers were by early 1819, and they were swelling each week, the majority of the populace remained in a state of uncomprehending or apathetic misery. They had to be stirred. Apart from the meetings, there was another channel through which they could be reached—the printed word. In the days before wireless and television the importance of the newspapers cannot be over-estimated. For even if thousands could not themselves read, they could be read to, and there were more than sufficient converts to perform this chore. There were six newspapers circulating in the Manchester area in 1819 which is an indication of the importance of the medium. They were all weeklies, selling at a price of sevenpence, fourpence of which was stamp duty. Four of the six were staunchly pro-Government, the *Manchester Chronicle*, the *Exchange Herald*, the *Manchester Mercury* and the *British Volunteer*. They varied from the reasoned but stodgy, to the unreasoned and downright boring. The fifth, the *Manchester Gazette*, for which John Edward Taylor wrote, followed the middle-class Radical line and was intelligent and interesting if above the heads of the masses. The sixth was the *Manchester Observer*. It was founded in 1818 to propagate the cause of Radical Reform. Joseph Johnson provided part of the money, the rest came from subscriptions from sympathizers and the pocket of James Wroe, who became its chief proprietor and editor. It was he who bore the brunt of the subsequent prosecutions. The subeditor, who wrote a great many of the leading articles, was John Saxton.

There is a tendency today to talk as if popular journalism, as well as mass circulation, came in with Northcliffe. A glance through a copy of the *Manchester Observer* would dispel this illusion. It had an outraged, emphatic, racy style. One adjective was never used when six would serve. It carried the common practice of *underlining* to a fine art. It used parody: '*The Prince Regent's*

Speech as It Ought to be. It is with regret that I have opened my eyes so late in the interest of myself and my people … I have learnt from experience that splendour is not happiness—that extravagance is not taste—that prodigality is not greatness—that pride is not magnanimity … I will no longer tolerate the robbery of the industrious for the luxurious support of the idle and debauched. I call upon you to examine … and to take into your first consideration, the great and vital question of Reform for which a million and a half of my subjects, I am informed, have petitioned' etc. It hit good and hard, 'The first thing that would be moved in an honest House of Commons, would be the IMPEACHMENT OF LORD SIDMOUTH for his recent conduct'. It had its poets' corner, full of verses such as:

> Let foes of freedom dread the name,
> But should they touch the sacred tree,
> Millions of willing swords shall flame,
> For COBBETT, HUNT AND LIBERTY.

It had its dialect columns, keeping in touch with local roots, a simple sample of which is, 'un woo, uts o'spark ofeelin' e-thur breast forth distresses othur fello creatures, isnut a reformer, in his hart?' It provided good foreign coverage: Napoleon's doings on Saint Helena,* Mungo Park's death in the interior of Africa, Simon Bolivar's declaration of the Republic of Venezuela, and numerous letters from the land of the free, the United States. They were mainly on the lines of one from 'Your Obedient Servant, Hugh Oldham, 367 Arch Street, Philadelphia', who wrote: 'We have no great pension to pay for people to govern or rob the poor; no gagging bills! No suspension of people's rights!

---

* As an ex-reformer, Napoleon was popular with the Radicals. He was accorded much the same respect by Napoleonic war veterans as was Rommel by the Eighth Army in the Second World War.

No occasion here to call upon the people to unite round the standard of liberty and freedom ... Nor no paying of £10,000 a year to a graceless son [the Prince Regent, of course] ... but may the sun of heaven shortly shine all its splendour upon my native land England, and expel the whole host of reptile vermin from their hiding holes! N.B. porter and Cyder as good as any in England, for three dollars, eighteen gallons, spirits and tobaccos for almost nothing.' That the *Manchester Observer* was a paper of dying Regency England, as opposed to oncoming Victorian England, is shown by a regular advertisement appearing on its front page. 'Dr Hallet's Anti-Veneral Merone Pills, sold in boxes at 2s 9d, 4s 6d and 11s each, duty included; and given gratis with each box a treatise on the Veneral Diseases; and so simplified that patients of either sex may cure themselves, without restraint or diet or hindrance, or even the knowledge of a bed fellow.'

The *Observer*'s main function was to spread the Radical message. To this task it applied itself with the utmost serious-ness. Either Saxton or Wroe was overfond of quoting Plato, the intellectual touch to impress the masses, but the editorials and lead columns had a tough pugnacious quality. Often they had depth and always they had readability. Whether relaying information about Hunt, Cartwright, Cobbett or local Radicals, whether attacking the Government, the magistrates or Nadin, the words had the vital urgency that carries the eye along. In Union Societies, in public and private houses, hundreds of eyes were carried along. They stored the message, the satire and the Lancashire version of schmaltz, and soon a thousand tongues were repeating them.

Week by week the *Manchester Observer* captured the mood of the moment. Week by week its circulation increased. By the time of Peterloo it was selling between three and 4,000 copies weekly which was a very high figure for the period. Its influence was not confined to Lancashire. By the end of 1819 it had agents from Glasgow to London, from Nottingham to Whitehaven. Hunt said it was 'the *only* newspaper in England that I know, fairly and honestly devoted to such reform as would give the people their whole rights'. This view and the extent of its influence was seconded by the magistrates, if hardly in the same words. Norris in particular was constantly sending copies to the Home Office, with equally constant bleats about the *Observer's* seditious effect. But until mid-1819 no action was taken against it, and the paper continued to make trenchant hay while the magistrates frowned.

The best the pro-Government papers could offer in response to the *Observer's* onslaughts was the gospel of patience and acceptance, synthesized by William Paley in his *Reasons for Contentment Addressed to the Labouring Part of the British Public*. Paley first delivered his *Reasons* as a sermon from the pulpit of Carlisle Cathedral where he was Archdeacon. That was in the year 1790 when the discontent was in its infancy, and they passed largely unnoticed. But as discontent grew, good reasons for content were in short supply, and by 1819 Paley's had been published as a tract, paraphrased in the pro-Government newspapers and parroted by sympathetic loyalists.

The tract is cogently argued. Paley starts by comparing human life to that most popular analogy, the theatre. From his analogy he draws the immediate conclusion that the wisest advice is never to allow one's attention to dwell on comparison. But if one must dwell it should be realized that providence, against which it is impious to complain, has contrived that while fortunes are only for the few, the rest of mankind may be happy without them. Indeed the rest of mankind is much better off without them, because the consequence of liberty induced by riches is the perplexity of choice. He then moves on to the active pleasures of being poor. What joy is there in taking from a large unmeasured fund? And there is the ease with which the poor can provide for their children which, according to Paley, is contained in two words, 'industry and innocence'. Whereas with the rich there is real difficulty in finding the jobs which will continue to support their children in the luxury to which they have been accustomed. There is the danger of indulgence through which desires become dead. Paley admits this is a danger to which the poor will never succumb, 'but the peasant whenever he goes abroad, finds a feast whereas the epicure must be sumptuously entertained to escape disgust'. Although the poor may envy the rich man in his house, they do not realize how little the rich appreciate the luxury of living in a big house. Religion, of course, soothes all inequalities because it unfolds the prospects which make all earthly distinctions meaningless. In conclusion, the life of labour has advantages which compensate for all its inconveniences. It keeps the body in better health and above all it is free from the anxieties that beset great men.

That Paley failed to appreciate that the old paternalistic structure—'God bless the squire and his relations/Who keep us in our proper stations'—had been shattered by the Industrial Revolution is understandable. That he believed in the structure is also understandable. On the practical level his *Reasons* simply would not do. There were thousands of spinners and weavers *prepared* to accept their lot by birth. But they could not follow the life of labour because there was insufficient work. Their chances of finding a crust of bread, never mind a feast, for their unjaded palates was growing less every month. Their children were dying without an opportunity of acquiring industry or innocence.

For the prepared-to-accept Paley's theme was developed by sympathetic loyalists and Tory newspapers into exhortations to be patient but a while longer and things would sort themselves out, or be sorted out for them by their anxiety-beset betters. But facing them was the grave. Urging them from the path of acceptance with much more exciting and enticing carrots were the Radicals. In the battle of words the Radicals won hands down.

All round, by the end of 1818, the Radical snowball was well under way. The failure of the strikes, and the continuing spread of misery and unemployment, was the well-spring on which they drew. But the buckets by which they hauled up the water owed nothing to chance and everything to organization. Despite the growth of Radicalism, by the end of the year Lord Sidmouth was feeling happier—at least about Manchester. 'The combination at Manchester is now nearly dissolved ... the arrest of Johnston, Bagguley and Drummond, the failure of the pecuniary supplies, and the admirable arrangements of Sir John Byng, in conjunction with the civil authorities, have effected this fortunate change.' He looked forward to an even happier New Year which shows how out of touch he was, spy system or no spy system.

Personally, Sidmouth was deeply unhappy. His younger brother, Hiley Addington, who for many years had been his confidant and had acted as a buffer for much outside hurt, whom he had loved as greatly as he was capable of loving, had died during the year. In fact, he wanted to retire, but unfortunately for himself, his memory and his country he was persuaded to stay on as Home Secretary. Had he retired would Peterloo have occurred? It would have needed a very strong-minded man to have changed the magistrate system within six months. Although a stronger, clearer minded, more liberal Home Secretary could have given the necessary clear directives to, and left less in the hands of, the magistrates. Who was there? Canning? Unlikely to be interested in the Home Office. The young Robert Peel? Huskisson? Both were strong possibilities and either would have been infinitely better. But the unhappy Lord Sidmouth remained in office.

There was one final event in the year of 1818 that could have changed the course of Peterloo had it been successful. This was yet another attempt to buy the manorial rights to Manchester from Sir Oswald Mosley. The oligarchy had been stirred into action by various scandals, unearthed by the Radicals, working and middle class, and by the activities of 'Nady Joe' in connection with 'the Hindley affair'. Two boys had been given stolen property by a minion of Nadin's named Hindley, and then arrested on charges of felony. After the affair was made public by the Radicals,

Hindley was dismissed. Although Nadin survived, this and other justified charges of bribery, corruption and incompetence led to a general feeling that the time had come for Manchester to have its own corporation. Mosley offered to sell the rights for £90,000, but this time the deal collapsed from the rearguard action of the oligarchy working on the fears of the small shopkeepers and ultra loyalists. Somebody would have to find the £90,000. Who would it be? Not the interfering Radicals who were mainly too poor to pay taxes but the small shopkeepers who were not. Thus ultimate control of Manchester remained in the magistrates' hands.

9

I ACCEPT WITH PLEASURE THE INVITATION OF THE COMMITTEE

1819 opened with what turned out to be a dress rehearsal for Peterloo. The fallible theatrical dictum of 'good dress rehearsal, bad show' this time proved true.

As the New Year dawned, the local Radical leaders held a meeting at which they decided the time had come both to test and prove their growing strength. Accordingly they wrote to Hunt asking for the honour of his attendance at a public meeting to be held on Saint Peter's Field on January 18th. The avowed purpose of the meeting was to petition the House of Commons for the immediate repeal of the Corn Laws. But the fact that Hunt accepted the invitation underlines the mounting importance of Lancashire in the Radical field. Because Hunt had never previously left the South.

The *Manchester Observer* ran both the full text of the invitation and Hunt's acceptance, which was in his usual fulsome tone. He began on a noble note: 'Although my absence from home at this time will be attended with considerable inconvenience to myself personally, yet I feel now, as I ever have, and I trust I ever shall, that no private consideration ought to prevail, when put in competition with a great public duty.' He continued by expressing his reluctance to be present at a meeting where yet another petition was to be considered for presentation to the House of Commons: 'A House is no respect differently constituted from the last, which treated the Prayers and Petitions of the People with contempt and derision'. Yet, 'the irresistable impulse to become better acquainted with the bravest of brave reformers, the men of Lancashire' impelled him to accept the invitation.

By means of the public correspondence, John Lees and the thousands of undecided Lancastrians learned that the famous 'Orator' Hunt was to honour their county with his presence. As a result of reading this information, or having it read to them, some people turned up from curiosity or interest. However, the attendance on January 18th was not high, about 10,000 people. But if the time of year is taken into consideration, together with the facts that Manchester is a cold damp place in early January, and that the Union Societies were in their infancy, it was not a bad figure. What was encouraging to the Radical leaders was the organized manner in which parts of the crowd arrived, with bands playing and banners fluttering. Such organization, which had not been seen before, provided further proof of the growing strength of the movement.

Hunt, not slow to note such proof, addressed the crowd with his usual confidence and magnetism. Pursuing the theme of his acceptance letter, he urged them to draw up a Remonstrance, addressed directly to the Prince Regent, rather than sending yet another petition to the House of Commons where it was sure to be kicked out. The idea was enthusiastically adopted, and a Remonstrance and Declaration were later drawn up. These two documents, which went far beyond the avowed purpose of the repeal of the Corn Laws, present the working-class Radical case at its coherent best.

After the meeting had dispersed peaceably, Hunt attended a dinner at the Spread Eagle Inn in Manchester. Such dinners were customary, serving both social and propaganda purposes. From the social angle an invitation gave local Radicals lower down the ladder a feeling of importance, and it might induce influential people sympathetic to the cause to contribute some much-needed money. From the propaganda angle, the speeches and toasts were fully reported in the *Manchester Observer*. Thus John Lees and the anonymous thousands like him learned of the growing importance of the movement, and its constant care for *their* problems. The toast after this January dinner was typical: 'The source of all legitimate power, the people; the Rights of Man; the immortal memory of Hampden, Sydney and Russell; the immortal memory of Tom Paine; the venerable father of reform, Major Cartwright; our banished countryman William Cobbett and may we all witness his speedy return; the beautiful Lancashire witches; the brave Reformers of Lancashire; the poor weavers of Lancashire, and may the day soon arrive when their labours may provide not only sufficient to supply their wants but to give them the comforts of life.' The only discordant note was the Lancashire witches, as sad a bunch of women as ever graced Lancashire soil. Was their inclusion a back-handed compliment to the Female Reformers? Or did they qualify because they had fallen foul of authority?

The dress rehearsal was an all-round success which means that the other side, the magistrates, behaved with good sense and restraint. In January, although they were alarmed by the entry of the gladiator Hunt into their arena, although they wrote copious letters to the Home Office, although they had troops standing at the ready in barracks on the 18th, they did not call upon those troops. Thus the meeting dispersed peaceably. For their forbearance and restraint they received Lord Sidmouth's highest congratulations. Throughout this first visit of Hunt to Manchester they continued to show restraint. He remained in the city for some time after the meeting, and his presence did not pass without further incident.

On the evening of January 22nd Hunt went to the Theatre Royal. As he entered the auditorium a large section of the audience gave him a standing ovation. As the people continued to stamp and cheer, the loyalist section called for the National Anthem to be played. After some indecision the band finally obliged. The loyalists then claimed that Hunt hissed during the playing of 'God Save the King'. This charge he denied and it does not sound in character. For one thing he had a prudent strain, and for another, one can imagine Hunt bellowing but not hissing. However, as a result of the alleged hissing, several officers of the 7th Hussars surrounded Hunt and forcibly ejected him from the theatre. He was not a man to be thus treated in any circumstances, but to do so in full view of his supporters was asking for trouble. Hunt reacted predictably and immediately. He sent for Bamford and asked him to supply a dozen or so stout Middletonians so that he could make a further visit to the Theatre Royal, with them acting as a bodyguard, should further insult be offered to his person. Bamford obliged. The word 'predictably', when applied to Hunt meant 'publicly', so that the whole of Manchester knew of his return visit. On the appointed night, Bamford and his bodyguard arrived to find the theatre closed on the magistrates' orders. A large crowd, having heard of the prospect of an alternative entertainment to that on stage, had gathered and were milling around the theatre. So were Nadin and his minions and the magistrate Sylvester. But no violence occurred. Neither Nadin nor Sylvester interfered when Hunt, never one to miss an opportunity, addressed the assembled throng.

During this address Bamford quotes Hunt as saying that the authorities only wanted a pretext to let the bloody butchers of Waterloo loose upon the people. One wonders if Hunt really said this, or whether the idea of January as a dress rehearsal for Peterloo also went to Bamford's head. The 'bloody butchers of

Waterloo', in retrospect, sounds almost too coincidental. After the uninterrupted harangue the crowd broke up. Bamford and his stout Middletonians went carousing until midnight, while Hunt returned to his lodgings at the Spread Eagle Inn. There he was again attacked by sundry officers of the 7th Hussars and the odd loyalist who entered his room and challenged him to a fight. Again nothing came of this incident, apart from Hunt writing to the Duke of York as Commander-in-Chief of the 7th Hussars, and taking out a warrant against one of his attackers for assault on his person—in both cases unsuccessfully. Shortly afterwards Hunt left Manchester. But there was to be a kick-back to the Spread Eagle attack. It occurred the day before Peterloo. It involved one James Murray who had participated in the incident, and it was not to improve the Radical prospects for that day.

The January meeting, and the various incidents described above, revealed new undertones to the situation. There was nothing illegal in suggesting a Remonstrance rather than a Petition, but it was more definite and aggressive. Whether Hunt actually used 'the bloody butchers' phrase or not, the language of the Radicals was also becoming aggressive. In this context Bentham was later to say that Radical language far outran Radical intentions and this, retrospectively, is true. But to the magistrates and loyalists on the spot, to whom a Radical was 'a libellous, seditious, factious, levelling, revolutionary, republican, democratical, atheistical villain'—to quote a contemporary letter—all the villains were growing too big for their boots and needed putting back in their places. The only way they could think of doing this was by violence, such as the attacks on Hunt. In January these were only the seeds of violence, but there was little indication that the Government, magistrates or loyalists would either uproot them or shrivel them to death from lack of water. It was from January that attitudes started to harden until the gap between loyalist and Radical was so wide as to be insurmountable, and led with sad inevitability to Peterloo.

At the beginning of the cold, wet month of February there were one or two small meetings to keep the Radical flag flying. Royton had one organized by the energetic William Fitton, to protest against the Corn Laws and paper money and to call for, needless to say, a radical reform of the House of Commons. But the next important meeting was held in mid-February on Sandy Brow in Stockport. It was organized by the Reverend Harrison, with John Knight and John Saxton also on the platform. This meeting was attended by the military, which perhaps indicates that the magistrates currently regarded Stockport as the premier sink of seditious iniquity, or were particularly frightened of Harrison's influence. After a Remonstrance, again not a Petition, had been passed, a further resolution was proposed to aid Messrs Johnston, Bagguley and Drummond then awaiting trial. Towards the end of the meeting a scuffle broke out, as some of the troops tried to seize a Cap of Liberty.* The attempt was a failure and, encouraged by their success, the crowd swarmed to the Wind Mill Rooms where the customary public dinner was to be held. The troops, constables and magistrates followed them. The crowd refused to disperse, so the Riot Act was read. As nobody took any notice the magistrates asked Harrison to use his influence to disperse the crowd, which he did, assuring them that neither he nor any of the leaders was in danger of arrest. The crowd then swarmed to the Market Place where the Riot Act was again read, and this time the troops dispersed them. But half an hour later the crowd had regrouped, and the Riot Act was read a third time before the day came to an end.

There was more than sufficient incident in this February day further to alarm magistrates and loyalists. Equally there was an indication of how rowdy meetings and post-meeting occurrences

---

* The Cap of Liberty had originally been the symbol of granting a slave his freedom in Roman times. It was increasingly carried by the Radicals as a symbol of their desire to be set free from misery and oppression.

could be kept under control, by the continued good sense of the magistrates, and co-operation between them and the Radicals. In Stockport even the *Manchester Observer* spoke of the demeanour of the magistrates being such as to entitle them to the thanks of the friends of liberty.

Unfortunately, the brows of Mr Norris and others, whose jurisdiction covered Manchester rather than Stockport, grew considerably more furrowed as a result of this meeting. Norris wrote a long letter to the Home Office in which he regretted the attempt to seize the Cap of Liberty, as to the Radicals it might have taken on the appearance of a triumph. As such they certainly regarded it. Lancashire and Cheshire's very own poet, Bamford, soon composed a set of commemorative verses, one of which ends with a particularly excruciating couplet.

> Then proudly let our banner wave
> Wi' freedom's emblem o'er it,
> And toasted be the Stockport lads,
> The lads who bravely bore it.
> And let the 'war-worn' Yeomanry,
> Go curse their sad disasters,
> And count, in rueful agony,
> Their bruises and their plasters.

In his letter to the Home Office, Norris thought he saw in the Stockport meeting a prelude to the repetition of last summer's dreadful occurrences. How right he was! But apart from tentatively suggesting that the Government might do something to alleviate the economic conditions, particularly those of the weavers, and by so doing remove the cause for their adherence to the Radical movement; and asking if the forthcoming Parliamentary debate on the cotton trade could not be postponed, now not being a good time to air and thus exacerbate grievances, he had no fundamental suggestions as to how the rot could be stopped.

Neither had Lord Sidmouth, who made soothing noises in reply. He regretted that assistance could not be afforded either by the legislative or executive branch of Parliament to the labouring classes, and that the cotton debate could not be postponed because of pressures from the Opposition. But he had the helpful thought that should Norris's fears about a repetition of 1818 be correct, the experience then gained would stand him and his fellow magistrates in good stead. Finally, as always, there was the comfort of the law: 'It should be proved by legal proceedings that a seditious speech is not to be made with impunity.'

For the next two months there was a respite from meetings, which did not mean that either Radicals or magistrates were idle—far from it. In March a declaration of the objects and principles of Harrison's Union Society appeared in the *Manchester Observer*, and the models mushroomed. Among them, at the end of March, was the Patriotic Union Society in Manchester. All the leading Radicals were members, with Johnson, then Knight, as its Secretary, and Wroe as its Treasurer. Its foundation was vital to Peterloo, as the fatal invitation to Hunt was issued by its members.

It was from the end of March that the magistrates began to be convinced, to quote Norris, 'that a general insurrection is seriously meditated'. Their conviction was probably linked with the spread of the Union Societies. Like a pair of bloodhounds Norris and Ethelston started sniffing for the weapons that would prove the revolutionary intent. The weapon they alighted upon was the pike which their spies were despatched to unearth. They had little success. By the end of April only one pike had been produced whose purpose could have been anything. But the lack of success did not deter Ethelston or Norris from their gloomy convictions of impending revolution. Many loyalists increasingly shared such a conviction on even less concrete evidence.

10

A GENERAL INSURRECTION IS SERIOUSLY MEDITATED

From the end of May the signs of impending revolution, in loyalist eyes that is, mounted weekly. For from May onwards the Radical activity not only revived, but grew in momentum. It was triggered off by Lord Sidmouth's refusal to present the Manchester and Stockport Remonstrances of January and February to the Prince Regent. People felt, and the Radicals obviously encouraged them to feel, that this refusal made clear the Government's indifference to their plight. The cry of Parliamentary reform acquired extra meaning. The snowball would have begun to roll anyway, given the growing strength of the Union Societies, the deepening distress, and the untiring efforts of Knight, Saxton, Healey, Bamford, Johnson and the rest. As it was, Radical organization, the fine weather and the refusal coincided. The result was a flood of meetings from Blackburn in the north of 'the affected area', to Macclesfield in the south. The purpose of most of them was the same, radical reform of the House of Commons. This was expressed in its highest form at a Blackburn meeting on July 5th: 'to unite in re-establishing a government in its pristine purity, which was founded on the principles of eternal justice and the Rights of Man'.

For using this pristine purity, among many other statements, John Knight was later indicted for sedition. Statements at a Stockport meeting on June 28th also led to indictments against Sir Charles Wolseley and the Reverend Harrison. However, the law as it stood was not wholly on the magistrates' side. Once indicted, provided he could furnish the bail demanded, the utterer of the seditious statements was free to go about his business uttering further seditious statements if he chose, until his trial came round. He was also legally able to postpone his trial and the practice was known as 'traversing in a misdemeanour'. It was a practice to which all magistrates objected strenuously. Of course if you could not furnish bail you languishd in gaol, as did Johnston, Bagguley and Drummond for months after their indictments in 1818. They were finally tried, and sentenced to prison in the spring of 1819 which removed them from the Peterloo scene.

The June Stockport meeting was the largest in the area outside Peterloo, over 20,000 people attending. This was not surprising considering Stockport's long-standing militancy, but the leap in attendance underlines the invaluable work done by the Union Societies. Wolseley made his customary reference to the storming of the Bastille—'and heaven knows I would assist in storming the English Bastille'—while Harrison urged the people to blow up, or down, the barrier of corruption. Both were speaking metaphorically, but the remarks could be interpreted as a call to arms, and by the magistrates they inevitably were.

Three meetings were held with different slants. Two of them had ominous undertones for the Government. The first of these was held at Oldham on June 7th, presided over by the tireless Knight. It was attended by deputies from twenty-two towns in Lancashire, North Derbyshire and the West Riding of Yorkshire. Their unanimous declaration was 'for the formation of Union

Societies in every town and village in the Kingdom, for the purpose of acquiring and diffusing political information, and also for the frequent holding of public meetings and district meetings in order to connect completely and harmonize their political understanding and feeling'. The words conjured up the dreaded combination of the working man on a much more formidable scale than before. At a meeting in Leeds the following week delegates came from Manchester, Rochdale, Huddersfield, Stockport, Oldham, Staleybridge, Wakefield, Macclesfield, Ashton-under-Lyne, Gee Cross, Lees, Moseley, Holmfirth, Failsworth, Heyside, Whitefield, Leigh, Middleton, Treakle Street, Barnsley, New Mills, Royton, Bury, Heywood, Todmorden and Blackburn. If the Leeds delegate himself is added, this was already seven up on the Oldham meeting. The feelings of cohesion and harmony were spreading fast.

The third meeting, which made no specific demand for Parliamentary reform, was held in Manchester on June 21st. It was organized by a non-political body of 'distressed weavers'. The weavers' plight by mid-1819 had reached a new level of desperation. The cotton trade was almost at a standstill. On the higher levels masters were making considerably fewer thousands. At the middle level luxuries were out. At the in-between level small-time masters or the more fortunate of the 'independent' spinners and weavers were struggling to make ends meet. While on the lowest rung the hand-loom weavers were sitting in their damp cellars with nothing, unable to buy more yarn because there was no market for the cloth they had already made. And those who still possessed a market were selling at such a low price that the week's wages barely bought a pound of potatoes and a loaf of bread. The most dreadful aspect of hand-loom weaving was that people were still pouring into it. The wages and conditions, the warnings of the articulate weavers, were overridden by a combination of the convictions 'I-shall-succeed-where-others-have-failed' and 'it-can't-happen-to-me', and by the desperate lack of employment.

At the June meeting the weavers asked either that some means be devised for the amelioration of their present conditions, with the old plea for a minimum wage, or that arrangements be made for their emigration to the northern states of America. The idea of emigration was viewed favourably by both Government and some Radicals, with one difference. John Knight was an advocate of subsidized emigration (so were the middle-class Radicals). If there was no work for people in this country, money must be provided for them in the far-flung Empire where they could establish model Radical communities. Lord Sidmouth agreed that 'the parts of the world to which the views of such persons should be directed are Upper Canada, Ceylon and the Cape of Good Hope'. But he—here lies the difference—did not agree about the subsidy. The destitute emigrants could find their own way to this interesting collection of countries. It was still a crime for an artisan to emigrate, so those who should direct their views elsewhere were the unskilled workers who would relieve the Government of an unwelcome burden. However, while the distressed weavers' leaders were addressing the meeting, John Saxton arrived on Saint Peter's Field and asked permission to speak. This being granted, he launched into a passionate tirade on emigration equalling transportation. He then urged the weavers to stay in Lancashire and fight the good fight at home, by means of Parliamentary reform. He met with great success, and the ease with which he swung the weavers from thoughts of America to support for the Radical cause did not lessen the loyalists' fears.

As July came in the two forces, Radical and loyalist, were ranged against each other like avalanches on twin peaks, both hanging precariously over the abyss of distress. Throughout July the abyss deepened, the Radical avalanche gained strength, and the loyalists became correspondingly convinced that it would come crashing down upon them. Or at least the local loyalists did. For each force was in two sections, national and local. Whereas the Radical sections were for once acting cohesively, the loyalist ones were not. Both Government and local loyalists were pursuing the same end of halting the Radical avalanche, but they did not pursue it in the same *spirit*.

It was the spirit of the local loyalists that finally and inevitably led to Peterloo. By the beginning of July they had a month of hectic Radical activity behind them. The emotion and reaction this induced was expressed by Norris: 'The working classes are beset by reformers, who by the licentiousness of the press and of their speeches, are inculcating every species of dissatisfaction and even insurrection and rebellion in which the whole may *very shortly* end … I fear it is now too late, and that the remedy for the present state of things must be (in the first instance) more violent than information or indictments.' Any awareness of these economic reasons, which made it possible for the Radicals to inculcate every species of dissatisfaction, reasons of which Norris himself had been aware not so long ago, had vanished. Gone, too, was any inclination to weigh what the Radicals were actually doing in the revolutionary stakes, against what they might infer in their wilder speeches. He could now only see a cauldron containing but one possible brew, insurrection and rebellion. Every action the Radicals took during July, mild or wild, judicious or injudicious, was pre-judged on the basis of impending revolution. Not by Norris alone. The ultra loyalists had reached his conclusion months before, and had been urging the violent counteraction he now favoured. As July wore on, more of the moderate loyalists, the men who also appreciated the economic roots and even something of the traumatic social upheaval that had overtaken Lancashire, were sucked into the general panic.

Searching for pikes had by the beginning of July become an obsessive occupation, and the knowledge of the caches that were supposed to litter the area did not soothe the more panicky loyalists. *Supposed* is the operative word. Post-Peterloo the Solicitor General's Office compiled a dossier on weapons, pikes in particular. To read it is high farce, for what it proves is that there weren't any. There were scores of *reports* from all points north, south, east and west of Manchester, typified by Ethelston's statement that 'The lead stolen the other day was to make balls, and the young man was employed by the Reformists to steal it.' But Ethelston produced no balls, nor any of the longed-for evidence. The conviction that such pikes and balls did exist was still firmly held by the magistrates however, even if it was not taken too seriously by the moderate loyalists.

One branch of Radical activity, also starting at the beginning of July, provided panic suction for even the moderates. This was the drillings. The magistrates were inundated with reports of men drilling in quasi-military fashion; 300 men on Oldham Edge, standing to attention, standing at ease; 500 men on Saddleworth Moor ditto; 200 men at Chadderton being instructed by old soldiers; in Royton hundreds being trained by beat of drum; in Middleton by bugle. What could the participants possibly be doing except training for insurrection, armed of course, with their pikes stuck somewhere up their jerkins? In fact there was no need for the spies to report. The drillings were held openly. Had anybody on the loyalist side stopped to think it would surely have struck them as being unlikely that anyone should train for armed insurrection in broad daylight, knowing that spies were watching from every gorse bush and jutting rock. But this sudden outburst of quasi-martial activity was a provocative act, calculated to make every loyalist ask the reason why. As most of them were past reasoning it was doubly provocative.

Provocation was not the intention. The drillings were linked with the decision to hold a mass meeting in Manchester on August 9th. This meeting was to be part of an all-out Radical effort, and the invitation was sent to Hunt by the Patriotic Union Society at the beginning of July. As soon as the invitation was despatched, the local leaders and the Union Societies set to work organizing the meeting. Uppermost in many of their minds was the manner of the crowds' arrival at, and their conduct during, the meeting. The problem was posed by Bamford: 'We had frequently been taunted by the press, with our ragged, dirty appearance, at these assemblages; with the confusion of our proceedings, and the mob-like crowds in which our numbers mustered; and we determined, for once at least, these reflections should not be deserved; that we would disarm the bitterness of our political opponents by a display of cleanliness, sobriety and decorum, such as we had never exhibited before.'

At the earlier January meeting on Saint Peter's Field, certain parts of the crowd had arrived in contingents with bands playing and carrying banners. Could not the idea be developed so that everybody arrived in contingents, marching on to the field like a military parade? But military discipline was not achieved by accident and the idea was hit upon of training a nucleus of volunteers in the military arts of keeping in step and marching in rank. There were sufficient ex-soldiers among the Radicals to make the scheme practical, with a disciplined nucleus the rest of the contingents would remain in order.

Nobody apparently considered the effect such martial activity would have upon their opponents. Or if they did they dismissed it as negligible. Or perhaps the originators of the scheme simply did not anticipate the enthusiasm with which it would be received. And when the volunteers turned up in their thousands they were swept into the general enthusiasm. People certainly did respond to the call. Sedentary spinners and weavers, incarcerated fourteen hours a day in the factories and cottages, leapt at the organized opportunity to breathe the high clear air of the moors and the sweet fresh air of the fields. The lure of the drum beat and the sound of the bugle were not without their attractions either. Among those who attended the drillings was John Lees. Desperation had finally driven the undecided, the indifferent and the non-political to the temporary shelter of the Radical fold. As a Waterloo veteran, John could well have been one of 'the old soldiers' who instructed the volunteers. By the end of July as many as 2,000 people were parading along the High Road from Manchester to Rochdale near Slattocks. There was no attempt at concealment, it would have been difficult to conceal 2,000 people anyway, but it was not a sight, seen or reported, to calm any loyalist.

In the event, on the fatal day, Bamford's hopes for the decorum of the crowds' assembly went beyond expectation. As for disarming the bitterness of his political opponents that, alas, did not succeed. The training period sent up loyalist temperatures, either because they did not know or simply could not accept the Radical explanation for it, while the effect of the disciplined arrival on the magistrates was disastrous. If the value of the drillings was doubtful, innocent as their intent, admirable as their organization might have been, the whole Radical organization behind Peterloo proved a two-edged weapon. When Hunt accepted the invitation to attend the meeting originally scheduled for August 9th, he asked that it should be 'rather a meeting of the county of Lancashire, than of Manchester alone ... I think by management the *largest assembly* may be procured that was ever seen in this country'. The request was made by Hunt the vain, Hunt the demagogue, Hunt the theatrical. It was a request to which the Lancashire Radicals, from Johnson, Saxton, Knight, Bamford and Healey down to the newest recruits such as John Lees, were only too ready to accede. Lancashire's pride as much as its desperation and reforming zeal was at stake. On August 9th its inhabitants would show to the rest of England a face battered but unbowed.

The manner in which the crowds would deport themselves was taken care of by the drillings. But the massive crowds which were to provide the largest assembly ever seen on England's soil had to be informed of the precise moment. The publicizing, and as it turned out re-publicizing of the meeting, was a major achievement of communication. Once informed of the meeting's date, assembly points had to be set up from which the people could march to Manchester in their disciplined contingents. Their organization was a magnificent piece of staff work. Each village was given a time and place to meet, from which its members would proceed to their named assembly points in the larger towns such as Oldham, Rochdale, Middleton, Stockport, and thence to Saint Peter's Field. The routes they would variously take were also worked out, although on the day several contingents took the wrong turning in the winding streets of Manchester. If funds permitted each contingent was to have a band, not only because music was stirring and festive but to help the marchers keep in step. Then there were the banners, for this was to be a serious as well as a festive occasion. The rest of England must know clearly why Lancashire was holding its meeting. Men and women set to work weaving and embroidering the banners, with all their native skill. Clothing was left to the individual. If one possessed a best suit it should be worn, but as thousands of the marchers were destitute the emphasis was on cleanliness and tidiness. Finally, there was the matter of the dispersal. The contingents would be arriving in phased order, but as thousands of people streamed off the field simultaneously there might be confusion. Half-way return points were therefore set up. Should a person be separated from the main body of his contingent, he should make for the half-way point, so that each group could march back into its respective town as proudly and in as good order as it had marched out. The emphasis on the discipline of the return journey was also to prevent any post-meeting eruptions in the streets of Manchester, or any diving into public houses.

About this meticulous organization the magistrates knew little, either while it was in progress or after the massacre had taken place. Three years after the event counsel was to ask, 'How was it known that you were to assemble on Oldham Green? By what means did you learn that?' The cagey reply he received was, 'I do not know. It was represented up and down the country.'

But if the magistrates were unaware of the thoroughness of the Radicals' preparations, as early as the first week in July they were sufficiently alarmed to hold a meeting at the Police Office. It was also attended by the Constables, the Boroughreeve, the church-wardens and other members of the oligarchy. After the meeting the following declaration was issued:

> We the undersigned being seriously impressed with a sense of Danger which threatens the community from the designs and practices of the disaffected, deem it indispensably necessary to declare our determination to support the constitution of the Country, and to co-operate with the local Authorities of these Towns for the Preservation of the Public Peace.

There then followed a list of reasons explaining why the patriotic citizen should carry out his duty and support the measures to be adopted. Of these measures the vital one was point six: 'To strengthen the Civil Power, a Committee be selected by the Magistrates for the Division, and the Boroughreeves and the Constables of Manchester and Salford, from the gentlemen who sign the declaration'.

Seven days later the Committee came into being. It was just such a self-defeating body as inevitably is organized in times of panic and unreason, rejoicing in the title of the Armed Association for the Preservation of Public Peace. It was more generally known as the Committee in Aid of the Civil Powers, and its first action was to implore loyal citizens to offer their services by enrolling at the police offices. Several hundred citizens of the ultra-loyalist variety duly enrolled. It was their action in supporting the Committee in Aid of the Civil Powers which precipitated Peterloo. The magistrates were in control, but they were subjected to six weeks of the Committee members and supporters, a cross breed yapping at their heels like terriers, baying revolution like bloodhounds, with the emphasis on blood. The *Manchester Observer*'s comment on the Committee was that 'Havock' was being cried and 'the Dogs of War' let slip. It was valid. After Peterloo the same view was upheld by John Edward Taylor, as spokesman for the middle-class Radicals, when he accused the Committee in Aid of the Civil Powers of being 'the original instigators of the massacre'.

While the Committee members were rushing around preparing to man the barricades, heightening the alarm in their rush, the Government was not entirely unalarmed or inactive. It knew of the planned all-out national Radical effort, and in the face of this, on July 7th, Lord Sidmouth sent a circular to all Lord Lieutenants ordering them to return forthwith to their counties. (Few Lord Lieutenants spent much time in the counties over which they presided.) To Lord Derby, as Lord Lieutenant for Lancashire, he wrote specifically asking him to put the Yeomanry Corps in a state of readiness, to assist the magistrates if required, though as usual he was equally emphatic in his hope that the civil powers would be able to cope without military assistance, amateur or regular. As a result of this letter, on July 12th, orders were sent to the commanders of the Liverpool Light Horse, the Aston Cavalry, the Oldham Cavalry and the Manchester and Salford Yeomanry Cavalry, 'to use their utmost exertions to have the Corps under their respective Commands in readiness, to obey the first call they may receive from the magistrates'.

For three years Sidmouth and the Government had been insisting that the deep-rooted Radical intent was revolution. Radical activity was manifestly increasing. So the decision to put the third force of law and order on the alert was not unreasonable. However, the Government did not act in the weeks preceding Peterloo as if it anticipated imminent revolution. Having apparently forgotten or allayed its own fears, it also forgot that those of the Manchester magistrates were far from allayed. The alerting of the Yeomanry Corps proved a most disastrous decision. For in the event the only one to be called upon was the Manchester and Salford Yeomanry Cavalry.

Since the Blanket March the members of the MYC had been prancing around Manchester on their ill-controlled horses. Ill-controlled because, being amateurs who had to work for a living, the MYC had insufficient time to acquire the equestrian arts. Their lack of horsemanship was crucial at Peterloo. But even more crucial was the attitude that had built up over the past two years. The MYC were not only disliked for their posturing and strutting and arrogance, but they were ridiculed. 'Stupid boobies of yeomanry cavalry' was among the milder epithets thrown at them. The *Manchester Observer*'s description, 'The yeomanry are generally speaking the fawning dependents of the great, with a few fools and a greater proportion of coxcombs who imagine they acquire considerable importance by wearing regimentals', was typical of much of the invective. Small men with small minds assuming superiority deserve ridicule. But once they are given power, the ridicule that burned them will scald the ridiculers.

At the first taste of power, on receipt of the letter from Lord Derby, the MYC leapt into action. *They sent their sabres to be sharpened.* That Sidmouth knew of this action before Peterloo is doubtful. What he would have made of it had he known is even more open to doubt. Being 200 miles away from the mounting hysteria in Manchester, unaware of the two-year buildup of hostility between MYC and populace, he would probably have considered the action a trifle over-zealous but showing the right spirit. After Peterloo it assumed deadly importance. No other yeomanry corps sent their sabres to be sharpened. The MYC had never sent theirs to be sharpened before, only to be cleaned. So what prompted the action other than hopeful bloody use of the sabres?

The only other specific action the Government took was at the end of July. This was to issue a proclamation in the Prince Regent's name condemning, though not banning, seditious assemblies and the practice of drilling. Occasioned by the Manchester magistrates' fears, it was an indeterminate action leaving everybody in the air as to when a meeting became seditious, and offering no reasons why drilling should cease.

11

MANCHESTER KNEW NOUGHT OF MISERY UNTIL NOW

The all-out *national* Radical effort consisted of four major meetings, in Birmingham, Leeds, London and Manchester, to take place in the months of July and August. They were to demonstrate how much *national* support the Radicals already had, and to attract as much further national attention as possible, so that the Government would be forced to take more than note. It will thus be seen that the only meeting to go down into popular history, Peterloo, was but part of a general plan.

The first meeting was held at Newhall Hill in Birmingham on July 12th. Major Cartwright and Wooler of the *Black Dwarf* were present, but Hunt was not. As the great Radical cry was Parliamentary reform, particularly for the unrepresented towns, the Birmingham Radicals decided to elect a 'legislatorial attorney' to underline the cry of 'all the unrepresented people of the Empire'. The legislatorial attorney thus elected in lieu of a real candidate, ready and waiting for his hour of call to the reformed Parliament, was Sir Charles Wolseley (not himself present as his mother had just died). The Government was surprised, not to say alarmed, by this move, and the Solicitor and Attorney General's offices were immediately put to work to consider its implications. Their considerations had a direct bearing on Peterloo. The Birmingham Radicals claimed that 60,000 people attended the meeting. As with all figures of the period it was an exaggeration, but it was a large and successful meeting, probably of about 30,000. Its success was counter-reactive, as was every step in these weeks, in sending Radical confidence and loyalist fears upwards. The *British Volunteer*'s comment on the election of Sir Charles Wolseley was, for a current Tory paper, nicely observed. As Birmingham 'had for so long been employed in manufacturing other descriptions of *counterfeits*, why so much displeasure at their making a Brummagem Member?'

The second meeting was held on Hunslet Moor, near Leeds, on July 19th. Of the four it was the least successful. It was held at midday which was said to be a bad hour for the workers. However, the time factor does not hold water as an alibi. Peterloo was held at the same hour and the workers managed to turn up there.

The third meeting took place at Smithfield on July 21st, with Hunt as the principal speaker. It was important, not just because it was held in London, but because of its resolutions. In the post-Peterloo trials the Government seized upon one of the resolutions, namely, 'that from and after the 1st day of January, 1820, we cannot, conscientiously, consider ourselves as bound in equity by any future enactments which may be made by any persons styling themselves our representatives, other than those who shall be fully, freely and fairly chosen by the voices and votes of the largest proportion of the members of the state'. The Government embroidered this claim as evidence of Hunt's revolutionary intent, that he intended to urge the Manchester crowds along the paths of anarchy as from January 1st, 1820. As he never had the opportunity of speaking at Manchester, nobody knows what he would actually have said.

It was also at Smithfield that the Reverend Harrison of the Union Societies was arrested, on charges arising from his Stockport speech on June 28th.* The Manchester magistrates were to adopt a similar proceeding at Peterloo, that is arresting a Radical leader from the hustings while the meeting was in progress, so it is worth noting that Harrison's arrest was effected without military assistance, because part of the magistrates' case after Peterloo was that they could not possibly have arrested the Radical leaders without military support.

Harrison's arrest was not only a shaky precedent for the magistrates. It had another repercussion, detrimental to the Radicals, inflammatory for the loyalists. Harrison was brought back from London to Stockport on July 23rd in the custody of a constable named William Birch. Nearing Stockport, Birch was shot. Lord Sidmouth learned 'with great horror ... the atrocious deed whereby the life of William Birch has been endangered if not destroyed'. The blame was immediately laid at the Radical door, as it happens unjustly, but as Hunt wrote to Johnson, gloomily regretting the incident, 'It will give the villains of the press such a handle'. It did. On July 31st the *British Volunteer* wrote that it had 'just received information that the assassination of Mr Birch was a preconcerted plot, on the part of about a dozen individuals'. The *Volunteer* was wrong on all counts. Birch was not dead. There was no preconcerted plot, nor were a dozen individuals involved. The shooting was the unprompted, solo act of a distraught and starving young weaver named William Pearson. By August 7th, the *Volunteer* was admitting that it had been wrong about a conspiracy against Birch, but the damage had been done. Ethelston expressed the loyalist reaction thus: 'I am not an alarmist but I think I foresee in this only a prelude to

---

* Wolseley was soon arrested on the same count. Archibald Prentice's comment was: 'Sir Charles and Harrison were ... found guilty of having breathed together and imprisoned'.

future Bloodshed'. In fact Birch recovered, and on August 13th His Royal Highness the Prince Regent was graciously pleased to grant him a pension of £100 a year. The wretched Pearson was sheltered by friends for a time, but on August 17th he was charged with maliciously shooting at William Birch with a pistol and subsequently hanged.

The shooting of Birch put a pint of boiling water in the already steaming cauldron. Several gallons more were added on July 31st when the official announcement of the intended meeting in Manchester appeared in the *Manchester Observer.*

It was Johnson who wrote the fatal letter to Hunt on behalf of the Patriotic Union Society of Manchester. It was full of foreboding and depression. 'Trade here is not worth following,' he wrote. 'Everything is almost at a standstill, nothing but ruin and starvation stare one in the face. The state of the district is; truly dreadful.' He also made the interesting and revealing statement that, 'I believe nothing but the greatest exertion can prevent an insurrection.' To an extent it backs up the loyalist contentions, but it also shows that the local Radical leaders were aiming to prevent such revolution. Inviting Hunt may have been one method by which they hoped to do this. He was the idol who could sway the crowds, stay the lurching avalanche and keep it on a stable, legal, Radical course. Hunt privately accepted the invitation, adding his hope that the meeting be made the largest assembly ever seen on England's soil, and that it be well publicized. His wishes were carried out. As we have seen, preparations started at the beginning of July. At the end of the month the official announcement appeared:

> The public are respectfully informed, that a MEETING will be held here on MONDAY the 9th August, 1819, on the Area near ST PETER'S CHURCH, to take into consideration, the most speedy and effectual mode of obtaining Radical Reform in the Commons House of Parliament, being fully convinced, that nothing less can remove

the intolerable evils under which the People of this Country have
so long, and do still, groan; and also to consider the propriety of
the 'Unrepresented Inhabitants of Manchester' electing a Person
to represent them in Parliament; and of the adopting of Major
Cartwright's Bill.

H. HUNT, ESQ. in the Chair.

It will thus be seen that Manchester had no intention of being
left behind Birmingham in electing a 'legislatorial attorney'. It
was this announced intention that led to the days of legal hair-
splitting, to the postponement of the original meeting, and in a
way to the disaster of Peterloo.

The Solicitor and Attorney General's offices had been considering the matter of the 'legislatorial attorney'. They passed their
findings on to Lord Sidmouth who then wrote to the Reverend
Hay, summarizing the legal position and conclusion. It was the
most crucial of the many hundreds of letters that passed between
the Home Office and the Manchester magistrates. The vital
section read:

I have now to acquaint you that the Attorney and Solicitor
General have given their opinion that the Election of a member of
Parliament without the King's Writ is the high misdemeanour and
that the parties engaged and acting therein may be prosecuted
for a conspiracy. Lord Sidmouth therefore hopes that if such an
election should be attempted at Manchester, measures will be
taken for bringing the offenders to justice. From the opinion of
the law officers it follows that a Meeting held for the purpose of
such an election is an unlawful conspiracy. But if the meeting
is not convened for the unlawful purpose, the illegality will not
commence until the purpose is developed and of course after the
crowd has been collected, when it must be a question of prudency
and expedience, to be decided by the magistrates on the spot,
whether they should proceed to disperse the persons assembled.

Lord Sidmouth has no doubt that the question will be judiciously
decided by the Magistrates of Manchester.

Thus Birmingham's decision to elect a 'legislatorial attorney'
unwittingly contributed to the disaster of Peterloo, because the
Radicals did change their plans so that the meeting was, without
any shadow of doubt, of lawful purpose, and to ensure that the
magistrates could not act until *after* the crowds had collected. It
hardly needs saying that Lord Sidmouth *should* have had doubts
about the judicious decisions the Manchester magistrates were
likely to take.

On the same day, July 31st, as the Radical announcement
appeared, the magistrates published their counter-blast, without having seen the official text, but assuming what its contents
would be and acting on the Home Office's advice.

Whereas it appears by an advertisement in the *Manchester
Observer* paper of this day, that a PUBLIC AND ILLEGAL MEETING is
convened for Monday, the 9th day of August next, to be held
on the AREA NEAR SAINT PETER'S CHURCH in Manchester. We, the
undersigned Magistrates, acting for the Counties Palatine of
Lancaster and Chester, do hereby caution all Persons to abstain AT
THEIR PERIL from attending such ILLEGAL MEETINGS.

The wording is interesting. If the last underlined sentence is
considered, the grammatical sense of abstaining at one's peril
is—go or else! Hunt, the *Manchester Observer* and the Radicals in
general were quick to seize upon the error which doubtless nowadays would be called Freudian. Ironically amused as the Radicals
were by the wording, they took the warning seriously. Their reaction too was legal. Everybody connected with Peterloo was so
busy trying to interpret the law that it can truly be said to have
been a most legal disaster, a wreck that smashed on England's
greatest strength and greatest weakness, the supremacy of the

established law. The Radicals sent John Saxton to Liverpool to consult Mr Ranecock, a counsel sympathetic to the cause, on their right to hold the meeting and of the magistrates to ban it.

In the meantime, the Home Office was bombarding the magistrates with further legal consideration and advice. Having again consulted the Attorney General, Lord Sidmouth was of the opinion that there was great difficulty in pronouncing the meeting of the 9th illegal beforehand, as the Radicals had not stated that they wanted to elect a representative to Parliament, but they merely wanted to consider it, which was not illegal. He therefore thought the magistrates should reconsider their ban. The next day the Solicitor General was considering when and how the meeting might become illegal, and whether the magistrates could use force in dispersing it. But in his next letter Lord Sidmouth, on reflection, was convinced 'of the inexpedience of attempting forcibly to prevent the meeting of Monday ... even should they utter sedition or proceed to an election of a representative, it will be wisest to abstain from any endeavour to disperse the mob, unless they proceed to an act of felony or riot'.

As it turned out, the legally bemused magistrates were saved from the ignominious position of having to retract and allow the meeting of the 9th to take place. Mr Ranecock had come to a different conclusion from the Solicitor General. He thought the Radicals were on tricky legal ground in considering the propriety of electing a representative. Accordingly, on August 4th, the Radicals published a further announcement to the effect that they had considered the magistrates' warning. Although they could see no reason why the meeting should be banned, they had decided not to hold it. They, therefore, requested the Boroughreeve to convene a further meeting. Not surprisingly the Boroughreeve, Edward Clayton, failed to respond to this call. On August 7th Norris received a letter from Lord Sidmouth congratulating him on the postponement of the meeting, which his Lordship thought the magistrates should regard as a personal triumph. His Lordship was already out of date. For on August 6th the Radicals called another meeting of their own accord. The amended text ran:

A REQUISITION having been presented to the Boroughreeve and Constables of Manchester, signed by above 700 inhabitants, requesting them to call a PUBLIC MEETING 'to consider the propriety of adopting the most LEGAL and EFFECTUAL means of obtaining a REFORM in the Commons Houses of Parliament', and they having declined to call such a meeting therefore the undersigned Requisitionists give NOTICE that a public meeting will be held, on the area, near St Peter's Church, for the above mentioned purpose on Monday the 16th instant—the Chair to be taken by H. Hunt Esq, at 12 o'clock.

Hundreds of signatures followed, with the final note: 'The signatures of Householders, who have since come to the Office of the Observer, have exceeded one Thousand, which for want of time and room, we are compelled to omit.'

12

THE TOWN HAS BEEN DELUGED
WITH PLACARDS

The stage was set for Peterloo. But several props had not yet been placed. A crucial one occurred on July 23rd. On this day, before any anouncements, postponements and re-wordings of intended meetings, the Select Committee of Lancashire and Cheshire Magistrates was formed. It was a protective, herd-instinct gathering of the clans. From July 23rd the Select Committee took control of the medieval market town of Manchester. It was therefore they who were at bed-rock responsible for Peterloo.

Their first act, on the day after their formation, was to file bills for seditious libel against James Wroe as editor of the *Manchester Observer*. Presumably togetherness gave them confidence, because Norris had been bleating about the seditious influence of the *Observer* for months. But the bills did not deter the *Observer* from its usual lively course. It continued to sound off at full blast. In the last weeks before Peterloo, the verbal warfare reached new heights. This battle was as important, and had as great an effect, as the physical preparations.

The *Observer* itself obviously devoted columns to the meeting, its cancellation, the correspondence with Hunt, and the reasons why the meeting was necessary. The reasons were covered from all angles and for all tastes. There were straightforward, serious editorials. There were pretty vicious, if amusing, attacks on the loyalists' incompetence and panic handling of the situation. There was a series of dialect discussions between such characters as 'Bill o'thowd Rappurs ut wur in th' Warkheawse un Sam Simple', in which the matter might be gift-wrapped but remained fiercely political.

The loyalist papers, until the last few weeks, devoted little space to the Radical activities. This was understandable and sensible. Why give the enemy more publicity? But when they were forced to enter the lists they did not canter forward with aplomb. Their lines of attack were either imitation Paley (Do not listen to the Radicals, accept your lot which will soon be improved) or, with the semi-realization that accepting your lot was at the moment difficult, vicious and unamusing onslaughts on the Radicals. Apart from their failure to present their own case skil-fully, there was an element of Nero fiddling while Rome burned. Much space was devoted in the *British Volunteer*, for example, to theatrical reviews of the Minor Theatre in Spring Gardens where such items as a new ballet dance called *Tommy Titmouse*, Miss Usher performing on a tightrope, and a rendering of 'The Monk's Cowl' were being billed. Grand balls at Carlton House received similar large coverage. Moments do arrive when that sluggish, unerudite, unintellectual body known as 'the people' demands something more than *Tommy Titmouse*, or Miss Usher on her tightrope, or the vicarious pleasures of reading about the toffs. Of such a moment the *Manchester Observer*, and the middle-class Radical paper, the *Manchester Gazette*, were aware. The loyalist newspapers were apparently not.

Apart from the newspapers attacking and counter-attacking, posters, squibs, bills and proclamations of various shapes and sizes were very much part of the scene. Just before Peterloo the *Observer* commented: 'The town, it is notorious, has, for the last fortnight, been deluged with Placards, some of which even Solomon, were he now living, could not possibly understand.' The *Observer* was referring to the attempts to blacken Hunt's character which it preferred *not* to understand. For in the placard war the loyalists were as active as the Radicals, and those that have survived are perfectly comprehensible.

Both sides used several methods of attack, and Manchester's citizens, gathering in groups where the placards were posted, or listening to the squibs being read in the public houses could take their pick. The reformers asked: 'Oh! ye sinking Manufacturers and Shopkeepers, is it the starving Labourers who have ruined you; or is it DEAR provisions and HIGH rents and taxes?' To this the non-reformers replied: 'Oh! ye sinking manufacturers and shopkeepers, is it these canting Reformers who will preserve you? or is it KIND MASTERS and plenty of employment?' There were the straightforward loyalist admonitions: 'TO THE REFORMERS at this critical juncture it is incumbent upon you most seriously to consider the consequences of the steps you take. Yet a little further and you will plunge the country into all the horrors of Civil Warfare. They began this way in the French Revolution—they wanted nothing but peaceable reform! and Liberty—reasonable Liberty! they ended by sinking into a tyranny morer galling than that which they had endured.' This, and a great deal more, was signed by one who 'thanked heaven above all mercies that he was born A BRITON'. There were the injunctions to such interesting subdivisions as the Men, the Poor, the Industrious, the Reformers, and the Women of England—the latter being admonished to reform their families without troubling with reforming the nation.

The most vicious, lively and prolific attacks were on Hunt himself. He was by now the devil incarnate, the man who would whip up the mob, produce the pikes and set insurrection ablaze.

Ergo he was the man on whom as much mud as possible must be flung. With Hunt it was not difficult to find the mud. The first obvious line of attack was his adultery. This was linked, by dredging back to 1807, to a matter of adulterated beer. In 1807 Hunt had gone into business as a brewer in Bristol. His beer was later condemned as being adulterated. Hunt admitted this, while claiming it was due to the malpractice of his partner and underlings whom he had trusted. The explanation sounds reasonable. Watering beer does not seem any more in character than hissing at National Anthems. That he was a poor businessman all Hunt's forays into business prove. The affair produced such attacks as, 'Sure this can never be our Orator, Henry Hunt. He, good man!!!, is honestly labouring day and night to keep our Constitution pure and unadulterated. The Brewer was day and night infusing poison into the Constitution of all his fellow subjects.' Lastly there were the imputations against the genuineness of Hunt's reforming zeal and his integrity as a whole. This produced the unlikely insinuation that Hunt was in the Government's pay. 'Is it not moreover strange that Sir Charles Wolseley, Harrison, Fitton and Knight—to say nothing of Bagguley, Drummond and Johnston—should be apprehended for words spoken at Public Meetings, and that Mr Hunt who at the late meeting in Smithfield, recommended you to resist the Payment of Taxes, should escape?'

Knight and Fitton were both indicted for words spoken at the Blackburn meeting on July 5th. Again presumably togetherness had given the magistrates confidence, because Knight and Fitton had been 'persons of turbulent and seditious disposition ... wickedly and maliciously devising and intending to excite tumult', to quote part of the indictment, for a considerable time. The charges did not affect the indomitable Knight's attendance at Peterloo, but Fitton did not lead the Royton contingent. Previously he had been as active as Knight, so possibly there was some other reason for his absence, but it seems probable that the charge kept him away. Incidentally, in the indictments, both Fitton and Knight were described as 'labourers', presumably to suggest that nobody of standing could be a Radical. The *Manchester Observer* redressed this by stating that Fitton was a surgeon and Knight a manufacturer, which the former was and the latter had been.

Continuing the theatrical analogy there was one vital prop whose absence greatly affected the day of Peterloo. This was Sir John Byng. Mr Donald Read* has said that the decision to dispense with Byng 'was perhaps the most important single decision leading to the bloodshed of Peterloo'. But how much of a *decision,* as opposed to an accumulation of emotion and circumstance, was it?

At the end of July, on the announcement of the meeting for August 9th, Norris travelled to Pontefract for a conference with Byng. One can imagine the confrontation. Norris had the baying of the Committee in Aid of the Civil Powers in his ears, plus his own conviction of imminent insurrection. Byng had his cool, practical eye on the situation. After the conference he wrote calmly to Lord Sidmouth: 'I have little expectation that Mr Hunt or his Associates will either say or do that which will authorize interference. They will be too cautious and fearful to try our strength'. His assessment was correct, although the Radicals would have said it was not fear that held them back, but good sense and legality. What Byng could not assess correctly was the atmosphere in Manchester entwined with the magistrates' state of mind. The former he failed to appreciate because he was not in Manchester, and the latter because it was beyond his cool, calm comprehension.

However, Byng realized something of the magistrates' fears and panic, as expounded and demonstrated by Norris, and he

---

* Donald Read, author of *Peterloo, the Massacre and its Background*, the first book to deal in depth with the circumstances leading up to Peterloo, as opposed to the day itself; a study invaluable to historian and student.

agreed to come to Manchester before August 9th to discuss the disposition of troops. (Incidentally, the 15th Hussars, whose role was so vital and fatal at Peterloo, were only moved into the area at the beginning of July.) In the event, Byng did not travel to Manchester. When the meeting of August 9th was cancelled, the magistrates immediately wrote to him telling him his presence was no longer necessary, but, curiously, not *why*. Then a few days later, they learned that Hunt was en route to Manchester. Jumping to the conclusion that the cancellation was a trick, that the meeting was to take place on the 9th after all, they again wrote to Byng requesting his immediate presence. Due to other duties Byng was unable to oblige, which was just as well, because the cancellation was genuine. Then on August 10th, Hay wrote a curiously apologetic, defensive and incoherent letter to Byng, even by his self-explanatory standards. After rambling explanations as to why the magistrates had first called for Byng and then told him not to come, the letter finished with the information that they definitely no longer required his presence. The final paragraph gives an indication of the letter's confused quality: 'Such was the aspect of things at the moment at which I applied to you, and I am happy to say that aspect has materially altered from reports which we have since received, and in such a degree as to do away with the propriety of applying to you in any further instance in the same vein as in the first instance we felt it our duty to do.'

A letter from Byng to Hay crossed the one from Hay to Byng. In this Byng opened with the tart information that he had a violent headache, due to the oppressiveness of the weather but not helped, one infers, by the behaviour of the Manchester magistrates. After presuming that the meeting of the 9th had dispersed peaceably so that his presence had been unnecessary, or that something had occurred so that dispersal forces had not been required, he asserted that he had the fullest confidence in the officers commanding the troops in and near Manchester. So that should a serious disturbance occur he could not see what good his presence would do. In a slightly more placatory tone, he asked the magistrates to believe that he stayed not where he was (in York) from the unworthy motive of avoiding the city that had given him so little pleasure in the past, but rather because he thought himself better placed where he was with a regiment at his disposal. As a footnote he added, with some astringency, 'My attention at this moment is being particularly called to two other quarters'. A reminder that Manchester was not the only disturbed area under his command.

Generally the impression gained is that Byng was not anxious to dash to Manchester. With reason, either he heard nothing from the magistrates—there were past bleats from the Home Office to the magistrates 'to make more frequent communication to the General, though you have nothing to impart to him, since it is important that in making the disposition of his troops in his extended district that he should know as well where mischief is *not* imminent as where it is'. Or he received frantic and unnecessary appeals to drop everything and descend on Manchester. Byng stated that he had the fullest confidence in his subordinates, so would his presence have made so much difference? The answer is undoubtedly 'yes'. He would have been with the magistrates, whereas the officer actually in command, Colonel L'Estrange, was not. Byng, as the officer commanding the Northern area, had an authority that Colonel L'Estrange, however efficient, did not. Byng would almost certainly not have sanctioned the action that started the havoc, the unleashing of the MYC on Saint Peter's Field. But whether the magistrates *decided* to dispense with Byng (a decision implying a certain resoluteness of mind), or whether the situation arose from a mixture of Byng's coolness, the magistrates' vanity, hurt pride and injured authority, safely ensconced in York Byng stayed, leaving the onus for August 16th on the unreliable shoulders of the Select Committee.

13

THE ALARM IN ALL THE NEIGHBOURING TOWNS BEGINS TO BE EXCESSIVE

For the last week before August 16th, the Select Committee had something else to raise their blood pressures. This was the presence of Hunt in Manchester, a presence which arose by accident, though the magistrates were not prepared to believe that anything Radical occurred by accident. On August 3rd Johnson wrote to Hunt to tell him of the decision to cancel the meeting of the 9th, but the letter failed to reach Hunt in time. He arrived in Stockport on August 8th, believing that the meeting was to take place on the following day. The manner of his arrival did nothing to decrease the magistrates' alarm. Hunt was greeted by large, enthusiastic crowds whom he promptly addressed from the Union Rooms. Similar large, enthusiastic crowds lined the route from Stockport to Manchester where he was to stay at Smedley Cottage with Mr and Mrs Johnson and their children. As soon as it was known that Hunt had reached Smedley Cottage, larger crowds gathered outside. The magistrates imagined themselves faced with the prospect of seven days of Hunt appearing here, there and everywhere, drawing the crowds like the Pied Piper. Remembering the drillings and those (undiscovered) caches of pikes, might he not sound the awaited call to insurrection during the week?

In fact, Hunt, on learning that the meeting was postponed until the 16th, decided to go back home and return for that day. Or at least he said that was his instinctive reaction. He also said he was reluctantly persuaded to stay by Johnson: 'And I can with great truth affirm that it was one of the most disagreeable seven days that I ever passed in my life.' It sounds reasonable. Johnson would have liked having the conquering hero in his house. He and the other local Radical leaders wanted interest in the meeting maintained at a high pitch, which Hunt's presence guaranteed. Whereas Hunt, whose vanity was only too aware of his interest value, with his inherent respect for the law, and a not unnatural desire to keep out of prison, had no wish to become involved in a possible contretemps before the meeting. (Hunt's respect for the law and fear of imprisonment were appreciated by the Home Office: 'All the demagogues feel extremely sore on the subject of criminal prosecution, and Hunt in particular observes extreme caution for the sake of avoiding them.')

For the seven days, although the magistrates ordered the constables to keep Smedley Cottage under close surveillance, there was little to report. On August 11th Hunt issued *An Address to the Reformers of Manchester and its Neighbourhood*, but apart from that he kept quiet. The Address was mainly a firm and restrained injunction as to how the people were to behave on August 16th.

You will meet on Monday next, my friends, and by your *steady, firm* and temperate deportment, you will convince your enemies, that you feel you have an *important and imperious public duty* to perform ... The eyes of all England, nay, of all Europe, are fixed upon you: and every friend of real Reform and Rational Liberty, is tremblingly alive to the result of your Meeting on Monday next. OUR

Enemies will seek every opportunity, by means of their sanguinary agents, to excite a Riot, that they may have a pretence for SPILLING OUR BLOOD ... Come, then, my friends, to the Meeting on Monday, armed with NO OTHER WEAPON but that of a self-approving conscience; determined not to suffer yourselves to be irritated or excited, by any means whatsoever, to commit any breach of the public peace.

This was not hypocrisy. Privately, Hunt was as sincere in his desire for a peaceful meeting as his public utterances indicated, and even the Home Office believed he meant to 'deprecate disorder'. The exhortation to come armed only with an approving conscience referred not so much to the possibility of pikes as to the known drillings. In a letter to the editor of the *Star* in London, published on August 14th, Hunt, after a deal of injured explanation as to the Radical innocence in the Birch shooting, said, '*playing soldiers* is said to be very much the fashion round here'. Later, after a description of the terrible distress in the area, he repeated the phrase: 'For want of better employment I believe it is too true that they, many of them, pass a considerable portion of their time in what they call *playing soldiers*'. Although he expressed his surprise that the manœuvres had only been hinted at in the Government newspapers, when they were being openly discussed in the Lancashire area, it is clear that he did not approve of 'playing soldiers', and that he was worried that such martial activity might include the odd weapon or two.

Hunt's temperate injunctions did nothing to soothe the magistrates or the majority of loyalists. They were but smoke to cover the deep-laid Radical fire of insurrection.

The final week-end before Monday, August 16th, therefore arrived with the two local avalanches facing each other: the Radical one, firm, confident, with only slight tremors; the loyalist one ready to crash at any minute. The Radicals had tremors because they knew that extra troops had been moved into the area. They knew that the Committee in Aid of the Civil Powers had been breathing fire for weeks. They could see Mayor Dyneley and his breed striding around Manchester, contemptuously eyeing 'the enemy'. They could see the members of the MYC swelling with power like mating roosters, their sharpened sabres glistening at their sides. The *Manchester Observer* expressed another fear on Saturday, August 14th: 'It is rumoured, but we trust it is merely rumour, that the meeting will not be permitted to take place; and that the military have orders to prevent it. Surely those in authority here, will never pursue measures so notoriously illegal as to attempt to suppress by force, a meeting held for the most legal purpose; we cannot think it—we will not believe it; until we have positive demonstration of the Fact. Should we, however, be deceived, we shudder at the probable consequences of such an improper inter- ference.' Their shuddering was to be only too justified, but the Radicals believed, from the leaders down to John Lees and the anonymous thousands who were preparing to attend Monday's meeting, that nothing *really* would happen. They were scratching their opponents as they had scratched them a hundred times in the past. That havoc was truly to be cried this time was inconceivable.

The main loyalist emotion during the final week-end was one of panic. Apart from the few extremists who were looking forward to possible bloodshed, to putting the bastards down once and for all, there were hundreds who genuinely believed that the Manchester Bastille was to be stormed on Monday, that the entry of thousands of Radicals into the city would plunge the streets into anarchy. Several loyalists sent their families to the safety of Liverpool, and the talk was of making a desperate stand for the values all true Britons cherished. But they were working from the premise that the Radicals would start the trouble, either by undisciplined accident or, more likely, from violent intent. That the havoc would be started by their representatives was as much beyond the loyalist belief, panicky or passive, as that of the Radical masses.

Over the final week-end, the Select Committee of magistrates sat in almost continuous session which cannot have done any of their nerves good. They would have been better employed getting some sleep. Almost to the end they continued to discuss the propriety and expedience of stopping the meeting. Was not a multitude in columns with flags a tumultous assembly in itself? But how were the columns, which would be approaching Manchester from every angle, to be stopped? From a practical point of view the idea of banning the meeting was dead, and on the late evening of August 13th a request was sent to Colonel L'Estrange for the assistance of the military on the 16th. Another idea which was being mooted by the magistrates was to arrest Hunt *before* the meeting. On this subject the Home Office had given its usual qualified advice: 'His lordship thinks that if you find good ground for issuing a warrant it will be advisable not to forbear from doing so in the expectation of his giving you a better opportunity, unless some other reason for forbearance presents itself'. In the end the magistrates chose to forbear, though Hunt himself presented them with a golden, if double-edged, opportunity on August 14th, by offering to surrender himself to them.

Hunt's explanation for going to the New Bailey, where the magistrates were, was that having heard of their plans to arrest him, he wanted to clarify the situation. Either they could arrest him, which he surely thought most unlikely, as the public reaction, although an unknown factor, would undoubtedly be a noisy and immense one (and his enemies said he only offered to surrender himself 'in order that his bail might be accepted on Monday before the meeting assembled'; or they could state that they had no charge against him. The latter was what happened: 'Mr Wright appeared surprised at my application [Mr Wright being one of the magistrates] ... and he called Nadin and asked him ... Mr Nadin who appeared surprised at the question said, "None whatever."' So off Hunt drove, back to Smedley Cottage, 'conscious of having performed an important public duty by depriving the authorities of every fair pretence for interfering with the meeting'.

On Sunday morning, August 15th, the kick-back from the January affair at the Spread Eagle Inn occurred. It took the form of an attack on John Shawcross, James Murray and a Mr Rhymer and his son. But principally the attack was on James Murray, who was a well-known and well-disliked special constable and spy, well remembered for his participation at the Spread Eagle, contemptuously referred to as 'Gingerbread Jack'. The four men left Manchester about a quarter past twelve on the Saturday night on the road to Middleton. At Harpurhey, about two miles from the city centre, they saw shadowy figures and heard voices in the darkness. They continued on their way for a further two miles, until they were on the edge of White Moss, where they again heard voices, and 'a great huzza' echoing from the silent, swampy ground. This time they decided to investigate, and followed the tracks across White Moss until dawn was breaking. As the full light of day spread, they were able to see four or five hundred men at their drilling exercises. Unfortunately for all concerned, the four or five hundred men could also see them. The Rhymers managed to escape, but Murray and Shawcross were set upon by the drillers. Both were kicked, beaten and knocked unconscious. Shawcross admitted that in his case it was only for a couple of minutes, after which time he scrambled from the hedge and proceeded back to Manchester and a surgeon. Murray's own testimony was that he was left unconscious for several hours, and that when he recovered his senses he prayed for his life and said, 'This conduct, gentlemen, does not look like Reform in Parliament. It appears to me to be wilful murder.' Which, in the circumstances of being knocked unconscious, and being surrounded by his assailants, was very civil of him. He was then asked, 'Will you beg pardon and never be a Kingsman again?' After declaring, under pressure of course, that he would have no more to do with King or constabling, he was allowed to make his escape. A post-Peterloo witness interrogated on the subject made the following comments:

Q. You found that he [Murray] was dead wounded?
A. He was gone, and they told me it was 3 o'clock he went.
Q. Nearly dead?
A. No, he walked home. He was seen afterwards staring out of a window.

Whether Murray was dead wounded or somewhat beaten up, there is no doubt that he was attacked, and that news of the attack was relayed to the magistrates whose fears and anger it only served to increase. The connection between the Spread Eagle affair and the beating-up was not discovered until later—not that the magistrates would have been impressed had they known this. An act of violence had occurred which was proof of the Radical intent, a sign of that imminent insurrection. The Radicals themselves greatly regretted the incident. Bamford wrote, '[it] probably eradicated from the minds of the magistrates and our opponents generally, whatever sentiments of indulgence they might have hitherto retained towards us'.

Just before midnight on August 15th, Norris penned the final pre-Armageddon letter to the Home Office: 'The magistrates, the military, and the civil authorities of Manchester have been occupied nearly the whole day in concerting the necessary arrangements for the preservation of the peace to-morrow, and for the safety of the town in case riot should ensue ... As at present advised, we do not think of preventing the meeting, yet all the accounts tend to show that the worst possible spirit pervades the country ... I hope peace may be preserved, but under all circumstances it is scarcely possible to expect it; and in short, in this respect we are in a state of painful uncertainty.'

As this letter represented the feelings of the entire Select Committee of Magistrates, who were in charge of the morrow's welfare, the auguries could not be called rosy. One person who was not troubled by pessimism or painful uncertainty was Lord Sidmouth. Early on August 13th he had departed for his favourite resort, Broadstairs although he was preparing to return to London on the night of the 17th, 'for the purpose of receiving on Wednesday morning the account of what passes at Manchester on Monday'.

1. Viscount Sidmouth. Painted in 1823 by George Richmond.

2. Viscount Castlereagh. Painted by Thomas Lawrence.

3. Samuel Bamford. This portrait was probably painted from sketches made at the York Trials in 1820.

4. Joseph Nadin, Deputy Constable of Manchester.

5. Henry Hunt. From a print made in September 1819 at the height of his national fame.

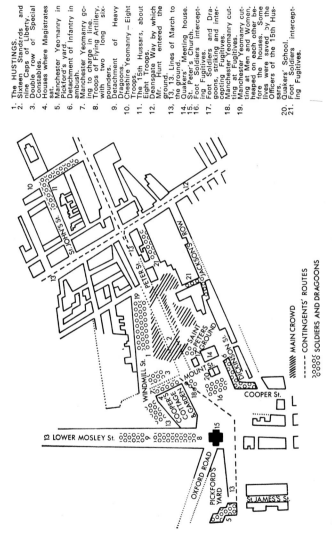

1. The HUSTINGS.
2. Sixteen Standards and nine Gaps of Liberty.
3. Double row of Special Constables.
4. Houses where Magistrates sat.
5. Manchester Yeomanry in Pickford's yard.
6. Detachment of Infantry in ambush.
7. Manchester Yeomanry going to charge in line.
8. Troops of Flying Artillery, with two long six-pounders.
9. Detachment of Heavy Dragoons.
10. Cheshire Yeomanry – Eight Troops.
11. The 15th Hussars, about Eight Troops.
12. Deansgate Way by which Mr. Hunt entered the ground.
13. 13, 13. Lines of March to the ground.
14. Quakers' Meeting house.
15. St. Peter's Church.
16. Foot Soldiers intercepting Fugitives.
17. Foot Soldiers and Dragoons striking and intercepting Fugitives.
18. Manchester Yeomanry cutting at Fugitives.
19. Manchester Yeomanry cutting at Men and Women, heaped on each other before the houses. Some lives were saved by the Officers of the 15th Hussars.
20. Quakers' School.
21. Foot Soldiers intercepting Fugitives.

6. Map of St Peter's Field, Manchester, as it appeared on 16th August 1819. Based on a contemporary drawing, with original legend, which appeared in the *Manchester Observer*.

7. A contemporary print of the 'Massacre' on the Field of Peterloo. Note the banners on the hustings whose captions would seem to be suggestive, rather than accurate.

8. The only surviving Peterloo banner – that of Middleton in green hand-woven silk with gold lettering.

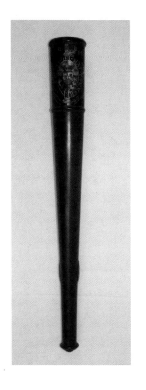
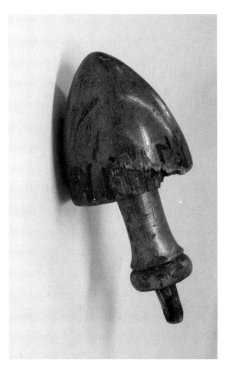

9. The only other relics of Peterloo: a heavy black constable's baton with the gold leaf of the royal insignia clearly stamped; the remains of a banner pole that carried a Cap of Liberty and which bears the faint inscription 'Hunt and Liberty'; and the red plume from a Hussar's helmet.

10. A vivid contemporary print entitled 'The Manchester Reform Meeting Dispersed by the Civil and Military Power, August 16th, 1819'.

14

THE MOST NUMEROUS MEETING THAT EVER TOOK PLACE IN GREAT BRITAIN

The thousands of people who threw open their windows, or stood on their doorsteps, or peered from their damp cellars, on the moors, in the hills and valleys and streets, at dawn on August 16th, must have thought the weather was on their side. The sky was a cloudless blue, and the sun was rising hotly. A grey sky and no sun would have been better, for fewer people would have made the long march to Manchester in cold soaking rain, and even at the eleventh hour Peterloo might have been a different story. But it was the sort of day the English like to imagine fills their summers. People dressed themselves and told their children to behave themselves and ate their breakfasts, meagre or more plentiful, and packed their dinners, if they had any, and started for the assembly points.

Among the thousands was John Lees. He left his father's house between 8 and 9 o'clock in the morning, and according to Robert Lees 'was hearty as ever he was since he was born'. With him went his step-brother Thomas Whittaker, for his father had recently remarried. The two young men walked to Oldham Green which was the main assembly point for Oldham itself, Lees, Saddleworth, Moseley and Royton. The Green was already overflowing with thousands of men, women and children in their most presentable clothes. The Oldham contingent was the best dressed of all. As a centrepiece it had 200 women in white dresses, which must have presented a very pretty spectacle, contrasting with and relieving the browns and blacks of the menfolk. Oldham also had what was generally agreed to be the most beautiful banner of the day. It was of pure white silk, emblazoned with the inscriptions *Universal Suffrage* and *Annual Parliaments, Election by Ballot* and *No Combination Acts, Oldham Union*.

Soon the Lees, Saddleworth and Moseley contingents came down from the high moors, led by 'Doctor' Healey. The Lees's banners had the inscriptions *No Boroughmongering* and *Unite and Be Free, Taxation Without Representation is Unjust and Tyrannical*. If Oldham's was the most beautiful banner of the day Saddleworth's was the most startling. It was pitch black, with the inscription *Equal Representation or Death* in staring white paint over two joined hands and a heart. When Bamford saw it a few hours later on Saint Peter's Field he said it was 'one of the most sepulchral looking objects that could be contrived', adding 'The idea of my diminutive friend [i.e., Healey] leading a funeral procession of his own patients, such it appeared to me, was calculated to force a smile'. It did not raise a twitch on the magistrates' lips, and the *Equal Representation or Death* lettering was later used as evidence of revolutionary intent against Healey. The Royton contingent, which had a large female section, had two banners, in red and green silk, with the wording *Liberty is the Birthright of Man* and *Labour is the Source of Wealth, Royton Female Union—Let us DIE like men and not be SOLD like slaves*.

At 9 a.m. the signal was given by John Knight, who had organized the Oldham assembly, and the columns swung off the Green and on the road to Manchester. En route they picked up the Failsworth and Chadderton contingents so by the time they reached Saint Peter's Field they were nearly 10,000 strong, the largest procession outside Hunt's.

Of the gathering in Middleton we have the most detailed account, recorded by Bamford. Middleton proper, as he called it, was the assembly point for the adjoining villages and hamlets of Back o' the Brow, Barrowfields, Boarshaw, Stakehill and Thornham, Hopwood, Heabers, Birch, Bowlee, Heatons, Rhodes, Blackley, Alkrington, Little Park, Tongue, Parkfield, Wood Street, Middleton Wood and Heywood (some of these names still exist, though all have been swallowed up by Middleton proper, Oldham or sprawling Manchester). By 8 o'clock the whole of Middleton was up and about, either to join the procession or to see it leave. Of the marchers every hundred men and women had a leader whose orders they were to obey. The leaders in turn were to obey the orders of 'the principal conductor', Bamford himself, who had a bugler to assist him in sounding the well-rehearsed calls to halt, right wheel, left wheel, etc. Each leader, Bamford included, had a sprig of laurel in his hat, to distinguish him, and as 'a token of amity and peace'. A few hours later the laurel was to litter Saint Peter's Field. Middleton had two banners, a blue one and a green one, both made of silk. The blue one bore the inscriptions *Parliaments Annual* and *Suffrage Universal* while the green one had *Unity and Strength* and *Liberty and Fraternity.* The latter was carried by Thomas Redford whose name was to go into the Peterloo annals. Middleton also had a Cap of Liberty which was of crimson velvet, with a tuft of laurel and the word *Libertas* on it.

Before the procession left, Bamford addressed the crowds. He left a long account in *Passages in the Life of a Radical* which two witnesses, one loyalist, one Radical, confirmed (although more briefly than he). 'Samuel Bamford stood, and said, "Friends and neighbours, I have a few words to relate. You will march off this place quietly. Not to insult any one but rather to take insult. I do not think there will be any disturbance or anything to do, if there is, it will be after we come back. There is no fear, for this day is our own.' Bamford finished his own account thus: 'I also said, that in conformity with the rule of the committee, no sticks, or weapons of any description, would be allowed to be carried in their ranks.' The Government was to try and make much of sticks after the event, to prove that the crowds were armed; and Bamford admitted that the committee had over-ruled his own feeling on the subject. This, bearing in mind the previous day's assault on Murray at White Moss, and its probable effect on the magistrates, was that they should carry cudgels, at the very least to protect 'the colours'. But more placid views than his prevailed and the Middleton contingent set forth, as Hunt had urged, armed only with their self-approving consciences.

Their procession was soon joined by the Rochdale one, 'and a shout from ten thousand* startled the echoes of the woods and dingles. Then all was quiet save the breath of music, and with intent seriousness, we went on.' On through Rhodes to Blackley, through the sun-filtered woods, up the mossy banks, down into the kloofs (the vernacular for a valley) to Harpurhey where they stopped for welcome refreshment. Here at the toll gates the roads forked to Collyhurst and Newtown. Although Bamford may have said, 'There is no fear, for this day is our own', he did have fears. He half anticipated that the magistrates might try to stop their entry into Manchester at the Harpurhey toll gates, as indeed the magistrates had considered doing. Once safely on the high road to Collyhurst his fears evaporated slightly, though his temper rose. The cause of his ire was two messages sent by Hunt, requesting Bamford's contingent to lead him on to Saint Peter's Field. Bamford said he received two such messages, though Hunt mentions only one. According to Bamford he ignored the first

---

* Exaggeration on Bamford's part. The Oldham contingent was the largest at 10,000. Middleton and Rochdale was about 6,000 strong.

request as he did not wish his column to become entangled in the long hollow road through Newtown, 'where, whatever happened, it would be difficult to advance, or disperse'. But when the second message arrived, 'to administer to the vanity of our "great leader"' he ordered the column to about-wheel and take the lower road through Newtown. Whether these were Bamford's emotions at the time, or whether it was his retrospective opinion of Hunt speaking, is a moot point, for pre-Peterloo nothing had occurred to reveal Hunt's feet of clay.

In Newtown, which was already an excessively depressed slum area, the poorest of the poor, the Irish weavers, came out to greet the procession. Many of the Irishmen looked adoringly at Middleton's green banner which was their national colour, the emblem of the homeland they had left in desperation only to find greater distress in Lancashire. As a nice gesture, before proceeding the Middleton band played *Saint Patrick's Day in the Morning*, and it is interesting to note that the Irish weavers were not among the participants at Peterloo. In the event Bamford's contingent took a wrong turning at Shude Hill in Manchester, thus missing Hunt's procession and forfeiting the honour of escorting their great leader on to the field, an error which did not displease Bamford. Or so he implies, though again one is not certain of his emotions at the time.

The first contingent actually to arrive on Saint Peter's Field was from the ever eager, ever militant town of Stockport, at about 11 o'clock (though individuals, and small unconnected groups, had been gathering since 9 a.m.). The Stockport contingent numbered 1,500 people according to loyalist witnesses, 5,000 according to the Radicals. It carried a Cap of Liberty and two banners, with the inscriptions *Annual Parliaments and Universal Suffrage, Vote By Ballot, No Corn Laws* and *Success to the Female Reformers of Stockport*. One of the loyalist witnesses of Stockport's arrival was a gentleman named Francis Philips. He had enrolled as a special constable in response to the appeals of the Committee in Aid of the Civil Powers, and was one of the few loyalists to rush into print after Peterloo. Philips, on duty at Ardwick Green, noted emphatically that 'nearly half the men carried stout sticks, and one particularly attracted notice from his audacious appearance, having on his shoulder a club as thick as the wrist, newly cut, with the bark on and many knots projecting'.

As the Stockport contingent took up its position, the narrow streets of Manchester were jammed with further oncoming processions. Countless witnesses later testified to the gaiety and discipline of the marchers. The solemnity with which the Middleton contingent, and presumably the others, had left their assembly points had changed to laughter and happy expectation as they neared their goal. Archibald Prentice, watching from a house in Mount Street which overlooked Saint Peter's Field, had never seen a gayer spectacle. Another eye-witness, also in Mount Street, was John Benjamin Smith, later Liberal MP for Stirling and Stockport. When he saw the children in the crowds taking their fathers' hands he observed: 'These are the guarantees of their peaceable intentions—we need have no fears.'

En route to the field, the Oldham contingent, with John Lees in their midst, passed the house of James Murray in Withy Grove. From the manner in which he leapt from window to window to observe what was happening Murray cannot have been as grievously wounded on White Moss as he tried to make out. At 10.30 a.m. the Oldham contingent passed by, but the Saddleworth section sounded the bugle to halt, right outside his house. They then proceeded to confer for half an hour, according to Murray, though it sounds a long time. After which lengthy wait the bugle was again sounded and the procession marched off, shouting, hissing, hooting and waving their sticks and banners at his house. One assumes 'Doctor' Healey gave an extra wave of the pitch black flag.

The barouche that was to take Hunt and the other leaders to Saint Peter's Field did not arrive at Smedley Cottage until midday. Why it was so late when the meeting was advertised to start at this hour is not clear. Perhaps the leaders believed the crowds would be unlikely to be assembled at the advertised time, or perhaps it was Hunt working on the principle of the late dramatic arrival. Neither side made an issue of the delay, though surely the magistrates could have made something sinister out of it? After agreeing that Johnson would move the Resolutions and Remonstrances, that John Knight would second them and that Hunt would be the only speaker, the party climbed into the barouche. From the start progress was slow as they were accompanied by, to quote Hunt, 'an immense multitude'. (It may have been as protection in case the multitude was less than immense that Hunt sent the message to Bamford, though equally he may, in his eyes, have been doing Bamford a favour by asking him to lead the hero's procession.) Hunt's procession was soon joined by the Manchester Female Reformers, headed by Mrs Fildes. The Manchester ladies, like the Oldham ones, were dressed all in white. The idea was that the ladies would precede Hunt on to Saint Peter's Field (presumably *after* the Middleton contingent). The ladies tried to walk in front of the barouche but this was soon found to be impractical, due to the immensity of the crowds and the narrowness of the streets. Most of the ladies therefore fell in behind the barouche, a position which they maintained 'with some difficulty the whole way to the hustings'. In the crush one can appreciate their difficulty, and tenacity. However, Mrs Fildes herself was lifted into the carriage at Hunt's suggestion, and rode by the side of the coachman bearing her colours—she was carrying a white flag bearing the words *Manchester Female Reformers* and a figure of justice—in most gallant style. 'Though rather small', Hunt commented, 'she was a remarkably good figure, and well dressed, and it was considered she added much to the beauty of the scene.' One notes his constant eye for showmanship, not to say female pulchritude.

Hunt's procession also went through Withy Grove, and the indefatigable Murray said he *thought* Hunt stood up in his carriage as it passed his house, and that certainly there was a tremendous hissing and hooting towards him, and an applauding of Hunt. Murray finished his testimony of the morning's dreadful happenings by stating that the direct route from Smedley Cottage to Saint Peter's Field was down Shude Hill to Nicholas Street, and that by passing his house and going down the Exchange and Deansgate, Hunt's procession went at least a mile out of its way. It seems unlikely that Hunt went out of his way in order to stand up in his carriage as he passed Murray's house, whereas it was highly in character that he should take the long route via the Exchange and Deansgate, two of Manchester's major thoroughfares. Quite what point Murray was making in this particular assertion, other than that he was a much maligned, injured character, is unclear. Perhaps it was to underline the loyalist contention that the Radicals wanted to intimidate the citizens of Manchester, if not seize the city. For after Peterloo, counsel was to ask another witness why the Oldham contingent took the long way round. The witness said because they did not know of any other. After further harrying on the lines of 'What! Not one among thousands of you knew the most direct route?', the matter was quietly buried.

While Hunt's procession, with its attendant thousands and ladies in white was making its slow progress, the long way round, to Saint Peter's Field, local leaders were addressing the crowds already assembled. As the hot sun beat down, the atmosphere grew more sultry; with no breath of cooling wind, the waiting crowds were ready to cheer anything and anybody. They cheered 'Doctor' Healey who told them to be steady and firm and waved his hat at them. They cheered Messrs Wild and Swift who also addressed them. Both these men were to stand trial after Peterloo, but not much is known about them before the day, except that Wild was a Methodist and his religion was used as further evidence of Methodism equalling sedition. Both spoke to the crowds on the lines of—Gentlemen, your worthy chairman will soon be here, and you must not attempt to create any riot or disturbance until his arrival. This was later interpreted by the magistrates as—but you may do so after his arrival. This was obviously not the intention, as all the speakers made sure that they underlined what Hunt had already urged, namely that the crowds should be steady, firm and temperate, and not let themselves be irritated. The loudest cheer, before Hunt's arrival that was, was given to the Royton contingent as it marched on to the field with its band playing *Rule Britannia.*

The general intention was to place the banners round the hustings to form a focal, proud and welcoming display for Hunt. In fact half the total banners—there were about sixteen in all, with many more Caps of Liberty—seem to have been round the hustings, and half with their contingents in the field. This may have been because the same thing happened to other leaders as happened to Bamford on his arrival. He found the hustings occupied by men whom he did not know, and who spoke to him sharply. If he, as a prominent local Radical, did not know them they could not be of import and, in a huff, he withdrew his banners. Being the romantic, ardent, volatile creature he was, Bamford's pique soon evaporated on contemplating the crowds, who had congregated together for the solemn purpose of improving the lot of their fellow men.

By 1 o'clock, Saint Peter's Field must have presented an impressive sight, thousands of people standing patiently in the stifling heat. Hunt himself, in more restrained prose than usual, was as much astonished and impressed, as personally gratified, by the scene that met his view as his barouche finally turned on to the field just after 1 o'clock. Only in his estimate of the crowd did he lean towards his customary exaggeration, giving the figure of between 180,000 and 200,000 people. For once he may be forgiven, because all the estimates vary wildly, and he was not alone in pushing the figure upwards. The lowest figure, given by the short-sighted magistrate Tatton, was 30,000. Bamford estimated 80,000, the

Manchester Observer 153,000. The *Annual Register* printed the figure of 80,000 while *The Times* gave both 80,000 and 100,000. It was Hulton, the chairman of the magistrates, who gave the figure of 60,000, and this became the generally accepted one. An astonishing figure it was too, being 6 per cent of the total population of Lancashire. Of the people in the south-east area of the county, upon which the meeting drew, about one in two were present.

As Hunt's barouche made its slow way through the crowds, to the accompaniment of the massed amateur bands' rendering of *See the Conquering Hero Comes* and a steady roar of 60,000 voices, as the banners were held aloft in the still air, the afternoon seemed set for the greatest Radical triumph to date. For truly the largest assembly seen not only on Lancashire's but on England's soil had been gathered together.

15

THEN YOU SHALL HAVE MILITARY FORCE

The thousands attending the meeting were not the only ones up early on August 16th. Lieutenant-Colonel Guy L'Estrange, the officer commanding the Manchester district, was also about at first light. Early on August 14th he had received the request from the magistrates for military assistance on Monday. On the 15th he received another communication stressing the urgent need for his assistance, which was probably induced by the attack on Murray at White Moss. Over the week-end he accordingly made his plans. He had available four squadrons of cavalry of the 15th Hussars, comprising about 600 men, with several hundred infantrymen in the whole of the 88th Foot and several squadrons of the 31st Foot (this being his own regiment). Then he had a detachment of the Royal Horse Artillery, Major Dyneley's regiment, with their two six-pounder guns. In addition he had the amateur Cheshire Yeomanry Cavalry at full strength with eight corps, at least 400 men, and three troops of the Manchester and Salford Yeomanry Cavalry, two of which, comprising 120 men, were actually used.

L'Estrange's plan was to ring the area of Saint Peter's Field with troops. The mounted detachments, amateur and regular, were to provide his first line to disperse the crowd (if necessary, of course). His infantrymen were the second line, should the situation turn to riot. Because, without horses or sabres, they would have to use firearms which he wanted to avoid. The artillery was only to be used in the extreme instance of the insurrection the magistrates, but not he himself, so gloomily anticipated. He disposed his forces thus: two squadrons of the 15th Hussars and one troop of the MYC were in Byrom Street; another squadron of the Hussars was in Lower Mosley Street, as escort to the Royal Artillery and their guns; with a final squadron held back at barracks. The 31st Foot was concealed in Brasenose Street, while the 88th were 'in ambush' in Dickinson Street. Most of the Cheshire Yeomanry were in St John Street, with one troop also held back at barracks. L'Estrange himself later testified that 'the remaining two troops of the Manchester Yeomanry were in Mosley Street under Major Trafford'. The Yeomanry's own deposition said they were under the command of Major Trafford in Portland Street. Their statement is more or less correct. More or less, because one troop was in Pickford's Yard commanded by Hugh Hornby Birley. The Yard was just off Portland Street, so one can forgive the slight mis-statement. Mosley and Portland Streets are close, so maybe they both meant the same thing to L'Estrange, though one feels a commander making a vital deposition after the event should have been strictly accurate.

From early morning of the 16th the plan was put into action. The Cheshire Yeomanry assembled on Sale Moor, an area of flat heathland on the Cheshire/Lancashire border, at 9 a.m. to ride to their positions in St John Street. The 15th Hussars paraded in field service at 8.30 a.m. before riding in at 10 a.m. to take up their positions in Byrom and Lower Mosley Streets. Among them, dressed in the blue uniform with yellow facings, the Busby bag with scarlet plume, was the nineteen-year-old

Lieutenant Jolliffe. The other forces had taken up their positions by mid-morning *with the exception of the* MYC. They, under their overall commander Major Trafford, did not assemble early. Once assembled they did not, alas, proceed to their allotted positions and wait patiently as the hours went by and the Radical processions streamed into Manchester. Members of the MYC, in their blue uniforms with white facings, were seen by countless witnesses in public houses, being entertained by Mr Birley or entertaining themselves. Whether Hugh Hornby Birley plied them with drink because he thought they needed Dutch courage, or to prove what a fine fellow he was, or to keep them out of mischief, one does not know. But it was an act a wise commander would not have performed. There is no evidence that any other troops, amateur or regular, were drunk, but that many members of the MYC were by the time they finally took up their positions is indisputable. It was considerably to add to the disaster of the day.

About 400 special constables, men who had responded to the call to aid the Civil Powers, were also about early. They assembled in St James's Square under the orders of John Moore, as senior of the two Constables whose official duty it was to preserve order in the town. Moore escorted 200 of the special constables to Saint Peter's Field, where he drew half of them up in a double row around the already erected hustings (consisting of two wagons pushed together); while the other half were formed into a line to provide an avenue of access between the hustings and a certain Mr Buxton's house, at 6, Mount Street. This house, situated full on to Saint Peter's Field, had been selected as the loyalist headquarters. The notorious Nadin was also involved in the organization of the special constables, presenting himself at Mr Buxton's house at midday, at which time the meeting was scheduled to start. Of the other 200 special constables, some were scattered around Manchester to protect vital property from possible attack, while others (as Francis Philips) were posted at the approaches to the town to report to the magistrates on the numbers and mood of the advancing Radical hordes.

The magistrates themselves, after their exhausting week-end, were at the Star Inn by 10 a.m. There they had an hour's discussion before proceeding to Mr Buxton's house to watch and wait for the contingents to arrive. They reached the house in time to see the first contingent from Stockport march on to the field, an area according to them as smooth and bereft of all inanimate objects as a billiard table. Prior to the 16th, on their instruc-tions, one Thomas Horrall who rejoiced in the title of Assistant Surveyor of the Paving of the Town, had employed scavengers to collect every stone, brick or possible missile from the field and surrounding streets. The scavengers also removed the lamp posts in Windmill Street, 'so that the Reformers might be destitute of every means of resistance'. The notion of the Radicals uprooting the lamp posts is a feasible one, there were some strong men among them. But the more interesting question is—resistance to what? The magistrates overlooked it when they later put forward Mr Horrall's activities as evidence that the Radicals must have come armed with their own stones.

The effect the oncoming contingents had on loyalists, as opposed to radical (though not necessarily Radical) witnesses, was divided. Some interpreted the cheerful, disciplined processions as evidence that the whole town of Manchester was in danger. Jere-miah Smith, the headmaster of Manchester Grammar School, sent the boys home after breakfast which must have pleased them, but shows that he acted before anything had happened. Other loyal-ists testified that they shut up their shops, closed their windows and bolted their doors after seeing the contingents go by, particu-larly Hunt's. However, Lieutenant Jolliffe, waiting patiently with the dismounted Hussars in Byrom Street, saw several Radi-cal processions pass along Deansgate, including Hunt's. He did not record anything about them that caused him to panic. The most reliable unbiased witness was the Reverend Edward Stanley,

Vicar of Alderley for thirty-two years, later Bishop of Norwich. He came upon the scene by accident, happening to have business with Mr Buxton on August 16th. He arrived at 6, Mount Street about 10 o'clock, and soon, much to his surprise, so did the Select Committee of Magistrates, Boroughreeve Clayton, Constables Moore and Andrew, Nadin and sundry other loyalists. Finding himself at the centre of activity he stayed to watch. He can be classified as the most reliable unbiased witness because he saw the whole scene from exactly the same position as the magistrates, and because of his background and temperament. From upbringing he was part of the Establishment, and he had no Radical affiliations or sympathies. Temperamentally he had a logical mind; he later became President of the Manchester Statistical Society. His account was only one man's view of Peterloo, but because of that background and temperament it was a most precious one for the Radicals on whose side it came down heavily.

Thus, to sum up, the position soon after 1 o'clock as Hunt's barouche finally arrived on the edge of Saint Peter's Field was as follows. Everything was concentrated on this area. The rest of Manchester was like a ghost town. The streets that had been filled with the Radicals' processions were empty and silent. Shops were shut, doors bolted, windows barred. On Saint Peter's Field, an area of roughly 14,000 square yards, were 60,000 men, women and children. The mass of the crowd was packed round and backwards from the hustings, so tightly that 'their hats seemed to touch'. Then there was a more open area, containing thick pockets but through which one could pass with reasonable freedom. On the outskirts of the field were heavy fringes of spectators, people who had come from curiosity to see how great the crowds were, what Hunt was like and what he would say. In No. 6, Mount Street, staring down on the scene, were the magistrates and other loyalists. Finally, there was the tight ring of 1,500 troops, mounted and foot, amateur and regular, with two six-pounder guns ready to rattle into action. It must be stressed that the crowds were not aware of the soldiers surrounding the field. The *Manchester Observer* might have spoken of the authorities preventing the meeting and shuddered at the possible consequences. Bamford might have experienced similar fears. But all the Radicals seem to have meant pre- or post-meeting trouble not a dispersal of the actual assembly.

It took Hunt a considerable time to make his way from Peter Street to the hustings through the adoring multitudes. It was approximately 1.20 p.m. when his barouche came within dismounting distance. Immediately there was minor trouble. Round the hustings was a double line of special constables armed with their stout black batons, bearing the royal insignia in gold, *Honi Soit qui mal y pense, Dieu et mon Droit, George III.* For a few minutes they refused to give way and allow Hunt access, but finally they cleared a small path. Among those who prepared to mount the hustings were Hunt himself, John Knight, John Saxton, Joseph Johnson, Mrs Fildes, Richard Carlile (the noted Devonshire Radical who had come up especially for the meeting) and several reporters. These included John Tyas of *The Times*, Edward Baines Jr of the *Leeds Mercury* and John Smith of the *Liverpool Mercury.* The presence of Tyas and Smith (for Liverpool was not a noted Radical town) shows the success the Radicals were having in their attempts at attracting national attention. This Manchester meeting was the first one to be covered by special correspondents from important distant newspapers.

As the Radical leaders stepped from the barouche, one of them noticed a heavily pregnant woman at the front of the crowd. Due to her condition, the stifling heat and the tightly packed bodies she was in a distressed, fainting state. He accordingly helped her into the barouche where she could rest and be safe. The gentleman could have been Hunt, ever gallant towards the fair sex, though it seems unlikely, as the woman, Mrs Elisabeth Gaunt, later said she did not know who put her into the barouche and even in a fainting condition she would surely have recognized the great leader. Whoever put her there did her the greatest possible disservice. She was to be far from safe and to pay for this chivalrous act with twelve days solitary confinement in prison. A late arrival on the hustings was Joseph Moorhouse, the Stockport Radical who had acted as host to Hunt in that town. Moorhouse had trapped his hand in the door of the barouche and stopped to receive medical attention. He may soon have wished that his injury had delayed him even longer.

Before Hunt finally mounted the hustings there was another minor incident, later blown up to great proportions by the magistrates. They claimed that the hustings were moved twice, once before, and then upon, Hunt's arrival. Their sinister interpretation of the first movement was that Hunt's strongest supporters, literally that was, had tried to get themselves between the constables and the hustings to block the avenue of access to Mr Buxton's house. The simple explanation of this first incident, never fully explained by either side, would seem to be that constables and stalwart supporters were jostling for position as near the hustings as possible. Of the second movement Hunt said that having surveyed the wagons he realized their position was such that, light though the wind was, his voice would be carried away from the crowd. He therefore ordered the realignment so that as many as possible of those who had come to hear him would be able to. Again the magistrates interpreted the move as an attempt to block the avenue of access. On this subject the Reverend Stanley's comment was: 'there seemed to be free and uninterrupted access to and from the hustings', at all times that was.

The realignment and/or movement of the hustings was in any case of academic interest, one of the water-sieving explanations remembered after the event. For the Reverend Hay stated: 'Long before his [Hunt's] arrival, the magistrates felt a decided conviction that the whole bore the appearance of insurrection, that the array was such as to terrify the King's subjects, and was such as no legitimate purpose could justify.' The magistrates had been pacing up and down at the windows of Mr Buxton's house since 11 o'clock, knowing that thousands of people would soon fill Saint Peter's Field, expecting riot and insurrection. But what terrified them as the crowds did fill the field was not the threatening rush of the mob, nor the producing of pikes, nor any sign of riot or insurrection. It was the reverse. It was the lack of 'natural violence'. It was the beautifully disciplined manner in which the crowds arrived and maintained their ranks while waiting for Hunt. By the bitterest of ironies, therefore, the very success of the Radical organization caused their doom, and made the magistrates take the first steps on, one can hardly call it the road, so quickly did events occur, but on the ravine to disaster. Only in the numbers can allowance be made for the magistrates' panic, and then not much, but probably neither side anticipated such a splendid turn-out. Having surveyed the scene for nearly two hours the magistrates reached their panicky conclusion. They were in control, they alone, and for God's sake they had to do something.

What they did was to justify the necessity for drastic action by getting one Richard Owen and thirty other loyalists (including Francis Philips) to swear and sign an affidavit for the arrest of Hunt and the Radical leaders, which they did by no means unwillingly. Thus, 'Richard Owen hath this day made oath before us, His Majesty's Justices of the Peace ... that Henry Hunt, John Knight, Jos. Johnson and—Moorhouse at this time (now a quarter past one o'clock) have arrived in a car, at the area near St. Peter's Church and that an immense mob is collected and he considers the town in danger'.

A conclusion had been reached. Hunt was to be arrested. The crowds would then disperse as had the Blanketeers after the arrest of Johnston, Bagguley and Drummond in 1817. The magistrates also had the more recent arrest of Harrison from Smithfield to comfort them. However, there were several factors they did not take into account. There were at least 30,000 more people on Saint Peter's Field than there had been in 1817. There was no Sir John Byng to disperse the crowds as skilfully as he had in that year. Harrison, chaplain to the poor and needy, stalwart hero of the Union Societies though he might be, was no Hunt, no nationally idolized demigod. And in any case the arrest of Harrison had not broken up the Smithfield meeting. Did the magistrates truly imagine that 60,000 people who had been preparing for weeks, who had marched miles into Manchester, would calmly watch as their demigod and everybody else on the hustings were hauled off to prison? Who knows? Perhaps the Radicals would have maintained their discipline. Hunt claimed emphatically that the arrests could have been peacefully effected *had not the military been used.* But it seems more probable that once the arrests had been decided upon, some sort of chaos and possibly bloodshed would have been inevitable. This was the first juncture at which the absence of Sir John Byng was regrettable. He would have taken the many different factors into account, and could well have counselled against the arrests.

First Hunt had to be arrested. Accordingly the Boroughreeve was called for. The shadowy personality of Edward Clayton emerged from the ranks of special constables round the hustings, and entered Mr Buxton's house. In his presence Hulton, as chairman of the magistrates, handed the warrants to John Moore, as senior of the two Constables whose job it was to preserve order. But Moore was not accustomed to doing the dirty work so he called for Nadin who was also down in the ranks of the constables. With the warrants in his possession, Nadin made a gesture towards making the arrests. He re-passed down the line of constables towards the hustings, and then quickly returned to Mr Buxton's house. With him came half the constables who were supposed to be helping in the arrest. All this to-ing and fro-ing between hustings and house seems absolutely to uphold the Reverend Stanley's statement that the avenue of access was never blocked. The to-ing and fro-ing, particularly of Nadin who always spelled trouble to the Lancashire masses, caused a slight panic among the crowd nearest the hustings. But a special constable called out, 'It is a false alarm.' However, another one said, 'Wait, you'll see something now.' This latter was sadly to prove true.

Back in Mr Buxton's house the following conversation ensued:

HULTON (with his hand on Nadin's arm, very chummy in the moment of stress). Is it not possible for the police aided by the Special Constables, to execute the warrant?

NADIN Never with those Special Constables, nor with ten times the number, nor with all the Special Constables in England.

HULTON Cannot it be executed without military force?

NADIN It cannot.

HULTON Then you shall have the military force. For God's sake don't sacrifice the lives of the Special Constables.

So the second conclusion was reached. The military were required to arrest Hunt, but there was no need to worry, had not the military also been required to arrest Johnston, Bagguley and Drummond? Hulton accordingly wrote two messages which were despatched forthwith, the first to Colonel L'Estrange, the second to Major Trafford. The message L'Estrange received read thus: 'Sir, as Chairman of the Select Committee of Magistrates I request you to afford those Magistrates military protection in the execution of their duty, as they conceive the Civil Powers wholly inadequate to keep the same. Wm Hulton'. The message Major Trafford received was slightly longer and politer: 'Sir, as Chairman of the Select Committee of Magistrates I request you to proceed immediately to No 6 Mount Street where the Magistrates are assembled. They conceive the Civil Powers wholly inadequate to preserve the peace. I have the honour to be Sir, yr. obt. humble svt. Wm. Hulton'.

A vital question, which was not answered in any of the later innumerable depositions, testimonies, inquest and trials, is *why* the magistrates sent *two* messages. L'Estrange was the commander in charge of the troops the magistrates were calling for. So why did they send a message to Major Trafford? There were several other officers as senior in rank as Major Trafford lurking around Saint Peter's Field, but they did not receive a separate message. This is the second juncture at which Byng's presence would have made a difference. It is unlikely that he would have authorized the message to Trafford. Did the magistrates send this second request because Trafford was the commander of their very own Manchester and Salford Yeomanry Cavalry? Was it a case of chauvinism? Whatever motive prompted this seemingly unnecessary second message, the fact that Trafford received the individual request was the final kick down the ravine. For now distance played a part. L'Estrange was in Byrom Street, while Trafford was in Pickford's Yard. L'Estrange had to organize his other troops, so although he started for Mr Buxton's house almost immediately upon receipt of Hulton's message, it was not physically possible for him to reach the field before the MYC.

On receipt of his request Major Trafford decided not to lead his brave men personally. It was a decision that saved him from much of the hatred and notoriety that descended upon the man to whom he designated the honour, his second-in-command, Hugh Hornby Birley. Given the order to advance by Birley, the MYC in Pickford's Yard were only too ready to oblige. They leapt, clambered or were pushed on to their horses, half or very drunk as most of them were, drew their sabres and, according to Birley, set off at an easy trot through Nicholas Street. Other witnesses were not so certain as to the easiness of the trot. As they turned into Cooper Street the trot, even according to Birley, became brisk. He says it was because they heard loud shouts coming from

Saint Peter's Field and therefore had to get to the magistrates' assistance as quickly as possible. At the head of the troop was Edward Meagher, the yeomanry's trumpeter, who was to earn as great a hatred as Birley for his subsequent actions. Another man called Tom Shelmerdine also loomed large in local infamy. But the yeomanry cavalryman who caused the first Peterloo death remains unnamed.

The main body of the MYC trotted briskly or 'galloped furiously as though they were flying', according to whether you were a yeomanry cavalryman or an onlooker, down Cooper Street. But one man, presumably more drunk than the rest, was left behind. Even the MYC admitted that the unnamed member, having been detained, was following on at a hard gallop. Among the passers-by in narrow Cooper Street was a Mrs Ann Fildes (no connection with Mrs Fildes of the Female Reformers). Ann Fildes had in her arms her two-year-old son William. She retreated against the houses as the main body of the cavalry swept past, clutching William to her. Assuming the rush over she stepped forward still clutching her son, whereupon, in the MYC's choice wording, she 'came into contact' with the horse of the lone rider. The contact threw her to the ground and stunned her, while William fell from her arms and was killed. Whether through hitting his head on the cobbles or being trampled upon by the horse with whom he had come into contact was not clarified. It did not matter anyway. He was dead. It was bitterly appropriate that the first death of Peterloo should have been that of a two-year-old child whose mother was not even at the meeting.

The majority of the MYC were obviously unaware of the child's death, but it is doubtful that they would have been perturbed had they known. Cooper Street led them straight into Mount Street. They drew up near Mr Buxton's house, about 100 yards from the hustings. Even Hulton admitted that they arrived 'in a certain degree of confusion'. He said it was because their horses were raw and unused to the field, but dozens of other witnesses attributed the confusion to intoxication. One Radical when asked why he had come to this immediate conclusion said simply, 'Because they rolled about on their horses.'

The time was now 1.40 p.m. Hunt had finally started to address the crowds who had been waiting so eagerly and patiently for him. Hunt himself said that he had scarcely uttered more than two sentences before the MYC arrived. Stanley agreed that he had only been speaking a minute or two, and a Radical witness more quaintly said: 'I could not have read two chapters of the Bible before the soldiers turned up.' The intent of what Hunt managed to say was inevitably queried. Although ear-witnesses' accounts vary slightly, there was agreement that Hunt told the crowds to continue to conduct themselves peaceably and quietly. But the magistrates' *later* interpretation—one firmly says *later* (Stanley, in the same room as they, and not known to be deaf, stated it was impossible to hear what Hunt said because of the noise from the crowd)—was that his exhortation to maintain order was a subtle form of incitement to riot. The *Quarterly Review*, for example, compared the words with Mark Antony's oration over Caesar's dead body: 'Good friends, sweet friends, let me not stir you up to mutiny'.

As the MYC galloped on to the field, there was a stir among the crowd. The first cry, before the horses were seen, was that the noise heralded the arrival of the Blackburn contingent. But this soon changed to a general cry of 'The soldiers, the soldiers', and the stir became something of a panic sway. Hunt reacted firmly and sensibly, shouting, 'Stand firm, my friends, there are only a few soldiers, and we are a host against them.' Then, pointing to the disordered halt of the cavalry, he laughed and again said, 'Stand firm, my friends. They are in disorder already. This is a trick. Give them three cheers.' The crowds responded happily to their leader's injunctions, a great cheer poured forth, and the panic subsided. Unfortunately, the magistrates chose to inter-pret Hunt's quick, firm action in suppressing incipient panic as yet a further sign of the riot that had not yet but must soon materialize. They heard the cheers as 'a most marked gesture of defiance'.

For a few minutes everything hung in the balance. The MYC were rolling about on, and trying to control, their frightened horses who were neither trained for, nor used to, the noise of battle, as were the steeds of the regular troops. The crowds were cheering and transferring their attention back to Hunt who was preparing to resume his speech. In these few minutes the magistrates themselves seem to have had doubts about the wisdom of sending the MYC to effect the arrests. Would it not be wiser to wait for the arrival of L'Estrange and the regulars? But they were worried by the removal of half the special constables from that contested avenue of access between the hustings and Mr Buxton's house. If they waited further might not the avenue be completely blocked? And the MYC were stout fellows so, after only a few minutes' pause, just after 1.40 p.m. they were ordered to accompany Nadin, Clayton, Moore and Andrew and the special constables to execute the arrests.

16

AH, BEHOLD THEIR SABRES GLEAMING

With sabres drawn, their sharpened blades flashing ominously in the shimmering sunlight, with Edward Meagher the trumpeter in the van, the sixty members of Birley's troop of the MYC advanced towards the hustings. But the famous avenue of access was only wide enough for pedestrian traffic. Between the MYC and the hustings were thousands of men, women and children jammed as tightly as fruit in a bottle. For a few paces an attempt was made to maintain order, to follow the officers in line abreast, but the further the horses were thrust into the dense throng the more frightened they became, and the less control the yeomanry had over them. The terrified animals reared and plunged while terrified people strove to get out of the way of their thudding hooves. But the very density of the crowd made such evasive action impossible. Men and women fell backwards into the arms of other men and women; the concertina pattern started; and the MYC lost any semblance of order. With ranks broken it was every cavalryman for himself, each vieing with the other for the honour of being the first to reach the hustings and drag the Radical scum into captivity.

Thus within seconds of the MYC's advance, chaos and panic began to grip the field. In the hurricane path people already lay dying and injured, crushed by the horses' hooves, slashed by sabre cuts. In the mad gallop there was no time to consider whether Radical scum or stalwart constable was being mown down or sabre hacked. Among the early casualties was Constable Moore, thrown to the ground and temporarily stunned by one of the cavalrymen who was supposed to be affording him protection. However, for the time being the chaos was limited to the area of the hustings, and the actual arrests were effected with comparative ease. Birley was among the first to reach the hustings. He approached Hunt and said, 'Sir, I have a warrant against you, and arrest you as my prisoner.' Hunt, at this point still urging the people round the hustings to keep calm, replied, 'I willingly surrender myself to any civil officer who will show me his warrant.' So Nadin, who had also arrived, stepped forward saying, 'I will arrest you. I have got information on oath against you.' He then repeated the words to Johnson. Hunt descended from the hustings of his own accord but others were not so fortunate in their manner of leaving. Yeomanry and constables dragged Moorhouse off by his ankles and Johnson by his legs. Mrs Fildes's white dress caught on a nail of the wagons and as she tugged at the material, frantically trying to free herself, she was 'slashed across her exposed body by one of the brave cavalry'. Having been unceremoniously or viciously hauled from the hustings, the Radical leaders were dragged equally unceremoniously and viciously back through the chaos to Mr Buxton's house.

Even at this point the worst of the disaster could have been averted if anybody had been in effective command of the situation; if the MYC had contented themselves with performing the job they had been sent on to the field to perform, i.e., the arrest of the Radical leaders; if Manchester had lived up to its later reputation as a permanent rain-sodden sponge. But there was nobody in authority to give sharp, sensible orders; the MYC were in no mood to trot tamely back to base; and it had not rained for days. Having tasted blood the MYC went berserk. The stifling heat worked on their wine-fuddled brains, the taunts and ridicule of the last two years swam in their seething brain cells. Now they had power. Now, once and for all, they would prove who were the masters. Leaving the task of escorting the prisoners to the special constables they turned their attention to the hustings, smashing the wagons, tearing the banners and Caps of Liberty. As they rampaged the dust rose from the hard-baked ground into the shimmering heat and there was no wind to dispel it. Thus what was, or was not, happening round the hustings was partially obscured from the fearful eyes of the watching magistrates.

In the meantime, and it was a very brief time, a few minutes at most, Colonel L'Estrange and the 15th Hussars had arrived on the field. At some point in this interval the Riot Act was read, once by Ethelston, once by magistrate Sylvester. Hay's account of Ethelston's reading is the essence of tragi-comedy, as during the reading the sabres were already hacking away. Hay said on oath: 'He read it with his head very far out of the window [i.e., of Mr Buxton's house] ... he leant so far out, that I stood behind him, ready to catch his skirts for fear he might fall over. Mr Ethelston is a gentleman who I have occasionally heard sing, and he has a remarkably powerful voice. When he drew his head back into the room after reading the proclamation, I observed to him, "Mr Ethelston, I never heard your voice so powerful".' Nobody mentioned the quality of Mr Sylvester's voice. He actually went out of 6, Mount Street to read the proclamation from a card, but he did not get far, either physically or with the reading, as somebody pushed him, not surprisingly seeing what was occurring round the hustings. On being pushed he returned to the house and abandoned his attempt. The Radicals later doubted that the Riot Act had been read at all. However, it was read. That hardly anybody in the crowd heard it, and that the statutory hour was not allowed before the dispersal started, is beyond question. The discussion was of more academic interest than that surrounding the movement of the hustings, because if the magistrates' 'decision' to disperse the crowd was justifiable, it was justifiable under Common Law which decreed that an illegal assembly could be dispersed without any reading of the Riot Act.

With L'Estrange's arrival dispersal was the decision taken. Peering into the clouds of shifting dust the magistrates became convinced that the crowd was attacking the yeomanry. Their brave cavalry must at all costs be rescued, and the only way to do this was by dispersing the mob. It was in fact Hulton who gave the order for the dispersal. He met L'Estrange as the Hussars rode in. L'Estrange asked what was happening and what he should do. Hulton cried out, 'Good God, Sir, don't you see they are attacking the Yeomanry? Disperse them.' Later Hulton had doubts as to the precipitance of his solo action but he said he knew he had the concurrence of his brother magistrates; a correct assertion as they were quite as much in a panic as he was. Lieutenant Jolliffe also believed that the dispersal was necessary. He saw the yeomanry as being in the power of those they had been sent to contain. The yeomanry were *not* in the power of the unarmed men, women and children, but they were now scattered. Having indulged in their orgy of destruction around the hustings they had ridden for the other banners, again each vieing with the other to see who could grab most as proof positive of glory. To the newly arrived Lieutenant Jolliffe, who had no idea what had occurred in the preceding minutes, it could seem as though the yeomanry were the attacked not the attackers.

Pausing only a few seconds to receive their orders Lieutenant Jolliffe and the Hussars charged on to the field. They charged from a position parallel with the hustings, having been led from their waiting stations off Deansgate not on the direct route via Peter Street, but on a circuitous one that brought them into a position facing the main body of the crowd. At this moment the main body was still in reasonable order. If this seems strange it must be remembered how swiftly everything had happened, how short a time had elapsed since the initial advance of the MYC. The panic round the hustings and the individual activities of the yeomanry were spreading like the ripples of stones in water. There was also panic on the outskirts of the field where the spectators who had been informed of what was happening round the hustings and of the Hussars' arrival, by those who had climbed on to higher ground for a better view, were trying to make their escape. But the majority of the crowd, though aware that something had gone radically (if not Radically) wrong with the proceedings, was totally unprepared for the dispersal. Everybody was anxious, craning necks, standing on tiptoe, trying to ascertain what was happening, turning to their relations, their neighbours, to fellow members of Union Societies, asking what had gone wrong, what the glistening dust meant, whether Hunt had really been arrested, demanding of their contingent leaders what they should do. Then suddenly the Hussars were in their midst, trained, disciplined, professional soldiers who had been given their orders and were carrying them out, with horses trained and disciplined for the task of removing the enemy from the field. With no time to collect wits, panic spread like a bush fire, the terrible panic of being trapped, of being enveloped in mass fear, in a maelstrom of falling bodies, rearing horses, trampling hooves and slashing sabres. In the Hussars' path the concertina pattern repeated and repeated itself, hundreds of people collapsing upon each other, while hundreds more were swept as though on tidal waves.

While the screams rent the sultry air, while the dust rose higher and higher towards the hot sun, while women with babies, men with children on their shoulders, young and old struggled to make their way from the death trap Saint Peter's Field had become, the MYC continued to indulge in their moments of individual glory. Thomas Redford, carrying Middleton's green banner, held it high in the air until the staff was cut from his hand and his shoulder was split open by a yeomanry sabre. Women crouched over their children's bodies, crying to the yeomanry not to hurt them and had their heads cleft by sabres. Many times attackers and attacked knew each other personally. An old woman saw Tom Shelmerdine, whom she had nursed as a child, riding down upon her. She cried: 'Nay, Tom Shelmerdine, thee wilt not hurt me, I know' but 'deaf to her supplications he rode her down'. As they plunged about their carnage the yeomanry underlined the message verbally, shouting: 'Damn you, I'll reform you'; 'You'll come again, will you?'; 'I'll let you know I'm a soldier today'; 'This is for Waterloo'; 'Spare your lives? Damn your bloody lives.' Many of the Radical menfolk, trying to protect their wives and children or their wounded comrades or the banners or simply themselves, wished they had come armed with something other than their 'self-approving consciences'.

Among the 60,000 struggling people was John Lees. He had what at the time seemed the good fortune to get himself a position near the hustings. As the yeomanry turned their attention from the arrest of Hunt to the battering of their enemies, John was slashed by a sabre, hit by a truncheon, and as he fell to the ground was ridden over by an MYC horse. The constable who lashed at him with the truncheon shouted, 'Damn your bloody eyes, I'll break your back.' In the chaos there was the inevitable miraculous escape that convinces people of fate, of your number being up or not being up. A man had brought a cheese for his dinner. Not having eaten it he put the cheese under his hat for safe-keeping. When the Hussars charged, like everybody else he tried to make his escape, but he found himself in the direct path of a yeomanry cavalryman. Up into the air went the MYC sabre, down it came on the man's head. There it embedded itself in the cheese. Whether the yeomanry cavalryman rode off with it stuck to his sabre is not recorded, but the cheese saved one head from being split open. An old man called Thomas Blinstone was knocked down by a galloping horse and had both his arms splintered as the hooves rode over his outstretched body. But it was not his wounds that disturbed him most. It was the loss of his spectacles. Months later, telling his story to the members of the Metropolitan Relief Committee, he said: 'And what is wur than aw, mesters, they'n broken my spectacles, an aw've ne'er yet been able to get a pair that suits me.'

The tides of humanity were swept towards the outskirts of the field. There further chaos met them. For the avenues of escape were wholly or partially blocked. The adjacent streets were choked at the far end with further oncoming Hussars and men of the 31st and 88th Foot, on one of the lower sides by the Cheshire Yeomanry Cavalry who had arrived with the 15th Hussars (though they were not used in the actual dispersal), and on the other by Major Dyneley bringing up his six-pounder guns at a hard gallop.

Much as the yeomanry started and contributed to the havoc, the dispersal proper was effected by the 15th Hussars. It was they who were responsible for the majority of deaths and injuries. Many Radical witnesses later testified that the Hussars *tried* only to hit with the flat of their sabres (not always successfully in the chaos), that they were not deliberately lashing out with their blades as were the yeomanry. Nevertheless most of the casualties were caused by the Hussars. For it was not the sabre cuts, vicious as their wounds were, much as the image of silver blades glistening in the sun and descending on defenceless heads that is associated with Peterloo, that wreaked the greatest havoc. More of the dead, and certainly of the wounded, suffered from being trampled upon by the horses or from the pressure of 'being literally piled up to a considerable elevation above ground level'—the description being Lieutenant Jolliffe's.

The place where the worst pile-up occurred was near the Friends' Meeting House on the outskirts of the field in a direct line from the hustings. There the greatest tidal wave of humanity was swept by the charging Hussars, and beached. In front of a nearby house one tongue of the wave was trapped. In simple, vivid language the female occupant of the house later described what happened. 'The people came in great crowds past my door, and a parcel of them beat down the fence. The stumps were all down on the ground, and also the stones were out of their places. There was a large stump with a stone at the bottom. It was an oak stump about twelve inches square. The people were so pressed against it that they could not get away. They [the MYC] kept cutting them in the corner, and the shrieks would astonish you, and they were laying on them all the time as hard as they could upon them, and an officer belonging to the soldiers [i.e., the Hussars] came up and said, "Gentlemen, gentlemen, for shame, forbear. The people cannot get away." Just as he was saying so the rail broke and let a whole number of the people into my cellar.' The person at the bottom of the falling pyramid was a Mrs Martha Partington of Eccles. She was 'took up dead'.

It was round and inside the Friends' Meeting House that the only pocket of resistance occurred. In front of the building was a pile of loose timber, carelessly overlooked by Mr Horrall and his scavengers. Behind the timber, a pile of stones and other missiles was found. Pressed and harried by the yeomanry as they were, many people seized upon the timber and stones to defend themselves. A considerable number found sanctuary inside the Meeting House. There is no doubt that missiles were flung at the yeomanry from near and inside it. Somebody threw a brickbat which unhorsed one of the yeomanry. Bamford, who had seen part of the tidal wave, said that somebody was 'a heroine, a young woman of our party, with her face all bloody, her hair streaming about her, her bonnet hanging by the string, and her apron weighted with stones', and that she kept her assailant at bay for several minutes before unhorsing him. It was also from the Meeting House that the one probable Radical shot of the day was fired. Loyalists later testified to hearing several shots, but nobody put 'the several' at higher than eight. The Radicals held on to the Meeting House for a short while, hurling as many missiles as they could find from its windows. Then a farrier of the 15th Hussars rode at a small door on the outer wall and his horse struck it with such force that the door flew open. Other Hussars rode in and resistance was at an end. As Sir Francis Burdett later said in the House of Commons, answering charges that as stones and missiles were thrown the crowd must have come armed: 'When once they were attacked what could you expect? Were people in the quiet exercise of one of their most undoubted privileges to be unresistingly bayoneted, sabred, trampled underfoot, without raising a hand, or (if the noble Lord would allow), without putting their hands in their pockets for the stones they had brought with them?' Of pikes not a mention was heard, not even from Norris and Ethelston.

By 2 o'clock, only twenty minutes from the moment the MYC had drawn up in confusion outside Mr Buxton's house, less than fifteen from the moment the 15th Hussars had charged, it was all over. The Field of Saint Peter was virtually deserted. The special constables were grouped round No.6 Mount Street, people were sheltering or tending their wounded on the outskirts of the field, Major Dyneley's six-pounders were rattling across the hardbaked ground, but the main 14,000 square yards had been emptied of humanity as if by magic.

To Lieutenant Jolliffe, 'The field and the adjacent streets presented an extraordinary sight; the ground was covered with hats, shoes and musical instruments. Here and there lay the unfortunates who were too injured to move away, and this sight was rendered the more distressing by observing some women among the sufferers.' Major Dyneley had 'I must not say the *pleasure* of seeing the field of Battle covered with hats, sticks, shoes, laurel branches, drum heads. In short, the field was as complete as I have ever seen one after an action.' But it was Samuel Bamford who wrote the most moving (and most paraphrased) description of the scene after the dispersal: 'Within ten minutes from the commencement of the havock, the field was an open and almost deserted space. The sun looked down through a sultry and motionless air ... the hustings remained, with a few broken and hewed flag staves erect, and a torn and gashed banner or two drooping; whilst over the whole field, were strewed the caps, bonnets, hats, shawls, and shoes, and other parts of male and female dress; trampled, torn and bloody. The yeomanry had dismounted—some were easing their horses' girths, others adjusting their accoutrements; and some were wiping their sabres. Several mounds of human beings still remained where they had fallen, crushed down and smothered. Some of these still groaning—others with staring eyes, were gasping for breath, and others would never breathe more. All was silent save those low sounds, and the occasional snorting and pawing of steeds.'

17

THE BATTLE OF
MANCHESTER IS OVER

If Saint Peter's Field was virtually empty by 2 o'clock, the dispersal was still very much in hand. In this the Cheshire Yeomanry, the 88th and 31st Foot, the other troops of the MYC and the 15th Hussars also participated—the Cheshire Yeomanry displaying some of the malign enthusiasm of their brethren in the MYC. Thousands of people, men carrying their wounded comrades, women with their terrified children, blood streaming down beaten and gashed faces, poured through the gaps into the adjacent streets. There they were further hacked and harried. Edward Meagher, the trumpeter, of whom it was simply said he spent the quarter of an hour murdering his fellow creatures, led a personal charge in Lloyd Street, two streets away from Saint Peter's Field, and filled with fleeing men, women and children.

As the human streams pushed their way from the centre of Manchester the main pursuit ceased. Once clear of the narrow streets the pace of the flights, north, south, east and west, accelerated. At a turnpike half a mile from the city centre, hundreds of people gave the keeper shillings and half-crowns, though the price was only a penny, and without waiting for their change dashed through the turnstile. Archibald Prentice, who had earlier left Mount Street to return to his home, heard 'a wailing sound … and rushing out I saw people running in the direction of Pendleton, their faces pale as death, and some with blood trickling down their cheeks. It was with difficulty I could get anybody to stop and tell me what had happened.' Many of the crowd continued their headlong flight, as if pursued by the Furies, until they reached the safety of the homes they had left with such solemn hopeful purpose only a few hours before. L'Estrange called off his troops once the orders had been completed and the mob dispersed, but the MYC continued to roam the streets and outlying districts, so the fear of the Furies was not misjudged.

Certain numbers of the contingents continued to show discipline, rallying at their half-way points into some semblance of order. About a thousand of the originally 6,000 strong Middleton and Rochdale contingent re-formed at Harpurhey. Led by Bamford, they wearily but defiantly marched home, with one saved banner, the blue one, fluttering limply, and the odd fife and bugle sounding forlornly, at their head. The Staleybridge band managed to keep together and save their big drum. They were on the last long haul upwards out of Stockport when they espied a group of marauding yeomanry, whereupon they scrambled over a hedge for safety. The big drum was thrown over first and, enter the never distant element of farce, one of the men landed right in the middle of it. But for most of the thousands, many of them wounded, who struggled home, five, ten, fifteen, twenty painful miles, the elements of shock, anger and tragedy were stronger.

None was more tragically wounded than John Lees. The crown of his hat had been cut off by a sabre slash, his shirt and coat were in ribbons. Underneath the visible signs of his encounter with the MYC there was a deep cut on his elbow which in fact had separated the elbow bone. There was a sabre gash on his left shoulder. The skin was off his right hip in two places, one foot was partially crushed, and the whole of his shoulders, back and loins were covered with bruises from the battering of the constable's truncheon and the weight of the horse's hooves. Somehow despite these injuries he struggled off Saint Peter's Field. His stepbrother Thomas helped him, although Thomas's shoes had been ripped off by horses' hooves and his feet were badly bruised. With other friends helping them the two young men walked the eight miles home to Oldham. They stopped at Newton Heath for a drink, which John must have desperately needed, but how long it took them to walk those long uphill miles is not recorded. John's stepmother saw him standing exhausted by the garden gate and, realizing that he had been injured, helped him into the house, gave him a warm drink and sent him up to bed.

In the meantime, Hunt and the others arrested had been dragged to Mr Buxton's house. In the mêlée both Hunt and Saxton could have lost their lives. Hunt himself said that one of the constables pulled off his white hat and made to strike at his bare head with a heavy truncheon, which would have split his skull, but Nadin (of all people) saved him from serious injury or possible death. Hunt's own testimony is always to be taken with a pinch of salt, but it was supported by that of John Tyas, *The Times* reporter. Tyas said Hunt was treated by the constables in a manner which was justifiable neither by law nor humanity. Saxton was attacked in the confusion round the hustings by two privates of the MYC. One shouted, 'There is that villain, Saxton, do you run him through?', to which the other replied, 'I had rather not. I leave him to you.' Thereupon the first private made a lunge with his sabre which Saxton just managed to avoid, receiving only a cut in his coat and waistcoat.

When Saint Peter's Field had been cleared of humanity, the prisoners were dragged out again. The magistrates intended to send them to the New Bailey by carriage, but finally decided to make them walk. When this became known to the special constables and loyalists surrounding the house there were shouts of approbation. As they emerged the prisoners were again badly treated, having to run a gauntlet of hissing, booing and beating. This behaviour caused the Reverend Hay some anxiety, and he urged the constables not to ill-treat the prisoners. They were then given into the custody of L'Estrange, and with two constables flanking each of them were marched to the New Bailey. Two staves, all that was left of some town's proud banners, were carried in mockery at the head of the procession.

Among those incarcerated within the New Bailey, thirty-five people in all, were Hunt himself, Johnson, Saxton, Knight, Moorhouse, Messrs Wild and Swift, a man called Jones, about whom little is known except that he was on the hustings, the heavily pregnant Mrs Elizabeth Gaunt who had been hauled from the barouche, a Mrs Hargreaves and John Tyas of *The Times*. As Hunt said: 'This circumstance I shall ever consider most fortunate. Mr Tyas is a gentleman of a most respectable family and connection ... and as he was totally unconnected with any of those who called the meeting, he was capable of giving and he did give, the most unprejudiced evidence upon the subject.' In a day full of blundering, panic-stricken actions the arrest of Tyas was certainly a major blunder on the magistrates' part.

When John Edward Taylor and Archibald Prentice heard that Tyas had been arrested, 'fearing that no relation of events would reach London, except what might be sent by directions of the magistracy, and coloured to justify their conduct', both sat down and wrote accounts of the day's proceedings. Taylor sent his copy to *The Times*, Prentice his to another London paper. Both stated firmly that the crowd had done nothing to justify dispersal and that the magistrates had panicked. Thus the first accounts to reach the capital of what had happened on Saint Peter's Field were sober, straightforward and untouched by loyalist justifications. For if Taylor and Prentice were radicals, they were not Radicals, and their byword was integrity. *The*

Times itself, which could not be accused of being either radical or Radical, did not take kindly to having one of its reporters arrested. With Mr Tyas, a gentleman who was 'as far as we can judge from preceding conduct towards this journal, about as much a Jacobin, or friend of the Jacobins as is Lord Liverpool himself', in prison, the august newspaper felt justified in querying 'the manner in which those who acted for the magistrates thought fit to exercise the power and to discharge the functions assigned to them'. When released from prison, the highly respectable, un-Jacobin Mr Tyas not only confirmed Taylor's and Prentice's accounts of what had occurred but asked other questions embarrassing to the magistrates.

On the evening of August 16th, the weight of *The Times* disapproval had not yet fallen on the magistrates. They had Hunt and most of the leading Radicals securely in gaol, but they were worried about the temper of Manchester's unruly inhabitants. Not because they considered they had taken any improper action on Saint Peter's Field, but because Manchester's populace was generally unruly and might take advantage of the afternoon's trouble to become more so. Consequently, they asked L'Estrange to supply strong pickets to support the few regular night constables and the special constables who were willingly remaining on duty. The strongest picket, consisting of two troops of the 15th Hussars and two companies of the 88th Foot, was posted in the New Cross area. As the long, stiflingly hot summer day turned into dusk the whole of Manchester was seething with stories and rumours, and there were those who were 'athirst for revenge'. Sure enough, as the twilight deepened, a crowd started to gather in New Cross. Whether reacting to the presence of the troops, or athirst for revenge, its numbers increased with the gathering night. Just before 9 o'clock missiles were thrown at the soldiers, then more missiles, and the Riot Act was read. Finally the officer commanding the 88th Foot ordered his men to open fire. The firing lasted about three minutes at the end of which the crowd had dispersed, one man was dead, and several people lay on the ground injured.

Major Dyneley was writing his report on the day's earlier proceedings when the New Cross disturbance started. In the report he noted that 'the first action of the Battle of Manchester is over, and I am happy to say has ended in the complete discomfiture of the Enemy'; that he had been 'very much assured to see the way in which the Volunteer Cavalry knocked the people about during the whole time we remained on the ground; the instant they saw ten or a dozen Mobbites together, they rode at them and *leathered* them properly'; and that both they and the Cheshire Volunteer Cavalry 'behaved uncommonly well, and a troop from *Stockport* cut their way through in form'. On receiving the news of further trouble he and his guns turned out immediately. But to his disappointment they arrived at New Cross as the crowd was dispersing, though he was glad to be able to report that 'the sight of us put them to the rout properly'.

While Major Dyneley was hastily penning his report—'I hope you will be able to read what I have written but I am sure you would excuse it all, could you see the hurried way in which I am writing'—the Reverend Hay began to write *his* report of the day's proceedings to Lord Sidmouth. He wrote because Norris, poor thing, was much fatigued by its harassing events. As the New Cross crowds dispersed, just before 11 o'clock, Hay finished his letter. The report began with the reasons why the magistrates had seen fit to arrest Hunt: no legitimate purpose, aspect of insurrection, terrifying all loyal subjects, town in danger, loyalists signing affidavits; and then went on to the dispersal of the crowd, marked defiance by the mob and attacking of yeomanry. He admitted that the dispersal had not been achieved without 'very serious and lamentable effects' which the magistrates deeply regretted, and 'that four women appear to have lost their lives by being pressed by the crowd'. But overshadowing these regrets were the death of a special constable named Ashworth, and the MYC man named Holme who had been struck by the missile and unhorsed, thus fracturing his skull, and for whose hopes of recovery there were none. (Ashworth was indeed a Peterloo victim, being crushed to death in the chaos round the hustings he was guarding. But Holme recovered so quickly that not even the MYC made great claims about his injury.) This emphasis on the men who had fallen in the execution of their noble duty, in the Government's service, detracted from the crowd's injuries. The impression that the meeting had grown completely out of hand on the Radical side, that the illegality had not commenced until after the crowd had assembled, that their magistrates had used their judicious prudence on the spot (as advised by the Home Office), and that the whole town of Manchester was grateful for the magistrates' firm, prompt, decisive actions was the one Sidmouth gained on returning from his holiday in Broadstairs.

Before discussing how implicit a reliance Sidmouth should have placed on the magistrates' version, there is a vital question to be asked: What were the casualties at Peterloo? How many people were killed and injured? It is a question that cannot now be answered with absolute certainty. The names and causes of death vary more alarmingly than the estimates of numbers present on Saint Peter's Field. Unlike the crowd estimate no casualty figure was ever commonly accepted. Working on the premise that if a person's name appeared several times from differing sources he or she died as a result of Peterloo, the list of killed is as follows:

Thomas Ashworth	Bulls Head, Manchester. Sabred and trampled. He was the special constable.
John Ashton	Cowhill, near Oldham. Sabred and trampled on by the crowd.

Thomas Buckley	Baretrees, Chadderton. Sabred and stabbed.
James Crompton	Barton. Trampled on by the cavalry.
William Fildes	Kennedy Street, Manchester. Rode over by the cavalry. This was the two-year-old boy.
Mary Heys	Rawlinson's-buildings, Oxford Road, Manchester. Rode over by the cavalry.
Sarah Jones	Silk Street, Manchester. No cause given.
John Lees	Oldham. Sabred.
Arthur O'Neill	Pigeon Street, Manchester. Inwardly crushed.
Martha Partington	Eccles. Thrown into a cellar and killed on the spot.
John Rhodes	Pits, Hopwood. Like John Lees he died several weeks later, and his body was dissected on the magistrates' orders to try and prove that death was not a result of injuries sustained on August 16th.
Joseph Ashworth	Shot. At New Cross.
William Bradshaw	Lilly-hill, near Bury. No cause given.
William Dawson	Saddleworth. According to one or two sources, sabred, crushed and killed on the spot.
Edmund Dawson	Also from Saddleworth. According to more definite sources died of sabre wounds in the Royal Infirmary.

Two Dawsons from Saddleworth *may* have died, but it seems more likely it was the same man. At the very most fifteen deaths. An anti-climax? Hardly much of a *massacre*! Yes and no. The definition of a massacre is general slaughter or carnage which was what occurred on Saint Peter's Field. It was by good luck, not the magistrates' or MYC's good management, that the slaughter was not greater. And as the Peterloo or Manchester Massacre the day certainly rang through the country. The numbers of injured make the term more viable. These again were contested but are more ascertainable. Once the storm broke various relief committees were set up. The main one, the Metropolitan Relief Committee, gave the numbers of injured as 420, and its account book is extant in the John Rylands Library in Manchester. A few extracts from the account book illustrate the seriousness of the injuries:

John Baker, 3 Pump Street. This poor man was beat by the constables but his principal injury was overstrain by carrying Wm Taylor of Boardmans Lane off the field who was wounded and lost so much blood.

40s final. £2 more.

Margaret Goodwin, 8 Bury Street, Salford. Trampled on by the horses. Her eye sight is much injured. Cut at by Shelmerdine. A widow with one child. Is much distressed.

20s final. 40s more.

Catherine Coleman, 40 Primrose Street. 3 ribs displaced in the right side and trampled on. 3 weeks totally disabled. Widow with 3 children.

20s. £2 more.

Mary Jervis, 17 Longworth Street. Trampled on and crushed dreadfully. The calf of the leg has been taken off. In consequence the Doctor's Bill is 4 guineas.

40s. £5 more.

William Butterworth, Stake Hill, Nr Middleton. A dreadful sabre cut on the right arm between the shoulder which was first false healed for want of proper medical aid but is still in bad state.

45s. £2 more.

William Leigh, 23 Queen Street, Deansgate. The boy who was so severely cut on the head. His mother a poor widow with 4 children living in a cellar whose husband does not live with her.

40s final.

James Mason, 22 Ledger Street, Blackley. Much trampled on and looks extremely ill. Has not been able to work since.

40s. £2 more.

The Radicals themselves produced a list of 500 injured. Hay's comment was that it contained 'some pretty notorious names'. It probably did. Almost certainly some scroungers who had not been injured at Peterloo obtained relief. But equally certainly many people were too frightened ever to seek medical attention. The later report of the Metropolitan Relief Committee commented: 'The extent of the terror that pervaded the district for many weeks after the outrage was considerable ... that if their names and descriptions had been published during the heat of the irritation and alarm they apprehended they would have been dismissed from their situations by their employers and thereby thrown out of bread'. Therefore upwards of 400 injured seems a reliable figure. And to be seriously injured in the days of limited medical knowledge and facilities, with no form of official unemployment benefit, meant great suffering and hardship and in many cases premature death.

When Hay wrote his report in the late evening of August 16th, the extent of the casualties was genuinely not so apparent to him, although he did admit towards the tail-end of the letter that Norris had just returned from the Royal Infirmary and there might be a few more casualties than he had earlier intimated. However, to the end of the furore created by Peterloo, indeed to the end of their days, the magistrates and the MYC refused to accept the casualty figures. Five, possibly six, deaths was the number admitted by the magistrates, and five by the MYC—although their list of names did not tally. The MYC refused to admit 'the instance of Fildes as it was clearly unconnected with the dispersal of the meeting'. A few score wounded was the most either allowed. The MYC said fifty-eight people were admitted to the Royal Infirmary; the magistrates that twenty-eight were admitted and forty treated as out-patients.

18

I NEVER SAW SUCH A CORPSE
AS THIS IN ALL MY LIFE

For the remainder of the week the atmosphere in Manchester was tense and taut, the town in a virtual state of siege. Armed pickets remained on duty at the possible trouble spots. There were barriers and troops covering the toll gates. On the day after Peterloo, Constable Moore spread the rumour that thousands of men armed with the inevitable pikes were marching on the town centre. The Exchange was abruptly closed, notices were posted ordering the people to stay indoors, and Major Dyneley was called out with his artillery to meet the advancing hordes. But as he reported in his customary racy style: '[We] came at a pretty sharp trot thro' the Town but I am sorry to say the report proved unfounded in respect of Pikes, and the Mob which were only gathering together, dispersed. It would have been a pretty thing to have caught them armed. I should of course have opened fire upon them immediately.'

The next day there was again a general turn-out for the troops, but by now even the ever eager Dyneley was growing chary of the alarms. He wrote: 'we had a thousand reports brought in from the country, one of which was that the mob intended to attack the Barracks, and seize the Arms. I was in consequence ready all night, slow matches lighted etcetera. We had a false alarm about 11. The rest of the night was quiet. We shall have the same bother I have no doubt tonight, little or any of our information can be relied upon.' Dyneley never had the longed-for opportunity to knock the enemy for six. There were sporadic acts of violence from 'the mob'. There was trouble in the New Cross area on the 17th, 19th and 20th, and there were riots in Stockport and Macclesfield on the 17th. But Dyneley either arrived too late or was too far from the scene of action, and the violence remained disorganized angry outbursts.

If ever the lack of revolutionary intent among the Radicals was proven it was in the days and weeks immediately after Peterloo. There was a core of the more angry, militant or outraged who considered the time was now past for self-approving consciences. It was they, together with the inevitable hoodlums, who threw stones at constables' houses and formed the mob Major Dyneley would have liked to have fired upon. But of disciplined, dedicated revolutionary action there was none. Nor was there concerted, lawful reaction. Bamford and some friends tried to organize a meeting on Tandle Hill shortly after the 16th to discuss what measures should be taken, but only a handful of people responded to the call. Thirty years later Bamford was to write passionately (and on this score he was still passionate however much his other views had changed): 'If the people were to rise and smite their enemies was not this the time? Was every enormity to be endured, and this after all? Were we still to lie down like whipped hounds, whom nothing could rouse to resistance? Were there not times and seasons, and circumstances, under which the common rules of wisdom became folly, prudence became cowardice, and submission became criminal? and was not the present one of these times and seasons? It was astonishing that men could eat and sleep and the voice of their brothers' blood crying from the ground did not make them miserable.' The season had not come because the English temperament is notoriously infertile revolutionary ground, although it can be brought to bloom, and because in this instance the seeds had neither been firmly planted nor nurtured. There were many who wept for the dead and injured, some who wept for themselves, but the majority were too stunned, shocked or frightened to take action. They suffered from mass concussion.

While their followers were thus suffering from concussion, the Radical leaders continued to languish in solitary confinement within the grim walls of the New Bailey prison. On August 24th they were joined by 'Doctor' Healey, arrested earlier in the day, and on the 26th by Bamford whose arrest was conducted as if he were Public Enemy Number One. He was wakened from his bed at 2 o'clock in the morning by Nadin who informed him that he had a warrant against him for high treason. Bamford dressed, said good-bye to Mima and his little daughter, and came downstairs to find a *posse* of foot soldiers and a group of Hussars waiting to escort him to the New Bailey. (Why the magistrates delayed a week before arresting such desperate villains as Bamford and Healey, was never made clear.) High treason was the heady charge the magistrates hoped to lay against the prisoners, but they were 'dissuaded' by important Treasury Solicitor officers hastily sent from London. This altering of the charge and preparing of a watertight case was the reason the prisoners were left for eleven days. Each had an individual interrogation on August 20th which produced one result. Being dragged off the hustings, beaten, insulted and flung into solitary confinement had proved too much for the unstable romanticism of Joseph Johnson. He offered to produce the private correspondence between himself and Hunt (they had avoided the official postal service when possible, knowing that the Government was intercepting and opening their correspondence). Hunt said there was nothing in the correspondence that would help the Government, and he was not afraid of anything he had written to anyone, but the idea of Johnson thus betraying him, turning King's evidence while he was under a charge of High Treason, was monstrous.

The magistrates wrote to Sidmouth to give him the good news about Johnson, and were cautiously told that they might inform Johnson that his case would be considered according to the information disclosed. But the magistrates' joy at (possibly) finding incriminating evidence against Hunt was short-lived. The correspondence was not delivered to them. On her husband's arrest Mrs Johnson, a young woman in her early twenties, immediately gave all his private papers to a lawyer. He refused to hand them over to the magistrates. On receiving this information, the Home Office told the magistrates that it was not deemed right to make any distinction between Johnson and the other prisoners. They also thought that if Johnson really wanted to show penitence he could use his influence as part owner of the *Manchester Observer* to stop the venom of that newspaper and its grossly libellous 'Peterloo Massacre' publications. Poor Johnson, who had neither the conviction of Saxton or Knight or Healey or Bamford, nor the courage (or arrogance) of Hunt, was released on bail before the other prisoners. For this he reaped Hunt's charge of deserting his friends and the censure that, 'among all the political apostates I have ever known, and they are many, and some of them very vile indeed, I never knew one that I believe would have been so poor and mean a creature as this Johnson'. But his lack of the necessary qualities to endure hardship and disaster did Johnson no good. He was indicted just the same.

On August 27th the prisoners were finally brought for examination, the charge being reduced to seditious conspiracy to overthrow the Government. Bail was allowed in such cases (to the chagrin of magistrates everywhere). But the sums required on August 27th were enormous. For Hunt and Johnson it was £1,000 each, with two sureties of £500, for the rest £500 with two sureties of £250. It was at this point that Johnson was released. So was Moorhouse, though at his door Hunt laid no charges of apostasy. Sir Charles Wolseley was ready to provide the bail money for Hunt but he was not given the opportunity. While Sir Charles was on his way to Norris's house to present the bail money, Hunt and the leading prisoners were put into a coach and sent off to Lancaster Gaol 'for want of bail'. Incidentally the heavily pregnant Elisabeth Gaunt was released. The magistrates had confused her with Mrs Fildes of the Female Reformers. After the poor woman had lain in solitary confinement for over a week they finally discovered their mistake and released her. Mrs Fildes, who could have been arrested for she was on the hustings and was a prominent Radical, escaped this fate. Having made one blunder, not overlooked by the Radical press and critics in general, the magistrates had not sufficient confidence to arrest the right woman.

Whether sending Hunt to Lancaster was a wise move is a moot point. The carriage was escorted by Nadin and a troop of cavalry with swords drawn. With this conspicuous bodyguard it attracted large cheering crowds for most of the fifty miles from Manchester to Lancaster. At Preston Nadin paid for the prisoners' meal from his own pocket, an action Hunt noted with surprise. The surprise was short-lived. Nadin quickly reverted to more accepted character. Just outside Preston the coach nearly overturned and Nadin, as Hunt recorded with some pomposity, 'poured forth a volley of oaths, which for atrocity and vulgarity exceeded all I had ever heard before or since; … I sat perfectly quiet during this disgusting scene, and heard with horror his beastly epithets and dreadful imprecations'. On arrival at Lancaster gaol the prisoners were conducted to, again to quote Hunt, 'a spacious dirty room' without a tap with which to wash themselves, and which all were to share. Hunt objected strenuously and was eventually given a separate cell. It was during the journey to Lancaster that Bamford recorded first glimpsing Hunt's feet of clay. He carried 'his earnestness and vehemence with him everywhere', which Bamford found both annoying and tiring. And the tremendous welcome that greeted them en route was 'cast like flowers at the feet of one who was excessively egotistical, and I really doubted whether he who loved himself could really love his country for its own sake'. Other more acid comments were to follow over the months and year.

In Lancaster the prisoners were treated to a visit from James Murray. He was brought into the communal cell to see if he could identify anyone as having been present on White Moss. None of them had been, and wisely Murray refrained from identification. They were also visited by Sir Charles Wolseley and Mr Harmer and Mr Dennison, the two solicitors who were to play a large part in the Radical attempts to indict the magistrates on legal grounds. Harmer and Dennison helped draw up charges against three of the constables for perjury, and against the MYC for maiming. But the Grand Jury refused to entertain the complaints. However, one true bill was admitted against Richard Owen, the man who had signed the affidavit for the Peterloo arrests, but it eventually came to nothing. At Lancaster the bail was reduced slightly, and met by Sir Charles Wolseley. Hunt and Knight were quickly released, the rest shortly afterwards. Sir Charles provided the bail money for nearly all the Peterloo arrested, not only the leaders but the lesser fry whom the magistrates had hoped to trap by the large sums demanded. As Hunt said: 'In this affair Sir Charles Wolseley did more to serve the cause of Liberty and the People, than was done by all the Aristocracy and all the Country Gentlemen of England put together.'

On the journey back from Lancaster Hunt's horse, Bob, died near Preston. The animal was buried under a weeping willow with a headstone inscribed, 'Alas! Poor Bob!!!' Thousands of people attended the funeral, almost as many as attended Peterloo, and left as weeping as the willow. (Rather gruesomely, seven years later, the remains of poor Bob were dug up, and his bones were made into snuff boxes. A special one was made from his knee cap, a silver lid was fitted, and presented to Hunt.) This unexpected demonstration of the English love for animals (one had thought it of more recent Victorian origin) prompts the question: Why did the magistrates never publish the *horses'* casualties at Peterloo? There was a complete list supplied by Colonel L'Estrange.

1 Officer's Charger cut by sharp instrument.

1 Troop Horse stabbed between the ears by a pointed weapon.

1 ditto cut in the head.

1 ditto wounded in the side by a pole with a spike.

1 ditto wounded in the side.

4 ditto struck by stones.

—

9 of the 15th Hussars.

—

1 Officer's Charger cut by stones.

2 Troop Horses cut by a sharp instrument.

8 ditto struck by stones.

—

11 of the Manchester and Salford Yeomanry Cavalry.

—

20 Grand Total.

—

Surely such touching information as wounded between the ears by a pointed weapon would have wrung a few hearts, converted some waverers to the official cause?

Hunt finally left Lancashire in the second week of September, but not before penning a farewell message to the Brave Reformers of Lancashire from, of all places, Smedley Cottage, the home of that vile apostate Johnson. In his message Hunt stated his pledge not to drink a drop of taxed beer, spirits, wines, tea or coffee until the murderers of Peterloo had been brought to justice. This affirmation was connected with several Radical plans formulated immediately after Peterloo, to hit the Establishment where it hurt most—their pockets. The idea of abstinence had been mooted before Peterloo. On the day before, the Reverend Harrison had preached a sermon in Stockport in which he said: 'The government have starved the people, and therefore it is fit that the people should starve the government.' (Such sentiments earned him an extra prison sentence on top of his indictment for the June Stockport meeting.) After August 16th the idea of boycotting taxed beverages was adopted with enthusiasm, by the Radical leaders anyway, and had it succeeded it would have deprived the Government of a large part of their income. But its adoption by the Lancashire masses, from the harshness of their lives notably heavy drinkers, was less than whole-hearted. Immediately after Peterloo it received limited support. At the Oldham Wakes, for example, the Radicals went so far as to brew their own beer. But Saxton expressed the common sentiment when he said that he would attend a meeting at any time, or make a speech, or move or second a resolution for Parliamentary reform, but a resolution for personal reform in the matter of a little cordial, he neither could nor would entertain. Surprisingly, Hunt, who liked the good life, kept to his pledge, extra proof of the sincerity of his Radicalism. He even produced an ersatz coffee made from roasted corn, but it was undrinkable.

Hunt's journey from Manchester to London was a further trail of 'Hail the Conquering Hero'. His entry into the capital on September 13th was greeted by the delirious enthusiasm of not less than 300,000 people, or so *The Times* estimated. He addressed the crowd, of course, urging them to remain peaceable however violently their feelings were justifiably running, reiterating his pleas for abstention from taxed beverages 'until public justice is done to the community, and the blood of the sufferers at Manchester is avenged'.

The blood of one Manchester sufferer finally slowed to a standstill in the early hours of 7th September. At 1.30 in the morning John Lees's fight for life ended.

The day after Peterloo, with those hideous injuries, he went to work. His father saw him at 8 a.m. standing at the top of the landing in the family factory. But he was obviously far too ill to work, his shirt was soaked in blood, so his father sent him home (the house was just across the street from the factory). Later in the day somebody in the Lees household decided John should see a doctor. Accordingly he went to the surgery. The doctor advised rest and poultices, and for the next eleven days John stayed in bed until 2 o'clock in the afternoon, struggling downstairs at this hour. His step-mother said he was 'very poorly', that he threw up everything he ate, that he suddenly grew very cold and could not stop shivering, and that he could find no ease from the pain of his wounds. By Saturday, September 3rd, he could no longer struggle out of bed, and leeches were applied to his temples. He had by this time lost the use of his left arm and the sight of his left eye. Slowly and agonizingly the life ebbed out of him. The woman who laid him out said she had seen many dead people in her life, but never such a corpse as his. The top of his right shoulder was absolutely black. His back was as if he had been tied to a halberd and flogged, not a piece of unbruised skin to be seen. His left foot was dotted with purple spots and lumps. The elbow bone was protruding from the arm. As he was put into the coffin the blood poured from him, and the next day his body was in a state of high putrefaction. The immediate cause of death, as certified by the local surgeon, was a suffusion of blood to the lungs.

It was John's stamina, ability to endure pain, and will to live that earned him his minor immortality. That and his father's anger and determination. There had already been several inquests on Peterloo victims, but these had occurred immediately after the day, the authorities had rushed them through with verdicts such as the one on little William Fildes—'fell from his mother's arms'—and the Radicals had been given no opportunity for intervention. As soon as it became known that the surgeon required an inquest on John Lees, his father was contacted and asked if he would allow the Radical solicitors to represent him, free of charge. Robert Lees understood the implications of this request, that an all-out effort was to be made, over the dead body of John, to prove that the magistrates had acted illegally at Peterloo. He entered the lists because he thought his son had been murdered and he wanted to help expose the culprits. His action required courage. Hundreds of Peterloo victims had feared to go to the Royal Infirmary because of what the authorities might do to them. Here was a humble cotton spinner defying authority. Agreed he had strong support from Messrs Harmer and Dennison, but Robert risked possible repressive action from the magistrates, or financial boycott or pressure from local loyalists.

The inquest opened at the Duke of York Inn, Oldham, on 8th September. From the start it was a tragi-comedy with moments of farce. The Radicals had rounded up four coachloads of witnesses and brought them from Manchester. The small room was packed with the jury, officials, reporters and spectators. The Radical intent was obvious to the authorities, and their first countermove was the delaying tactic. Mr Harmer opened the proceedings, addressing himself to the gentleman in the presiding chair.

HARMER	I presume, Sir, you are the Coroner?
BATTYE	No. I am clerk to the Coroner, Mr Ferrand, who is at Lancaster.
HARMER	Then you attend to take the Inquest as his Deputy?
BATTYE	Yes, I came to take it in his stead.
HARMER	Are the jury sworn, sir?
BATTYE	Yes, they are sworn.
HARMER	May I be favoured with their names?
BATTYE	No, I shan't tell you. I should like to know what is your name?

HARMER	My name is Harmer. Now I presume you can have no objection to tell me your name or to give me the names of the Jury?
BATTYE	I won't answer any questions.
HARMER	What motive can you have for refusing your name, or keeping those of the Jury unknown to me?
BATTYE	I shall answer no questions.
STRANGER	(calling out from the packed assembly) His name is Battye.
BATTYE	Yes, that is my name, and I tell you I shall not proceed upon this Inquisition now. I shall adjourn it until Mr Ferrand comes.
HARMER	I think I have had trouble enough upon this business. I have rode 18 miles and gone to Manchester, all to oblige you, and you are not satisfied even now. You have all behaved very ill to me. I do not know what you would have.

What Mr Battye would have, acting under orders, was adjournment. The proceedings were duly adjourned until September 25th when they were to be resumed at the Angel Inn in Oldham. There Mr Ferrand, the Coroner, presided and immediately made his bias evident by ordering that no notes of the proceedings were to be published until after the inquest and any possible further legal proceedings had been concluded. The injunction was to prevent any publicity damaging to the magistrates. It led to some spirited exchanges between Mr Ferrand and various gentlemen of the press:

FERRAND	Who are you taking notes for?
REPORTER	I am taking notes for the *Statesman*.
FERRAND	I thought I told you that you were not to take notes.
REPORTER	I never understood, Sir, that your injunction applied to me.

FERRAND   Have you sent your notes to London?

REPORTER   I have.

FERRAND   Have they been published?

REPORTER   I hope so. I sent them for that purpose. I can't answer
             whether they have been published or not.

FERRAND   Then I shall not suffer you to take another note.

The reporters for *The Times* and the *Morning Chronicle* were both expelled from the court-room (the local authorities were most injudicious in their dealings with *The Times*). Despite, or because of, these injunctions, evidence most damaging to the magistrates began to spread. The aim of the authorities was, in the first place, to prevent any such evidence being given. In addition to the stalwart efforts of Mr Battye and Mr Ferrand, they were supported by a barrister named Ashworth, briefed by Constables Andrew and Moore and Boroughreeve Clayton. Ashworth parried the Radical attempts to show that troops had attacked the crowd by constantly saying that until it could be proved who had struck John Lees, it was not permissible to bring in further witnesses on the theme of attack. 'Shew me a principal and then I will accede to the possibility of there being accessories'. But a principal proved impossible to show. Dozens of people could say they had been near John Lees, or had seen him injured, but none could name the MYC member responsible. Despite the efforts of Ferrand and Ashworth, despite the squashing tactics—

'Did you know John Lees?'

'No.'

'Do you know anything of his death?'

'No, I do not.'

'Then what do you know?'

'I only know of myself being wounded.'

'That is not evidence and I shall not hear it.'

—the witnesses continued to get in their statements about standing peacefully on Saint Peter's Field one minute and being slashed, hacked and trampled under foot the next. In fact the Radicals tended to call too many witnesses who had no connection with John Lees. On one occasion Harmer, who was a Londoner, stepped straight on Ferrand's Lancashire pride by strenuously objecting that this was not how the law was interpreted in London. Despite these minor Radical aberrations, the proceedings continued to go badly from the magistrates' point of view, and on October 7th Ferrand transferred the inquest to the Star Inn, Manchester. When this effected no improvement, on October 13th he ordered an adjournment until December 1st. His excuse for this inordinately long delay was that the jury were tired and needed a rest. His reason was to prevent further damaging evidence being given. With a month and a half to think things over he hoped many Radical witnesses would fall by the wayside.

The Radicals immediately applied to the King's Bench for a mandamus to compel the Coroner to proceed forthwith. They might have obtained it, for Ferrand had no valid reason for calling an adjournment. However, during the course of their application, an irregularity came to light. It was shown that Ferrand and the jury had not viewed the body of the dead John Lees *at the same time*. This irregularity, the bench concluded, made the proceedings of the inquest null and void. As Archibald Prentice commented: 'The Coroner, by omitting to observe the law, placed himself above the law!' Although many signatures were collected in Manchester protesting against the employment of Ashworth by the Boroughreeve and Constables on the grounds that his fees were to be paid from the rates; although several jury members wrote to Ferrand and said that if a verdict had been asked for they would have returned one of wilful murder; although Robert Lees presented a petition 'To the Honourable the Commons of the United Kingdom of Great Britain and Ireland, in parliament assembled', requesting that the case of his dead son be re-opened and re-examined, it never was.

19

SHAME! WIND YOUR BLOOD SPRINKLED SURPLICE AROUND YOU

The general mismanagement and smothering of evidence at John Lees's inquest added further to the storms of protest that had been rolling round the magistrates' heads since the week of August 16th.

In the days immediately following Peterloo the magistrates were to a degree protected. As the *Manchester Mercury*'s publication day happened to be Tuesday, the first newspaper view was strongly on their side. On August 17th it pontificated: 'The results of yesterday will bring down upon the name of Hunt and his accomplices, the deep and lasting execrations of many a sorrowing family. With a factious perverseness peculiarly their own they have set open defiance upon the timely warnings of the magistrates, and ... daringly invited the attendance of a mass of people which ... may be computed at near 100,000 ... Yesterday's proceedings showed that the Revolutionary attempts of this base Junto was no longer to be tolerated.' This approbation, together with the fact that by being safely immured in their large houses, surrounded only by sycophants and rabid supporters, they were physically divorced from the atmosphere in the town, may account for the magistrates' curious behaviour. For if the Radical masses were suffering from concussion, the magistrates behaved as if they had been stricken with blindness and deafness, a sudden paralysis of these senses which made them unable to see or hear the effects of their actions.

On August 17th they published a notice thanking the MYC for 'the extreme forbearance exercised when insulted and defied by the rioters'. By the 18th, Hay and Thomas Boardman, an ex-Boroughreeve and prominent loyalist, were in London to give a first-hand account to Lord Sidmouth. The reason for this precipitate descent on the capital may appear to be the obvious one that the magistrates realized their actions were open to doubt and wanted to make certain they were understood and accepted. But their general oblivious behaviour, including the ill-judged publication of the vote of thanks to the MYC, strongly suggests that they were not prepared for the storm that was about to break over their heads. They anticipated Radical denunciation obviously. From past experience they knew that the Radicals had heavy literary guns, were excellent at making mountains out of loyalist molehills, and throwing seditious dust in everybody's eyes. But that their actions were to be denounced, or at least disapproved of, by sober respectable citizens does not seem to have entered their heads. Therefore Hay and Boardman descended on Lord Sidmouth not so much to get their version in fast, but because the magistrates were weak, timid men who had taken great decisions upon themselves and wanted his Lordship's approbation.

This they received. Sidmouth accepted their version *ad hoc* and immediately transmitted it to the Prince Regent who was currently disporting himself on his yacht, *The Royal George*, anchored off Christchurch. The Prince Regent did not leave the yacht but he sent a reply to Lord Sidmouth, which was published as 'AN IMPORTANT COMMUNICATION TO

THE PEOPLE OF ENGLAND.' In it his Lordship said he had been commanded by His Royal Highness to express the great satisfaction derived from the magistrates' 'prompt, decisive and efficient measure for the preservation of public tranquillity', and for the assistance afforded on the occasion of the 16th August by Major Trafford and the Manchester and Salford Yeomanry Cavalry.

The fur coat of approbation was ripped from the magistrates on the same day as the 'Important Communication' was published, on Saturday, August 21st. For Saturday was the day on which the *Manchester Observer* came out and it stormed into the attack with all guns firing. The onslaught came in two parts. The first, under the demure heading 'Manchester Political Meeting', was, for it, a restrained account of the sequence of events. It noted that 'the women seemed to be the special objects of the rage of these bastard soldiers' (i.e., the MYC). Its casualty figures proved surprisingly accurate: 'From all the inquiries we can make, there appear to be five or six dead,—as many mortally wounded, and not less than 300 severely and slightly wounded'. And it was in this section that the word Peterloo first appeared. In fact it was originally printed as Peter Loo: 'It is rumoured … that orders have been sent to an eminent artist for a design to be engraved in commemoration of Peter Loo Victory.' Who coined the sobriquet one does not know, not Saxton because he was in the New Bailey, perhaps Wroe, but it was a stroke of journalistic genius. Soon it was PETER-LOO MASSACRE in banner headlines, then the hyphen disappeared, and Peterloo was being written and heard all over the country. The Radicals had gained that most precious of weapons, an instantly identifiable emotive label, and English history a day to remember.

The second part of the *Observer*'s onslaught was devoted to its IMPORTANT COMMUNICATION TO THE PEOPLE OF ENGLAND. Never a newspaper to miss an opportunity, and this one was presented on a plate, the *Observer* seized upon the Prince Regent's smug, complacent, ill-informed congratulations and tore them to pieces. It hastened (after two long paragraphs) to give the barbarous narrative of the day's proceedings, 'however abhorrent to our own minds, or however harrowing the detail may prove to our readers'. The details included such rabidly, luridly readable descriptions as, 'a scene of murder and carnage ensued which posterity will hesitate to believe, and which will hand down the authors and abettors of this foul and bloody tragedy to the execration of the astonished world ... Men, women and children, without distinction of age and sex, became the victims of these sanguinary monsters.'

In the meantime, *The Times* (among others) had joined the attack. Their language was more temperate than the *Observer*'s, but from August 19th onwards Peterloo was given extensive coverage. The questions posed by the non-Radical *Times* and its un-Jacobin reporter Mr Tyas proved highly embarrassing for the magistrates. Had the crowd come in a hostile mood? Had it behaved in an ugly, riotous fashion thus warranting dispersal? Or had the magistrates panicked and unleashed upon unarmed men, women and children, peaceably exercising the right of every true-born Briton to voice discontent at a public meeting, the ferocity of the sabre wielding MYC and the weight of the 15th Hussars?

Apart from the unexpected attack from such newspapers as *The Times*, the magistrates experienced a shock on another front. They had a strong feeling of being let down by the Government. The very fact that Lord Liverpool and his ministers did not censure them was regarded by the country at large as approbation. But the magistrates themselves felt such approbation was too negative. In view of the widespread condemnation they needed positive praise and positive action. What they received, initially anyway, seemed to them lukewarm to say the least. For instance, Hulton wrote to Sidmouth requesting permission to publish his letter of August 18th in addition to the 'Important Communication' from the Prince Regent.

Sidmouth's first response to Peterloo contained such sentences as: 'I am gratified equally by the deliberate, spirited manner in which the magistrates discharged their arduous and important duty on that occasion ... I do not fail to appreciate most highly the merits of the two companies of Yeomanry Cavalry and other troops employed on this service ... It may be deemed a matter of surprise and congratulation that the casualties have not been more numerous.' Not unnaturally Hulton wanted to make these statements public. But by August 23rd even Sidmouth doubted the wisdom of such outright approval. 'His lordship presumes that it can no longer appear to the magisrates of any consequence to give publicity of his letter of the 18th inst., and his lordship would accordingly prefer that it should not be published.' A small palliative occurred simultaneously in that Sidmouth, in the light of Peterloo, finally agreed to the request Norris had been making for months, namely that permanent barracks be erected in Manchester. The consolation they derived from this concession, and the barracks could not be erected overnight, did not last long.

The magistrates demanded new or amended laws to give them stronger weapons against the Radicals. From their viewpoint this was a reasonable demand. It was, for instance, hardly a satisfactory state of affairs when Hunt could be arrested on a charge of High Treason, have it reduced to conspiracy to overthrow the Government, nevertheless still a grave offence, obtain bail and go free for months on end. This, as we have seen, was a longstanding grievance but Peterloo gave it added meaning, and in the early autumn months of 1819 there was no sign of the Government's rushing to remedy the legal defects.

The magistrates thus had to endure national condemnation, as they felt little support from their ministerial masters, in addition to local hostility and hatred. Not that they took any actions likely to improve their local image. For example, early in October there was an incident involving Edward Meagher, the trumpeter. His Peterloo activities, spending the quarter of an hour murdering his fellow creatures, caused intermittent crowds to collect outside his house. They did nothing but hiss and boo but one night, being very drunk, Meagher fired on them from his window. He did not kill anybody but, as with the MYC's activities on August 16th, it was more by good luck than good management. The magistrates merely bailed him for a misdemeanour and a month later acquitted him completely on the grounds that he had been in great danger. In the next edition of the 'Peterloo Massacre', a series of pamphlets issued under the auspices of the *Manchester Observer*, John Edward Taylor commented, 'We are not surprised at anything nowadays.'

If the local populace had ceased to be surprised, the magistrates had not ceased to feel outraged hurt. Throughout the autumn months Hulton, Norris and Hay wrote long letters to the Home Office expressing their dismay at the lack of help from the Government, and their general dislike of their jobs as magistrates. Sidmouth's replies had a considerable asperity. Although he did not doubt that the current position was invidious and harassing, certain passages (i.e., one of Norris's letters) contained such strong reflections upon the conduct of the Prince Regent's ministers that he did not feel himself authorized to reply to them. As for the magistrates' accusations of Government neglect, the town of Manchester had during the last three months 'engaged more of the attention of the Ministers, and received more proofs of that attention than any other part of the Kingdom, not excepting the Metropolis itself'. Constables Moore and Andrew also found the depths to which their reputations had sunk hard to endure. They wrote a combined, virtuously explanatory, long-suffering letter to Lord Sidmouth in which they said: 'The difficulties in collecting rents from those of the lower orders who are able to pay, increases daily, and serious depression in the value of property is consequently taking place. We also have reason to fear, that numbers, whom we had looked upon as neutral with respect to Mr Hunt are becoming partisans ... The sacrifice of wealth and comfort which the magistrates have willingly made, can only be appreciated by ourselves; and we are bound to declare, that nothing but the purest patriotism could have influenced or supported them. An anxious desire to serve the public faithfully, has completely exhausted our worthy colleague, the boroughreeve ... and indeed, we ourselves are much worn out, that we should shortly become unequal to our duty.'

Not all the magistrates suffered greatly from the hostility resulting from Peterloo. Hugh Hornby Birley rode the storm with aplomb. Given the same circumstances he would act in the same manner. His critics were either making political capital or were Radical trash. For short-sighted Tatton it was all a great big fuss about nothing. But the condemnation certainly ate into the soul of the Reverend Hay. He kept many of the vicious letters he received after Peterloo until his dying day. In his surviving papers there are also, significantly, several pieces copied from such authorities as Lord Ellenborough justifying the use of the military in certain legal circumstances.

One of the letters Hay received makes hilarious reading, although its intent was serious. It was dated September 8th, 1819.

Dear Sir,

I hereby give you notice that it is in contemplation to pop you off between this and the next sessions and that arrangements are made for that purpose. Your motions are closely watched, and as soon as opportunity offers, a Ball will be sent to your head. I would not be the hand to do it, but would glory in hearing of an *arbitrary scoundrel* being *levelled in the dust*. The fittest place for all rascals who tread upon the *rights* of the *people* ... This will be a glorious day and thousands will rejoice and be glad ... I write merely that you may *set your house in order* and pray to God to forgive you for your lawless conduct.

The DEED may be considered DONE.

A Friend to Order.

Not all were anonymous. James Neville writing from Scotland Road, Liverpool on September 5th said: 'Shame! Shame! that a clergyman should head a band of privileged murderers, and invite them to acts of bloodshed and massacre. Is this like the conduct of the heavenly master whose cause you expect to espouse? Shame! wind your blood sprinkled surplice around you, retire from a station of which you are unworthy, and if too lost and sunk in crime to ask pardon of an offended heaven join the [indecipherable] bands of the benign Ferdinand the Seventh and there like a vampyre you may glut your accursed appetite until you disgorge blood.'

No official account from the magistrates' angle was ever published. It was initally said that the magistrates did not wish to interrupt the course of justice by discussing details before the trial of Hunt and his associates. It may also have been felt that it was beneath the dignity of magistrates to explain their actions, they being self-evidently justifiable. But the stunning silence was widely intepreted to mean the contrary. There *was* no justification, therefore the magistrates *had* to take refuge in silence.

Privately there was no lack of vindicating accounts. Hay, of course, wrote to Sidmouth on the night of the 16th, but this was followed by two further lengthy reports in November 1819 and April 1820. In these the grounds for alarm, the mounting Radical agitation, the spread of the Union Societies and of public meetings, the drillings, the attack on Murray at White Moss were hashed and re-hashed. The matter of the crowd being armed was dealt with. Mr Horrall had completely cleared the area of Saint Peter's Field before the 16th, and after the dispersal he found large quantities of sticks, stones and bricks lying in all directions, 'as many as would have filled a large cart and more'. This proved that the crowd had come armed. The magistrates' explanation for the two most serious charges levelled against them, (a) that they had deliberately allowed the crowd to assemble so that they could attack it and (b) that the Riot Act, if read at all, was incorrectly read and the statutory hour for dispersal not given, had a modicum of justification. For they acted on the Home Office's advice in permitting the crowd to assemble, and the Riot Act was a red herring because an illegal assembly could be dispersed under Common Law. The question of whether the assembly had become illegal was wrapped in the mists of sticks and stones and a conviction that the whole town of Manchester had been in danger. The magistrates' case was never strong because they had panicked, but a version could have been presented that was acceptable to some people.

L'Estrange also wrote a full account of the day's proceedings from the military angle. It was a straightforward one and avoided political implications and self-vindication. He also gave the numbers of troops injured, which amounted to sixty-seven, amateur and regular, all of whom had superficial wounds. The MYC provided their own report which was full of injured innocence, virtuous indignation and outraged feeling. They struck at no one en route to the hustings, not a sabre was used until they were assailed by the mob, the avenues of escape were never blocked, and so on. As yeomanry cavalrymen they did not feel it necessary to defend their conduct, for they had done no wrong, but as men and gentlemen they were forced to answer the various calumnies which had been so maliciously and wickedly propagated against them.

Their answers never saw print, which was in their case just as well. But the failure to present any official version was an error of judgment. In 1821 even Bootle Wilbraham, the magistrates' spokesman in the House of Commons, admitted that 'the country had, perhaps, been led to draw an inference unfavourable to the magistrates of Lancashire, on account of the silence they had thought proper to preserve'.

In the unofficial stakes the magistrates were again badly served. Apart from the sterling efforts of the press, the Radicals had *An Impartial Narrative of the Late Melancholy Occurrences in Manchester*, a sober account published in Liverpool in late 1819. It was published anonymously, though it has been suggested that the author was John Smith, the reporter from the *Liverpool Mercury* who was on the hustings. In 1820 John Edward Taylor published *Notes and Observations, Critical and Explanatory, on the Papers Relative to the Internal State of the Country recently presented in Parliament; To which is intended a Reply to Mr Francis Philip's Exposure.* This was the most serious, intelligent pamphlet written by either side; the magistrates only having the effort of Francis Philips to which Taylor replied. Philips who had been active as a special constable and signed the affidavit for Hunt's arrest, published his pamphlet in late 1819, as an *Exposure of the Calumnies Circulated by the Enemies of Social Order and reiterated by their Abettors against the Magistrates and the Yeomanry Cavalry of Manchester and Salford.* He first demolished the conception of Radicalism: 'As to Universal Suffrage, Annual Parliaments and Election by Ballot, the first is madness, the second child's play and the third roguery and intrigue'. The Radical methods were equally deplorable, seducing children (i.e., morally), inculcating defiance of all Government and contempt of all religion. He spent a considerable time on the matter of the sabres being sharpened. Really there was nothing to it. They just needed re-sharpening. On specific charges he put up heavy smoke screens. He injured his cause by presenting figures that were grossly inaccurate even by the current partisan standards. As for the dispersal it was his solemn belief that if the crowd had given way no cuts would have been received. Neither as an exposure, nor a defence, was Philips's pamphlet a brilliant exercise.

Peterloo also spawned a shoal of doggerel, lampoon and verse. At this level there was no great dipping of pens on behalf of the magistrates. On the Radical side the *Manchester Observer* was, as ever, first into the fray. On August 28th it published the following.

This is the field of Peter-loo,

These are the poor reformers who met, on the state of affairs to debate; in the field of Peter-loo.

These are the butchers, blood-thirsty and bold, who cut, slash'd and maim'd young, defenceless and old, who met, on the state of affairs to debate; in the field of Peter-loo.

This is *Hurly Burly,* a blustering knave, and foe to the poor, whom he'd gladly enslave, who led on the butchers, blood-thirsty and bold, who cut, slash' d, and maim'd young defenceless and old, who met, on the state of affairs to debate, in the field of Peter-loo. These are the just-asses, gentle and mild, who to keep the peace broke it, by lucre beguiled, and sent Hurly-Burly, a blustering knave, a foe to the poor, whom he' d gladly enslave, to lead on the butchers, blood-thirsty and bold, who cut slash'd and maim'd young, defenceless and old, who met on the state of affairs to debate; in the field of Peter-loo.

The cumulative house-that-Jack-built style proved popular. Many more in similar vein followed. There were also the schoolboy parodies such as *The renowned achievements of Peterloo, on the Glorious 16th of August 1819,* by Sir Hugo Burlo Furioso di Mulo Spinissimo Bart, M.Y.C and A.S.S. And there were the furiously ironic efforts:

And the heroic host no more shall boast,

The mighty deeds of Waterloo,

But this henceforth shall be the toast

The glorious feats of Peterloo!

O would'st thou Albion still be free

And bid to every fear adieu;

Call to thy aid the M.Y.C.

They fought so well at Peterloo!

Bamford, naturally, added his own composition, *A Song of Slaughter*, to the flow. The last three verses are:

> Ah, behold their sabres gleaming,
> Never, never known to spare,
> See the floods of slaughter streaming!
> Hark the cries that rend the air!
>
> Youth and valour nought availed!
> Nought availed beauty's prayer!
> E'en the lisping infant failed
> To arrest the ruin there!
>
> Give the ruffians time to glory!
> Theirs is but a waning day;
> We have yet another story,
> For the pages of history.

Hunt helped to circulate this poem from Ilchester gaol. He sent it out with his own weekly addresses to Radical Reformers with the information 'N.B. This song is the exclusive property of Samuel Bamford, for whose benefit it is published separately, price One Penny'. Thus however much Samuel grew to dislike his erstwhile idol, the idol remained faithful to him, though it must be admitted that Bamford published his defamatory comments on Hunt after the latter's death. Ultimately the Radicals had *The Masque of Anarchy* on their side. Shelley, resident in Italy by 1819, received the news of the massacre on 6th Septem- ber. He wrote to his publisher, 'The torrent of indignation has not yet done boiling in my veins. I wait anxiously to hear how the country will express its sense of this bloody, murderous impression of its destroyers. Something must be done. What, yet I know not.' What he did was to sit down and write *The Masque of Anarchy*. The reference to Castlereagh has already been noted:

> I met Murder on the way,
> He had a mask like Castlereagh.

In stanza six, Sidmouth was dealt with:

> Like Sidmouth next, Hypocrisy
> On a crocodile came by.

The final rousing cry to the men of England was:

> Rise, like lions after slumber,
> In unvanquishable number!
> Shake your chains to earth, like dew,
> Which in sleep had fallen on you!
> Ye are many–they are few!

Although the whole poem is carried along on the tide of passion, such emotion seldom makes for great works of art. Leisure and the cooling of passion more often produce masterpieces. Shelley certainly worked under pressure. By the end of October he had despatched the completed work to Leigh Hunt for publication in *The Examiner.* But Leigh Hunt, who had suffered considerably in the cause of freedom of the written word, decided he could not risk publication of this libellous, angry, republican poem. It was 1832, with Shelley ten years dead, and the Reform Bill passed, before *The Masque of Anarchy* was finally published. It remains the most powerful indictment of Peterloo because men of genius are rare blooms, but it is far from Shelley's greatest work.

In the middle of the nineteenth century, Mrs Linnaeus Banks best-selling novel, *The Manchester Man*, appeared. Her description of Peterloo is most accurate and interesting because she knew Mrs Fildes of the Female Reformers personally. Fifty years later the Radicals had yet another best-selling novel on their side, Howard Spring's *Fame is the Spur*, in which a Peterloo sabre is the hero's initial spur. Mr Spring's description of the day has surely made more people aware of Peterloo than any other book, or history lesson.

On the magistrates' side one of the only verses that circulated, and that not specifically about Peterloo, was:

> Blithe Harry Hunt was a sightly man,
> Something twixt giant and runt,
> His paunch was a large one, his visage was wan,
> And to hear his long speeches vast multitudes ran,
> O rare Orator Hunt.

Nobody produced any lines in support of the MYC.

20

WHAT DO REASONABLE PEOPLE THINK OF THE MANCHESTER BUSINESS?

The weight of condemnation fell as heavily upon the Government as upon the Manchester magistrates. For who was in ultimate control of the country's well being? Who was ultimately responsible for the actions of their servants? Lord Liverpool and his administration.

From Sidmouth's flying start the Government continued to uphold the magistrates' actions, at least to the extent of accepting their version. As Castlereagh cheerfully admitted the Government's sources of Peterloo information were Hay, L'Estrange and Sir John Byng (who was not present). More important for the magistrates, though still not in the autumn months of 1819 sufficient to soothe them, was the stone-wall manner in which the Government refused to take note of anybody else's version. The Government may never have published an official account of the magistrates' justification, but equally it never permitted an enquiry into Peterloo to be held, despite constant demands.

Privately, however, the Government was not nearly so enthusiastic in its approbation. Sidmouth remained true to character by publicly hoping that 'the proceedings at Manchester would prove a salutory lesson to modern reformers'. The Duke of Wellington told him with relish: 'Lord Sidmouth, the Radicals will impeach you for this, by God they will!' And Sidmouth's recent excellent biographer, Philip Ziegler, has written that his complete upholding of the magistrates showed, 'his insensitivity, lack of political acumen and underdeveloped social conscience'. Lord Liverpool made no such public utterance as Sidmouth's. Privately he wrote to Canning that the magistrates' actions were 'most injudicious' and 'when I say that the proceedings of the magistrates at Manchester on the 16th were justifiable, you will understand me as not by any means deciding that the course which they pursued on that occasion was in all its parts prudent.' Canning himself expressed the Government's view more cynically. 'To let down the magistrates would be to invite their resignation, and to lose all gratuitous service in the Counties liable to disturbance for ever'. While Lord Chancellor Eldon, that most devout upholder of the *status quo*, said 'Without doubt the Manchester magistrates must be supported; but they are very generally blamed here.'

Lord Carlisle, no noted Radical, said of the Government's behaviour after Peterloo that it was 'characterized by downright insanity'. If there was little tact or deftness, no impartiality or feel for the public's sense of outrage, there was method in the madness. It consisted of we're still in charge of the boat, boys, so let's ride the storm. The Government's actions after Peterloo demonstrated a firmer grip on the helm. By sending Mr Bouchier of the Treasury Solicitor's office to Manchester they also showed that the day had at least convinced them of one thing—that further reliance should not be placed upon any judicious decision the magistrates might take. Officially Mr Bouchier was sent to help collect evidence against Hunt and the others arrested, but undoubtedly his job was to keep the magistrates out of further trouble. Had Mr Bouchier, or someone of equal authority, been sent before the 16th to 'advise' the legally bemused, panicky magistrates there could well have been no trouble to keep the magistrates out of.

A friend of Canning's comment on the Governmental behaviour was: 'The House of Commons seems equally determined upon two points; first that it should always stumble; second that it shall not fall.' To the opposition, Radical, radical, or Whig, Peterloo presented the most excellent stick with which to try and trip the Government into a fall. For one of the important aspects of 'the Manchester Massacre' was that it marshalled 'reasonable' censure, i.e., as opposed to committed Radical attack. By early September the weight of this reasonable censure had started to mount. The first most important poundage was *The Declaration and Protest* issued from Manchester. This stemmed from a meeting called by the ultra loyalists on August 19th at the Police Office in Manchester. The meeting, which was organized and chaired by Francis Philips, was quickly adjourned to the Star Inn where a vote of thanks was given for the magistrates' actions. It was supposed to be a public meeting of the inhabitants of Manchester and Salford and the surrounding neighbourhood. The vote of thanks was supposed to represent the views of numerous and highly respectable citizens. But the adjournment to the Star Inn made certain it was a private meeting where the views only of the ultras were expressed. Just what was said, as opposed to what was published, was only made public because John Benjamin Smith, an eye-witness of Peterloo, and later Liberal MP, somehow managed to gain entry.

The *text* of the *Declaration and Protest* ran thus:

> We, the undersigned, without individually approving of the manner in which the MEETING held at St. Peter's on Monday, the 16th August was constituted, hereby declare, that we are fully satisfied, by personal observation or undoubted information that

it was *perfectly peaceable*;–that no seditious or intemperate harangues were made there;–that the Riot Act *if read at all*, was read *privately*, or *without the knowledge of the great body of the Meeting*; and we feel it our bounden duty to protest against, and to express our utter disapprobation of, the *unexpected and unnecessary Violence by which the Assembly were dispersed.*

We further declare, that the Meeting convened at the Police Office on Thursday, the 19th August, for the purpose of thanking the Magistrates, Municipal Officers, Soldiery etc. was strictly and exclusively private;–and in order that its privacy might be more completely ensured, was adjourned to the Star Inn–It is a matter of notoriety, that no expression of dissent from the main object of the Meeting was there permitted.

We therefore deny that it had any claim to the title of a *'numerous and highly respectable Meeting of the Inhabitants of Manchester and Salford, and their neighbourhood'*–and we hereby invite those who have presumed so to style it, to join with us in giving the Inhabitants at large of Manchester and Salford, and their neighbourhood, a public opportunity of expressing their real opinion upon the subject.

The invitation was not accepted, even though the undersigned numbered 5,054 people. The importance of the *Declaration and Protest* was that it was organized by the middle-class Radicals and its signatories could not be dismissed as Radical riff-raff, for they included many solid respectable citizens, previous supporters, whether actively or passively, of the oligarchy. Among them were over a hundred of those big, bad wolves, the cotton manufacturers. All felt that this time the magistrates had gone too far. Among the cotton masters and other businessmen who signed many felt angry not wholly or solely on account of the loss of life on August 16th. They felt strongly that by their precipitate actions the magistrates had aggravated the already bad economic situation. With the town still in a virtual stage of siege, with hostility and fear on every side, a vacuum had been created that made normal business impossible. One action that had particularly infuriated the businessmen was the shutting of the Exchange on August 17th on no other evidence than Constable Moore's panicky, and as it turned out unfounded, report that thousands of pikemen were advancing on the town. A further way by which the respectable citizens demonstrated their disapproval of the magistrates' actions and their sympathy for the Radicals (in this instance) was by generous contributions to the various Relief Committees.

The activities of the middle-class Radicals were not confined to organizing the *Declaration and Protest*. With Saxton in prison, it was John Edward Taylor who edited the pamphlets of 'The Peterloo Massacre' issued under the auspices of the *Manchester Observer*. The pamphlets, which appeared for fourteen consecutive weeks from August 28th, price twopence, contained eye-witness accounts, details of the prisoners' examinations and indictments, the throwing-out of the bills presented at Lancaster against the Manchester authorities, and the inquest on John Lees. They had a wide circulation and did much to spread 'the true story'. All the middle-class Radicals were active in the various relief committees, collecting and distributing money to buy food for those unable to work through injury, and assisting with the legal expenses of the less important of those indicted.

Above all Peterloo acted as a political catalyst for them. It took the 16th August to spur them into action, but they did not miss the opportunity presented. The eyes of England were currently focused on Manchester. The cause was a righteous one, so onward Christian soldiers. By exposing the panic actions of the magistrates, they also exposed the antique structure of Manchester's government, a national disgrace in the Liverpool era. By obtaining over 5,000 signatures to the *Declaration and Protest* they underlined the gap, not only between the antique structure and the masses it had mown down, but between it and the solid, respectable citizens. Peterloo brought them firmly into local politics, and once in, they worked with tenacious grip. The massacre also presented them with the opportunity to plead the cause of moderation. Although Hunt was not to be blamed for the actual attack, although he had shown personal courage and restraint on the day, had not his methods led inevitably to the tragedy? With moderate, reasoned, intelligent, radical leadership Peterloo would not have occurred, and there would be no possibility of its repetition. While personally abhorring the tragedy, politically they could not but welcome it.

To the Whigs Peterloo also presented a splendid opportunity. To what had seven years of Liverpool's administration led? To the slaughter of the innocents of Saint Peter's Field. It has been nicely said that Peterloo stirred the Whigs from their 'sulky hibernation'. However, the emerging hedgehog, with the face of Lord Grey, had to inch forward with extreme caution for the Whigs were even less of a political entity than parties then were. Grey himself headed the largest faction and was official Leader of the Opposition, but there were several powerful splinter groups and Grey's task was to create a party, keep the various factions happy *and* condemn and utilize Peterloo. It was an impossible task and en route the most right-wing faction, headed by Lord Grenville, broke away, giving their whole-hearted support to the Government. (Lord Liverpool found the support of his former adversary most comforting, as well he might.) Long-term this was an undoubted blessing for the Whigs. They had spent far too many years trimming their sails to the unstable whims of Grenville. Once this shackle was finally unchained, and they found they could survive without it, their traditional liberal tenets swam to the surface. But short-term Grey manoeuvred within the existing framework and was thereby considerably hampered. In addition to the strangling effects of the Grenvilleites and his other right wings, Grey had a further bit and bridle on his post-Peterloo activities. This was shared by everybody riding the Whig horse, himself most definitely included. It was a dislike and fear of the Radicals as great as the Government's. If the Whigs tore too hard into the magistrates and Government's conduct they might seem to be approving of, and thereby creating support for, the Radicals. Yet they had to condemn this conduct, so some over-lapping with the Radicals was inevitable. The Government, in its turn, was not slow to attack and condemn such association as political opportunism. Lord Chancellor Eldon wrote contemptuously: 'They are fools enough to think they can overturn the administration with the help of the Radicals, and that they can then manage the Radicals.' This was not in fact Grey's strategy. He aimed to attract support *away* from the Radicals and to overturn the Government without their help. And when the Radicals tried to associate themselves with the Whigs they met short shrift. But because the focus of attention was Radically inspired, because of the inevitable over-lapping, it was a difficult course for Grey to steer.

However, by September the Whig hedgehog was on the move. Meetings were organized to discuss the massacre, but great stress was laid upon the fact that there should be nothing in the conduct of the meetings to suggest an imitation of Hunt's mass efforts. The most important Whig-backed meetings were held at Norwich on September 23rd, in York City on September 27th, in York County on October 14th and in Durham County on October 21st. In Norwich, 2,626 people 'exclusive of a list containing nearly 100 names which some malicious and evil disposed person has stolen from the Town House Tavern', signed and contributed to a subscription list for 'the Manchester sufferers'. The contributions ranged from £5 to 2d and the signatures included A Friend to Humanity, An Enemy to Despotism, A Friend to the Poor all over the world, A Poor Man, A Radical Reformer and A Cavalry Man Who Detests Murder. The York County meeting was graced by the presence of the Lord Lieutenant, Lord Fitzwilliam, and the Duke of Norfolk, among other notables. The tone of the speeches was as cautious as the general Whig attitude, particularly in regard to the magistrates' conduct, which necessitated 'a strict enquiry' but nothing more censorious. On the less difficult ground of the throwing-out of the bills against the constables and the MYC, and the conduct of John Lees's inquest (and the final quashing blow was yet to come), the attack was stronger. The presence of Lord Fitzwilliam did much to convince that section of popular opinion, which had not already been convinced, that Peterloo had been an outrage. For his attendance, for betraying the duties of his office, Fitzwilliam was dismissed from his Lord Lieutenancy. This action increased popular conviction that the Government was trying to disperse a nasty stench, and made him into a temporary hero. To the Whigs it appeared as further proof of the Government's increasing despotism. Since when had England been a country only of the authorized version?

Apart from trying to associate themselves with Whig activities, the Radicals were busy of their own accord. They, too, held protest meetings, starting with one in Westminster on September 2nd. At this Sir Francis Burdett, hauled off his fence by Peterloo, was the main speaker. His theme was that the Manchester meeting had been entirely legal, that the crowd had been wantonly attacked, and that such attack was the natural consequence of a non-representative Parliament. It was from this meeting that the Metropolitan and Central Relief Committee, the most important of the relief organizations, emerged. Other meetings, attended by crowds of up to 50,000, were held in Paisley, Birmingham, Leeds and Newcastle.

In November the Radicals were strengthened by the return of one of their heaviest guns—William Cobbett. By October Cobbett had decided the hour had come for resettlement in his native land. Accordingly he booked a passage from the United States, the ship being due in Liverpool on November 20th. On receiving this great news the Manchester Radicals planned a grand reception. However, the magistrates stepped in immediately and, with strong 'guidance' from the Government, firmly. There were to be no more 'unusual processions and multitudes of people'. On landing in Liverpool Cobbett was greeted by enthusiastic crowds *and* a strong warning to avoid Manchester. Wisely he accepted the warning and altered his route. There was an element of grisly farce attached to Cobbett's return. With him from America he brought the bones of Tom Paine. The American authorities had refused to allow the body of Paine, the atheist revolutionary, to be buried in hallowed ground. Cobbett decided this was monstrous. He also came to the conclusion that thousands of Englishmen would welcome the opportunity to pay homage at the shrine of the begetter of the Rights of Man. Accordingly he dug up the bones and brought them back to England. The first difficulty was encountered at the Liverpool customs. It was with extreme reluctance that the customs officers allowed this peculiar piece of baggage entry. Having secured re-admission for Tom Paine, Cobbett found that nobody was interested in re-interring him. Over the years Cobbett tried to raise funds for a national mausoleum, and in the end his son finally sold the bones (for very little) when he was clearing his father's debts. The whole subject became a macabre joke. Byron was among the many who joined in the black comedy:

> In digging up your bones, Tom Paine,
> Will Cobbett hath done well;
> You'll visit him on earth again.
> He'll visit you in hell.

21

THERE IS AN END TO LIBERTY

In the autumn of 1819 the Radicals appeared to be in a stronger position than ever. True, their leaders were awaiting trial for conspiracy. True, the Government showed no signs of repentance or lessening of their repressive grip. But the weight of public opinion was with them. Attack and condemnation poured on the Government from all sides. Cobbett was back in their midst. Hundreds of people had joined Union Societies as a result of Peterloo. Many new societies had been formed, particularly in the Midlands and North-East. Thousands more people, if not advocates of Radical Reform, accepted that something must be done to alleviate the distress, and reform the structure of Parliament. The wind of change was blowing hard. It was the Radicals who had started the breeze that Peterloo had fanned. It was they who would rightly and righteously continue to mark the path until it reached Eldorado.

Such was the *appearance* of the Radical movement. In fact dissension shattered its fragile coherence almost from 16th August. The Radicals realized that Peterloo had presented them with the greatest opportunity of all, but how they should react, what steps should be taken to seize the sad opportunity to further the grand design, were matters on which they could not agree. The dissension, apart from the usual personal quarrels such as the choice of route for Hunt's triumphal entry into London in September, and who should pay for the subsequent dinner, was between those who advocated a violent, and those who urged a non-violent response. The former were led by the Spenceans, Thistlewood and Doctor Watson. Protest meetings at which the actions of the magistrates were condemned, however strongly, and demands for an enquiry did not satisfy them. They called for simultaneous meetings throughout the country, and recommended that the crowds should come armed. Hunt was strongly opposed to such an idea. He agreed that at any immediate mass meeting the crowd would have to be armed to prevent another Peterloo. But, as he did not want the blood of more innocents on his head, the sensible course was not to hold any such meetings. The Huntite faction (much the stronger) won the day. If ever Hunt's *personal* lack of revolutionary zeal and intent was in doubt, it was quashed by his actions after Peterloo. He put his faith in Parliametary redress. The pressure of public opinion, kept well on the boil by the Radicals, would force Liverpool's administration to hold an enquiry, would see that the leaders had a fair trial, and would lead to Parliamentary reform. The *Manchester Observer* followed the Hunt line—it was not entirely devoted to passion-rousing descriptions of Peterloo—urging its readers to support all moderate condemnations, such as the *Declaration and Protest.*

There was a hot-headed element in Lancashire, which is not surprising as the Lancastrians had been the recipients of the magistrates' conduct at Peterloo. This element was fanned along by Thistlewood and Watson, and it started breakaway Union Societies. (The Union Societies were Huntite.) But the new societies did not attract many members and, although they tried to organize simultaneous meetings on the Spencean lines, they met with little success. Joseph Johnson expressed the majority view when he said: 'The Manchester Reformers see the necessity of resting on their oars, and waiting the decision of Parliament on that subject [i.e., Peterloo] before they meet again.' On the matter of the meetings the *Manchester Observer* urged its readers to 'Stay at Home and spare the effusion of blood'.

If the inherent defects of the Radical leaders, their lack of revolutionary intent, their inability to face the challenge of potential power, and the practical signs of breakdown were *present* in the autumn of 1819, they were not as yet *apparent*.

When Parliament reassembled on November 23rd, the Government gave strong evidence that it still regarded the Radicals as a potent, coherent force. With the reassembly, the Huntite expectation of Parliamentary redress was firmly quashed. For one week later, on November 30th, the first of the famous (or infamous) Six Acts was introduced. Lord Chancellor Eldon was a prime mover in their drafting; Sidmouth actually introduced them; while it was the unfortunate Castlereagh whose name become most linked with them and on whom the greatest popular hatred fell.

The Six Acts were the *Training Prevention Bill*, which made any person attending a gathering for the purpose of training or drilling liable on conviction to transportation for a maximum of seven years or imprisonment for a maximum of two; the *Seizure of Arms Bill* which gave the magistrates 'in certain disturbed counties', very firmly including Lancashire, on the oath of only one witness absolute power to search any property or person for arms and seize any found therein or on; the *Misdemeanours Bill* which prevented delay in the administration of justice; the *Seditious Meetings Prevention Bill* which prohibited the holding of public meetings of more than fifty people without the consent of a sheriff or magistrate. In addition, even if official consent were obtained, the people then attending had to live within the area and were prohibited from carrying banners or flags, or arriving in military array. Should the magistrates decide to disperse such a meeting the people had fifteen minutes only in which to obey their command before it became illegal. Finally there was the *Blasphemous and Seditious Libels Bill* which provided much stronger punishment, including banishment for publications judged to be blasphemous or seditious; and the *Newspaper and Stamp Duties Bill* which subjected 'certain publications', i.e., sheets such as 'The Twopenny Trash' and the Radical tracts which had previously avoided stamp duty by publishing no hard news, *to* such duty. It also imposed further regulations to check 'the abuse arising from the publication of blasphemous and seditious libel'.

By the end of 1819 all the Acts were law, the last two being rushed through Parliament on 30th December. It has been suggested that the Acts could have been more repressive. It is true that Habeas Corpus was not again suspended. But the Acts provided a virtually water-tight blanket over the Radical activities. They could no longer legally hold meetings, and their press was truly muzzled. The only section of Radical activity that was not directly affected was the Union Societies. The Government, although most anxious to break this backbone, had been unable to think of a specific proposal against them. But in any event the Societies were crippled. Cheap tracts were part of their disseminating life-blood, and these were taxed out of existence by the Newspaper and Stamp Duties Act.

The Government's reasoning behind the Six Acts was simple. The mass of the people were not at heart seditiously inclined, which was true, to wit the lack of revolutionary upsurge post-Peterloo. They had merely been deluded by the Radicals, which was less true. So what was needed were measures to prevent access to the Radical delusions. Deprived of such access the people would cease to dabble in matters which they did not understand and leave them to the men who did, and England would return to its good old Tory paternalism. Lord Ellenborough expressed this view succinctly: 'He would say that he saw no possible good to be derived to the country from having statesmen at the loom and politicians at the spinning jenny.'

The influence of the Manchester magistrates' demands for positive action were visible in the Acts. The Government consulted them about the Seditious Meetings Prevention Bill, in their capacity as Peterloo experts. The Misdemeanours Bill was influenced by their demands for a swifter administration of justice in such cases as Hunt's. The magistrates were sent early copies of the Six Acts for their approval. Their opinions were not decisive, but they were much appreciated by the Government. Conversely, the Government's anxiety to consult them did much to soothe their injured feelings of being left to hold the Peterloo baby. In January 1820, the Government added the final soothing touch by appointing Hay to the rectorship of Rochdale, which was then one of the richest livings in the country. The fact that Hay had applied for the position early in June 1819 when the living was not actually vacant (though the vicar was seriously ill), and had returned from his interview in London most unhopeful of getting it, made the appointment doubly provocative. Everybody, rightly, interpreted the move as the Government's seal of approval on the magistrate's actions at Peterloo. The appointment demonstrates how secure, only five months after the event, the Government suddenly felt, and with apparent reason.

The Grey/Whig reaction to the Six Acts was inevitably qualified. They opposed the three Bills against the holding of public meetings and the muzzling of the press with a vigour they had not shown in years. They made a valuable amendment to the Misdemeanours Bill so that lengthy delays on either side were no longer possible. That was the extent of their opposition.

The heaviest Parliamentary attacks came from a renegade, radical Whig, the Honourable H.G. Bennet, member for Shrewsbury. The interest of Bennet to this story was his association with the middle-class Radicals. It was Bennet who presented Parliament with a petition from Manchester requesting an enquiry into Peterloo, a petition signed by nearly 7,000 people, 'good, rational and sincere men, of deep religious impressions, and of sedate and sober character'. But it was Taylor, Shuttle-worth, the Potters, Prentice and company who organized these rational, sedate, sober Mancunians into signing the petition. It was they who supplied Bennet with the accurate information, the irregularities of the magistrates' conduct, and the accumulation of proven discrepancies in their statements, that gave weight to the petition.

Early in December 1819, Bennet introduced another important motion. This was for an enquiry into the state of the manufacturing districts, covering the Glasgow area and the West Riding of Yorkshire but with the focus on south-east Lancashire. Much of what Bennet said in his very long speech reflected the views and remedies of the middle-class Radicals; the urgent need for a revision of local government; the rising standards of education that made the people no longer prepared to accept oppression and suffering without hope or explanation; their turning now, as never before, towards a Parliament in which they would have a voice. Bennet did not, of course, get his enquiry, or one into Peterloo. He was an able, sincere, intelligent man, with strong reforming instincts (he had been a fierce opponent of the suspension of Habeas Corpus, had helped expose Oliver and had introduced Bills to curb the employment of boy chimney sweeps). Many of the views and remedies he would have reached of his own accord. But the meeting with the Manchester reformers occasioned by Peterloo pushed him along the road and made him an early spokesman for the later, formidable 'Manchester School'.

The Acts were accepted by the Huntites in a spirit of resignation. Parliament had failed them so what could they do? Apart from violent reaction, or holding meetings, now illegal, which would inevitably lead to bloodshed, there was little they *could* do. But the meekness with which the Radicals resigned themselves to the inevitable was another matter. The calls in their hour of darkness could have been a deal more clarion than they were. Hunt urged his followers to cherish the principles of liberty, to show patience, forbearance and fortitude, and to despair not. For, 'if our cause be just, Heaven will yet assist us in obtaining that cause'. When politicians start invoking heaven, and nothing else, disaster is on hand.

By the beginning of 1820 the Radical movement as such had virtually ceased to exist. It had been a most spectacular collapse. Six months before it had half England rousingly, fervently within its ranks and now there was next to nothing. The Six Acts provided the death blow, but a strong movement should have been able to survive them. The root answer lay within the leadership. They were *not* men capable of leading the country. They could rally discontent but they could not hold it together when faced with disaster, or a slight lessening of the distress. This was another factor that went against the Radical movement. By early 1820 business had heaved itself out of the vacuum in Manchester. Over the country as a whole the economy picked up slightly. Conditions were still bad, but they were not now sufficiently bad for the waverers to retain interest in Parliamentary reform. With no clarion calls, no staunch leadership to guide them, thousands of people slipped back into apathy. Even the depressive, panicky Manchester magistrates began to take heart. Norris said, 'The great body of radical reformers seem to retire from their work of disturbing the peace.'

However, if only the stalwart kept their beliefs, the Radicals remained in the public eye throughout 1820. The first of the eyecatching events occurred at the end of February. It was the Cato Street Conspiracy, that ridiculous, absurd, wild, tragic counterpoint to Peterloo. The instigators of the plot were Thistlewood and Watson, and they later claimed that their intention was to avenge the innocent blood shed in Manchester. The scheme they devised in their role of avengers was drastic to say the least. It was to kill all the members of the cabinet while they were at a working dinner. However, the Government was forewarned. They had an informant, and the question whether he turned informer or was an *agent provocateur* on the lines of Oliver was raised. Certainly the Government knew of the plot well in advance because in January the Duke of Wellington had 'just heard that Lord Sidmouth had discovered another conspiracy!' Anyway, a false cabinet meeting was arranged, the conspirators were arrested in a stable in Cato Street off the Edgware Road, and duly tried and executed.

The Cato Street Conspiracy should have presented the Government with a glorious vindication for their diagnosis of, and measures against, the Radical canker. For Thistlewood and Watson were noted Radicals, and nothing could have been more revolutionary than a plot to annihilate the entire cabinet. To an extent it did. The final Spencean outrage convinced some moderates what the earlier Spencean/Huntite quarrels had led them to suspect, namely that no Radical could be trusted. But the conspiracy had another effect which reflected on the good sense of even more of the moderates. Not all the conspirators were Spencean devotees of violence, one or two being 'reasonable' men. That the effect of Peterloo could have been so traumatic as to plunge them into the melodrama of Cato Street, made many people re-ask the basic questions. What circumstances within the country had led to Peterloo and then, the conspiracy? And what was the Government doing to remedy these circumstances? The answer was nothing. True, it had reacted with new-found vigour to the concrete circumstance of Peterloo. But the Six Acts were negative insomuch as repressive, coercive action is by self-definition. Not one step had been taken to consider or meet the conditions in the manufacturing districts on which the Radicals had battened and fattened. Towards what everybody, Government included, agreed was the root cause, i.e., the parlous state of the country's economy, the Government's attitude remained what it long had been. The depression was the result of the French wars. It was unavoidable and irredeemable. It must run its course and could not possibly be affected by Government interference. Liverpool's administration soldiered serenely on after Cato Street, but the questions remained unanswered and the conspiracy, curiously, helped rather than hindered their ground-swell.

The next event was the trial of 'Hunt and his Associates'. This opened in York on Thursday, March 16th, and closed on Monday, March 27th, 1820. Indicted were Henry Hunt, John Knight, Joseph Johnson, John Thacker Saxton, Samuel Bamford, Joseph Healey, James Moorhouse, Robert Jones, George Swift and Robert Wild, for an 'Alleged Conspiracy to Alter the Law by Force and Threats and for Convening and Attending an Illegal, Riotous and Tumultous Meeting at Manchester on Monday, 16th August 1819.' Mr Justice Bayley presided. The nature of the indictment made certain that no discussion of the magistrates' right to disperse the meeting, or of the MYC's actions during the dispersal, would be entertained. The trial was concerned only with the motives of 'Hunt and his Associates' in convening the meeting and the manner in which it had assembled.

Several of the accused walked from Manchester to York for the trial, among them Bamford and Healey. Admittedly both were great walkers, but lack of funds prompted the long march as much as love of fresh air. One hundred and forty still ardent Radicals also walked to York to appear as witnesses for the accused. Bamford and his witnesses went as a body, and he recorded that the ascent of Blackstone Edge, 'the backbone of the English Alps', tried the marching qualities of the women, and by the time they reached Leeds two of them were exhausted. At Leeds they were joined by other foot contingents from Stockport, Hyde, Ashton-under-Lyne and Staleybridge, and Healey's brigade from Saddleworth. From Leeds the two exhausted females, and others, male and female, lame from the haul over the Pennines, were sent on by coach. But the majority 'passed through Tadcaster and arrived at York in a compact body at night fall on Tuesday, March 14th'.

Healey had a bad cold throughout the trial, probably caught on the windy Pennine uplands. He sat, as Bamford recorded, 'opposite the judge, with a handkerchief thrown over his head, the corners drooping on his shoulders, exactly as the flaps of his lordship's wig drooped on his'. It was to alleviate his cold that Healey had the snuff he passed so freely round the court-room, and which Scarlett, the chief prosecuting counsel, politely declined.

The Radicals defended themselves, Hunt most ably. Sydney Smith, who attended the trial, was 'much struck by his boldness, dexterity and shrewdness', in his own defence speech. But, typically, Hunt had to make a further speech which did not help. Mr Justice Bayley believed that he would have been acquitted had he rested his case after his defence speech. Before the verdicts, there was a widespread belief that Hunt would go free. Bayley's summing up was in favour of an acquittal, for all the accused. However, he laid stress on the drillings and banners. It was almost certainly those well-intentioned, but ill-advised, drillings, together with the proud banners with their cries for *Equal Representation, Let us Unite and be Free, Let us die like men and Not be Sold like Slaves*, that frightened the jury, as they had frightened the magistrates.

Saxton, Moorhouse, Jones, Swift and Wild were acquitted—Saxton's plea that he had been on the hustings as a reporter rather than a Radical being accepted. But Hunt, Johnson, Knight, Healey and Bamford were found guilty on the count of assembling with unlawful banners at an unlawful meeting for the purpose of exciting discontent. They were not, however, sentenced until May 15th, after a motion for a new trial had been refused. The appeal and sentence were heard and given in London, which meant further walking and further expense. Before he left, Healey had some circulars printed which announced that 'Joseph Healy* would be under necessity of taking his departure for London, to receive judgment in the court of the Kings Bench; and he was

---

*   Healey's name was spelt with or without the final 'e'.

entirely without funds to carry him up, he would thankfully receive whatever sums the friends of reform contributed for that purpose'. Bamford considered this an outrageous, begging gesture but the friends of reform rallied round to the extent of £20, proving yet again that he who ask outrageously often receives.

Once in London, Bamford's disapproval of Healey did not lessen. When they were called to the bench Healey cried out in the manner of Luther, 'My name is Doctor Healey. I will never flinch, so help me God.' Such dramatics Bamford considered misplaced. But there was worse to come. Each man had to read his own appeal, but Healey of course could barely read. Each time he stumbled, he looked supplicatingly at Bamford and hissed, 'Prompt, Bamford, prompt.' In the end Bamford, unable to endure this mortifying example of North Country ignorance in front of southern witnesses, shouted, 'Throw down that paper, man, and speak off-hand.' This Healey cheerfully did. A final action of Healey's, unconnected with the court-room, justifiably earned Bamford's condemnation. For Healey (and Joseph Johnson) attended the execution of Thistlewood which occurred while they were in London. Bamford, apart from being ahead of his time in disliking public executions, rightly said that such a spectacle, the death of a fellow Radical (however much they personally disliked and disapproved of the Spenceans) was the last place a respectable Radical should be seen.

The sentences finally passed on the Radicals were as follows: Hunt, two years and six months' imprisonment in Ilchester gaol, Johnson, Bamford and Healey one year in Lincoln. All four prisoners had to give security for their good behaviour for five years after their release. John Knight was not actually sentenced on the Peterloo charge. He received two years' imprisonment for his attendance at a meeting in Burnley on November 15th, 1819.

Apart from the Radicals directly connected with Peterloo, the Government was busily imprisoning other leading figures. By the middle of 1820 Sir Francis Burdett had been fined £2,000 and sentenced to three months' imprisonment for his post-Peterloo pronouncements. Sir Charles Wolseley and the Reverend Harrison were sentenced to eighteen months each for their speeches at Stockport prior to Peterloo, with Harrison receiving a further two years for his sermon urging abstinence from taxed beverages. James Wroe, the editor of the *Manchester Observer*, was sentenced to twelve months' imprisonment, plus £100 fine for seditious publication. Richard Carlile, one of the few on the Peterloo hustings who escaped arrest, had this oversight rectified in the shape of a three-year sentence for publishing the works of Tom Paine. Finally, after a long delay, Wooler of the *Black Dwarf* and Major Cartwright were sentenced for their parts in the election of Birmingham's 'legislatorial attorney'. Wooler received fifteen months' imprisonment, but Cartwright escaped with a fine of £100. Maybe his advanced years made the Government show clemency or maybe they were simply exhausted.

22

RISE LIKE LIONS AFTER SLUMBER IN UNVANQUISHABLE NUMBER

The quick-fire despatch of their demigod Hunt and other former heroes to prison was received with remarkable equanimity by the mass of the people. There were protests of course. The scathing parallels were drawn. If you ordered the murder of innocent people the reward was the rectorship of Rochdale, while if you fought for the rights of your fellow human beings the sentence was two years in Ilchester gaol. But for most people King Hunt and his entourage if not dead were the next best thing, out of sight, so long live ... the Queen and her affairs.

The Queen was Caroline, the Prince Regent's wife. Between these two sordid, immoral, selfish human beings there was little to choose. But the Prince Regent equalled the Government, Tory despotism and repression, so when he finally decided to divorce Caroline she equalled liberalism, radicalism, the rights of man, liberty, equality and fraternity. In short, any anti-Government, pro-populace cause you cared to mention. It was with no great enthusiasm that the Government undertook the divorce action on the Prince Regent's behalf. They first offered Caroline, who had been out of England for years, £50,000 if she never set foot in the country again, and foreswore her title to Queen. But Caroline's blood was up. She wanted to be Queen of England and she saw the chance of larger prize money. Encouraged by the Whigs, she landed in England on June 4th, 1820. She was greeted with the hysterical enthusiasm that had been bestowed on Henry Hunt in the previous year.

In July, Sidmouth introduced the Bill of Pains and Penalties to deprive Caroline of her royal title and dissolve the marriage. Six noisy weeks elapsed before her trial opened in Westminster Hall. If fixed bayonets had been necessary when the Corn Bill was passed, an army was required to keep the people at bay during Caroline's trial. Witnesses were brought from Italy, Switzerland and Germany, to give the lurid details of Caroline's love affairs with foreign persons 'in her service in menial capacity', of the orgies in which she had danced half naked. Everybody had a splendid, salacious, titillating time, revelling in the public washing of the royal dirty linen. What a wash it was and what dirt it produced. Nothing like it had ever been heard before, and is never likely to be heard again.

Eventually, the Divorce Bill was carried by twenty-eight votes, dropping to nine votes in the Lords. But it was then abandoned as it could not be taken to the Commons with so narrow a majority. Parliament was prorogued amidst scenes of wild disorder. For three nights London was illuminated by thousands of bonfires in which effigies of anti-Caroline witnesses were burned. Members of the Government were attacked. Sidmouth's house was stoned, and he and Castlereagh had missiles hurled at their coach. With nice irony, for once, Sidmouth observed, 'Here we go, the two most popular men in England.' To which Castlereagh replied, 'Yes, through a grateful and admiring multitude.' With his insensitivity and certainty of judgment, Sidmouth sailed through such unpopularity, but the strain was taking its toll upon Castlereagh.

At the end of 1820 it looked as though the Government might fall, but they again displayed their powers of survival. Six months later Caroline was dead, to nobody's sorrow. For by this time, with her stupidity, her rapaciousness, her vulgarity, her inability to accept anybody's terms, she had become as much an embarrassment to her supporters as to the Government.

What the 'Queen's Scandal' showed was how unstable the country still was, how quickly the working-class tiger could be re-roused and *how lost was the Radical cause.* Agreed most of its leaders were securely in prison and its press muzzled. But Cobbett was at large (if up to his ears in debt), and the Queen's affair could have been utilized to further the grand Radical design. The *Political Register* was filled for months on end with Caroline's business. But Cobbett, ever personifying the common man, exhibited the English veneration for, and devotion to, the conception of monarchy. Genuinely, with sad lack of judgment, he believed in the Queen as an ill-used person and his columns were written from a personal angle. The chance to marshal the re-roused passions to useful Radical purpose was dissipated.

It was the last chance. By 1821 the working-class Radical movement was dead. One by one the Union Societies collapsed through lack of funds, Stockport, the vanguard, being the last to go under. There was a Union resurgence based on Harrison's formula which became Hunt's Great Northern Political Union. This lasted until 1824 and then formed another basis for the trade unions. But these were off-shoots, not part of the old framework. In mid-1821 the *Manchester Observer*, with Wroe in prison and bankrupted by fines, ceased publication. It was revived, merging with Wooler's *British Gazette*, which survived a further year, but things were not what they had been. Even the first anniversary of Peterloo roused little enthusiasm. Saxton organized a memorial meeting on Saint Peter's Field but only about a thousand people turned up. In

Oldham an intended grand procession to the grave of John Lees produced but a handful of spectators.

However, there was one final direct legal consequence of Peterloa. Despite all pressures the Government resolutely refused to hold an enquiry into the conduct of the magistrates, or the behaviour of the MYC. So in 1822 Thomas Redford, who had carried Middleton's green banner and had had his shoulder split open by an MYC sabre, brought a personal action for assault against Hugh Hornby Birley and three other yeomanry cavalrymen, including Meagher the trumpeter. It was personal to the extent that Redford fought for, and brought, the action in his own name, but it was a test case such as the unfortunate inquest on John Lees had been, and was backed morally and financially by Whigs and Radicals. For example, Scarlett, the chief prosecuting counsel, wrote just before the verdict at York was given: 'If there is a conviction it will not touch the case against the Magistrates or the Yeomanry. The nature of the charges did not involve the propriety of their conduct, which will be still open to inquiry and in my opinion will call for an inquiry as much as ever if all the defendants are found guilty.' Scarlett was a Whig.

The action opened at Lancaster in April 1822 and lasted five days. The defendants' plea was that the assault had been properly committed in the dispersal of an unlawful assembly. The Radicals produced scores of witnesses, including such respectable, politically uncompromised figures as the Reverend Stanley, who stated that the assembly had been peaceful; while the defence produced only eight uncompromised witnesses, none of them of any standing. The burden of the defence was borne by such biased witnesses as Hay, Ethelston, Tatton, Nadin, Constables Moore and Andrew and Francis Philips. They made much of the state of Radically induced terror that had held Manchester's respectable citizens within its grip, and therefore justified the dispersal. But not one of Manchester's terrified, respectable citizens appeared to support their claim. However, the jury accepted the plea and the defendants went triumphantly home, all expenses paid by the Government. To celebrate the happy occasion the MYC presented Hugh Hornby Birley with an inscribed sword 'in testimony of their esteem for him as a soldier and a Gentleman'.

If Peterloo represented the high water mark of Radicalism, after which its tide went out with alarming rapidity, if the movement was never the same afterwards, neither was any other party. The effect of Peterloo was not that of an earthquake, it did not move political mountains. But it did prove to be a watershed. A nice, neat little massacre occurring within a quarter of an hour. No long-drawn out horror to numb the sensibilities. Not too many casualties, but sufficiently occasioned, with sabres slashing, chilren screaming and horses trampling, to shock. (It is to the credit of maligned English tolerance and sense of justice that people were outraged by Peterloo and called it a 'massacre'.) As we have already seen, the day galvanized the middle-class Radicals, prodded the Whigs and stiffened the Government into action.

The middle-class Radicals continued relentlessly with their attacks on the antique structure of Manchester's government. Although it was not until 1838, twenty years later, that the town was incorporated. It is interesting to note that in the final agitation for its reform Richard Cobden recalled Peterloo: 'Peterloo could never have happened if the Borough had been incorporated. Why? Because the magistrates of Lancashire and Cheshire, who entered the town and sat at the Star Inn to take command of the police, and order the soldiers to cut down and trample upon unarmed crowds, would have had no more jurisdiction over Manchester than Constantinople.' Peterloo was also responsible for the foundation of one of the world's most renowned newspapers, the *Manchester Guardian*. In 1821 the middle-class Radicals decided they needed a mouthpiece to consolidate their new position in local government and further the cause of rational reform. The great effect exercised by the *Manchester Observer* in the old working-class Radical cause had not escaped their attention. John Edward Taylor was the guiding spirit behind this venture, and with financial and moral support from a growing number of middle-class Radicals, in May 1821, he launched the first edition of the *Manchester Guardian*. The dying *Manchester Observer* nobly urged its readers to transfer their support to the *Guardian*.

The Whigs continued to move with extreme caution. Slowly what Grey had hoped came to pass. The masses did slip away from the Radical grasp, and the Whigs, revivified by Peterloo, were able to attract them and to a small extent heal the breach between 'the upper and lower classes'. It was, of course, Grey who introduced the Reform Bill in 1832. Again a long time elapsed, and the Bill fell far short of the Radical aspirations. For example, Lancashire, the home of the agitation, the most densely populated area in England, received only ten more members, making the still meagre total of twenty-six. But 1832 was the first major reform of Parliament, and Peterloo was a spur that set the horse if not exactly galloping at least trotting.

Manchester itself obtained representation before the Reform Bill. In 1820 first the Grampound then the Penryn seats were transferred to the town. An immediate result of Peterloo? Did the pressure of the day make the Government in one instance act fast? No, it did not. It was the Pittites led by Hugh Hornby Birley who played a large part in the transfers. They made it clear that business interest rather than Parliamentary reform was their spur. It was hardly necessary for Birley to clarify his beliefs. They were obvious from his position on August 16th, 1819. But indirectly Peterloo had an effect even on this transaction. For many of the businessmen who signed the *Declaration and Protest* were behind the agitation for Manchester's representation. If their interest in things Radical died quickly, and their interest in things cotton was the impulse, the interest was stimulated by Peterloo. Previously they had shown little but apathy. Now, for whatever motives, they took action.

Peterloo was as much a watershed for the Tories as anybody else. It was not apparent for several years that the repressive Six Acts were the death rattle of the old rigid, reactionary, uphold-the-*status-quo* Tory guard. But they proved to be just that. It has been suggested that Lord Liverpool himself was responsible for and paved the way for the new 'Liberal Toryism' that in a short while was to turn into the Conservative party. This author has no great belief in Liverpool's inherent Liberalism. But he remained in office until 1827, and significantly before that year the Combination Acts and the Test and Corporation Acts were repealed. The wind of reform was blowing hard and Liverpool had the political sense to bow before it, but that is not to say that he instigated it. It should also be remembered that it was the working-class Radicals, however great their defects and dubious some of methods, who fanned the gale. Nobody surrenders power willingly, though occasionally politicians arise who accept a gale force considerably earlier than did Lord Liverpool. And without the working-class Radical agitation the much needed reforms, including Catholic Emancipation in 1829, the Reform Bill in 1832 and the Abolition of Slavery in 1833, could have been delayed several more decades.

The first anniversary of Peterloo may have attracted meagre support, but for the rest of the nineteenth century, whenever there was reforming agitation in Lancashire, the memory of the day was brandished. In 1829 the Duke of Wellington was greeted by hostile Mancunian crowds with placards bearing the words REMEMBER PETERLOO. After the passage of the Reform Bill, when its terms proved so unsatisfactory for the working classes, at the first great Chartist meeting in Manchester, Peterloo banners were carried in procession. Throughout the Chartist agitation, it was said that nothing excited the Lancashire crowds more than the word Peterloo. In 1874 the Liberals were still using the name in their election pamphlets: '[Peterloo] was Tory justice, and is what they would repeat should they ever come to power again'.

What became of the leading and supporting characters in the day's drama? How did their lives turn after the 16th August, 1819?

For Hunt, as for the Radical movement, Peterloo was the high water mark. He served his two and a half years' sentence in Ilchester gaol, being released on October 29th, 1822. Sir Charles Wolseley met him on release and provided the surety money for his good behaviour. While in prison Hunt wrote his ill-advised *Memoirs* which he dedicated to Radical Reformers everywhere, but particularly those in Lancashire. He also composed weekly letters to Radical Reformers which were headed thus—Ilchester Bastille, 1st day, 3rd month, 2nd year of the Manchester Massacre without retribution or justice. (Or whatever the appropriate date was.) The reference to Ilchester Bastille was not without justification. Hunt's treatment in prison provoked questions in the House of Commons, though nothing came of the discussions. After his release he continued the good fight, though he never regained his former power or following. In 1826, he contested Somerset as a Radical and lost, but in 1830 Lancashire proved faithful, the citizens of Preston electing him. As an MP Hunt was a disaster. His vain, arrogant, quarrelsome temperament made him unable to accept the vital political art of compromise, and he was constantly voting the way he felt, not the way that would have furthered the cause he was supposed to be supporting. Consequently in 1833 the electorate of Preston kicked him out, and he retired from active politics. But he was to the end *consistent*. By 1832 he was the only champion of the working classes, every other major Radical having agreed to the compromise of the Reform Bill. He remained a champion of women's rights, introducing the first Parliamentary motion for female suffrage in 1830. Early in 1835 he died, aged sixty-two. He was buried in the family vault of his mistress, Mrs Vince.

Bamford had a much pleasanter time in Lincoln gaol. His wife came for week-end visits. He was allowed out, and apart from not being able to go home, the only serious annoyance was Healey, with whom he initially shared a cell. Bamford soon found that at close quarters Healey's personal habits left a great deal to be desired. Eventually, they had a fierce quarrel, Healey came at him with a poker which ended another lovely friendship. Soon after his release, after giving hearty thanks to the governor for his kindness, Bamford began to see the error of some of his ways. During the Chartist agitation, which had the identical aim of working-class Parliamentary reform, for which he had gone to prison, he actually became a special constable. It cannot be said that he ever turned Tory, the radical instinct was too strong for that, but during the 1830s and 1840s he was taken up by local, wealthy citizens. He enjoyed hob-nobbing with the rich and influential, and he enjoyed their creature comforts. It was during this period that he wrote his two most lasting books, *Early Days* and *Passages in the Life of a Radical*. The former gives an invaluable picture of rural Lancashire before the deluge. The latter presents the best, most readable first-hand account of working-class Radicalism. However, the ambiguity of Bamford's position at the time of writing is apparent. Some modern writers have accepted *Passages in the Life of a Radical* as the Peterloo gospel, but it should be remembered that it is the long view, that it was written thirty years after the event by a man who had changed. In his last years Bamford reverted to earlier type. He became a local character, striding around Middleton and Manchester with a flowing beard, and thick grey hair falling on his shoulders. He was the recognized authority on working-class politics; Liberal admirers gave him a small pension and local Middletonians considered him 'work-shy'. He had, after all, done nothing to earn a living for years, except write. He died in 1872, aged eighty-four years.

On his release from prison Healey withdrew from public life, though he took an interest in a local Radical society. He died in 1830, and on his tombstone were written the simple words: 'Died at Bent Grange, Joseph Healy of that place, a very eminent doctor, aged 50'. Johnson, whose young wife died while he was in Lincoln gaol, and whose funeral the governor (nice as he may have been to Bamford) refused to let him attend, remained semi-active in politics for a while. He played a minor part in the agitation for the Reform Bill, but gradually drifted away from his former beliefs, and when he died, in the same year as Bamford, his obituary notice said he had become 'a Tory *sui generis*'. John Knight worked as tirelessly as ever in the Radical cause until his death, aged sixty-five, in 1838. Saxton and Harrison also continued the good fight. Harrison played a prominent part in the agitation for the repeal of the Combination Laws, as might be imagined, and a less prominent one in the Chartist agitation. Both had slipped from the public eye by the time of their deaths. Major Cartwright battled on to the end, dying in 1824 at the ripe old age of eighty-four. Sir Charles Wolseley remained active for several years, and the Radicals indisputably owed a great deal to his generous financial aid. From 1826 he gradually withdrew from the political arena, and in 1834 he found a new faith, becoming a Roman Catholic, which it is to be hoped gave him solace until he died in 1846, aged seventy-five.

That contentious man, William Cobbett, also battled on to the end, up to his ears in debt, libel suits and trials for seditious publication. He stood as a Radical candidate for Coventry in 1820, and came bottom of the poll. In 1826 he contested Preston which he also lost. But in 1832 he was returned as the member for Oldham to the reformed Parliament. Before he died in 1835, battling against the new Poor Law, he managed to open a seed farm in Kensington, write the classic *Rural Rides* among many other books, besides fighting the libel suits, conducting his own defence in the sedition trials, trying to keep the *Political Register* solvent and raise the money for Tom Paine's mausoleum. *The Times* obituary said he was 'a more extraordinary Englishman than any other of his time'. It also said he was 'an episode' because he did not fit into any pattern, which was true, at least the bit about the pattern was. Cobbett was a prophet of the Old Testament who accepted the role of an apostle of the New.

On the other side of the fence, by 1821 the wind of change had blown Sidmouth from the Home Office. However, he remained in the cabinet, without a post, until 1824. He resigned over Canning's intention to recognize the South American countries that had broken away from Spain, and call the new world into existence to redress the balance of the old. The resignation caused little interest. Sidmouth's visits to the House became less and less frequent, only such matters as Catholic Emancipation and the Reform Bill making him attend. He voted against both, of course, and to Grey he said: 'I hope God will forgive you on account of this bill; I don't think I can.' He lived forgotten in retirement until he died in 1844, aged seventy-seven, a political dodo.

Liverpool remained in office until February 1827 when he suffered a severe stroke. He lingered until December 1828, seldom regaining consciousness, being fifty-eight at the time of his death. The unfortunate Castlereagh committed suicide, slitting his throat with a penknife in 1822. The verdict was suicide while insane, so that he could be buried in hallowed ground. Even in death popular hatred followed him. Byron composed a wicket epitaph:

> Posterity will ne'er survey
> A nobler grave than this,
> Here lie the bones of Castlereagh,
> Stop, traveller, and–.

Of the magistrates, Hay remained comfortably as vicar of Rochdale for many years, though he gave up his chairmanship of the Salford Quarter Sessions in 1823. He died in 1839 aged seventy-eight. Norris and Ethelston soldiered bravely on as magistrates, the former dying in 1838 aged about sixty-four, the latter in 1830 aged sixty-three. But Peterloo proved altogether too much for Boroughreeve Clayton who withdrew from public life with what would now be called a nervous breakdown. Hulton also suffered from pangs of conscience. When in 1820 it was suggested that he stand for Parliament in one of the safe Tory county seats, as a mark of esteem 'intended to counteract the hostile deportment of his opponents', he did not accept the offer. Finally, in 1831, when remarks were made in Parliament about the unjustifiable loss of life at Peterloo he resigned from public office, pathetically claiming that only two people had been killed. He died in 1864 aged seventy-seven. Hugh Hornby Birley and Nadin both survived remarkably well. Birley became the first President of the Manchester Chamber of Commerce, and later worked with Sir Robert Peel to introduce the Saturday half-holiday. He died in 1845 aged sixty-seven. Nadin retired from his post as Deputy Constable in 1823. He had by this time amassed a nice fortune. With it he bought a house and land in Cheshire where he lived in some style until his death in 1848, aged eighty-three.

On both sides of the fence the Peterloo veterans were, by and large, long-lived. So were the two men on the opposing fringes, Sir John Byng and Sir Francis Burdett, who followed opposing courses. Byng crossed from his cool Establishment position to become a Whig MP in 1831, and thus was one of the few generals who voted for the Reform Bill. He was created Earl of Stafford in 1847, and died in 1872 aged ninety-two. Sir Francis Burdett ceased to be a Radical after the Reform Bill, and ended up as a Tory MP for North Wiltshire. He died in 1844, aged seventy-four.

The middle-class Radicals achieved more of their aims than life normally averages, underlining their strength, dedication and intelligence. Before his death in 1844, aged fifty-four, John Edward Taylor had made the *Manchester Guardian* into a leading and influential provincial newspaper. Archibald Prentice successively edited the *Manchester Gazette* and the *Manchester Times*, both to the left of the *Guardian* in Radical vigour. He was prominent in the agitation for the Reform Bill, and in 1838 he helped found the Anti-Corn Law League. On his retirement he wrote *Historical Sketches and Personal Recollections of Manchester Intended to Illustrate the Progress of Public Opinion from 1792 to 1831* which, if it suffers from slight moral indigestion, is most readable, and gives an invaluable account of the middle-class Radical activity of the period. Prentice died in 1857 aged sixty-five. Richard Potter became the first MP for Wigan in the reformed Parliament and spread the middle-class Radical word nationally. His brother Thomas helped reorganize Manchester Grammar School, became the first mayor of incorporated Manchester, and was later knighted. Shuttleworth played a major part in the Reform Bill agitation. He and Richard Potter also played a vital part in getting the Bill passed. During the last dramatic phase, when it seemed as though the Lords were about to throw out the Bill, Shuttleworth organized a meeting in Manchester at which a petition was drawn up urging the Commons to refuse supplies until the Bill was passed. He and Potter led the deputation which took the petition to London. Shuttleworth later became one of Manchester's first aldermen. Potter died in 1842, aged fifty-four, Shuttleworth in 1864 aged sixty-eight.

What of the anonymous thousands who formed the backbone of Peterloo? They never bestowed quite the same enthusiasm or solidarity upon any other movement as they had upon the Radicals. But they emerged battling throughout the nineteenth century, in support of Chartism, in the anti-Corn Law agitation, in support of Lincoln and the Northern states during the American Civil War, and during the recurring cotton slumps. The spinners remained militant and Lancashire, as we have seen, was a cockpit of trade unionism. The weavers, alas, grew more and more depressed. In an era of industrial suffering theirs was the greatest and most prolonged. Well past the middle of the nineteenth century the hand-loom weavers were still struggling to scratch an existence, still refusing with that blind obstinacy that is the despair of reformers and is yet part of the human spirit, to accept the industrial facts. In the long run both spinners and weavers benefited from the division of attitudes and interests, evident in 1819, between the magistrates/landowning class and the new-style manufacturers. The more socially conscious of the manufacturers had no desire to be called slave drivers and inhuman monsters by the industrially disinterested landowners. Helped by the efforts of the reformers and philanthropists, then of the sensible and socially conscious, conditions and wages improved. But it was, to misquote the Duke of Wellington, a damned long run thing.

POSTSCRIPT

One hundred and fifty years after Peterloo, in the Manchester of 1969, there are few memories of the day. Until recently there was no official recognition, successive generations of city councillors, Tory, Liberal and Labour, shying away from the political implications. However, the Free Trade Hall, that bastion of Manchester's reforming Victorians, was blitzed in 1940. When it was finally rebuilt in 1951, a mural commemorating Peterloo was commissioned. But as the attendant who first showed it to me said, 'It's nowt mooch to look at.' And, as it has no inscription, you need to be well-versed in Manchester's history to know immediately what scene it depicts. Apart from this belated, unsung acknowledgement of one of the most memorable of Mancunian days, the only other time you will hear the name mentioned officially is when you are unable to obtain a Manchester number on the telephone. Then you are connected to the Peterloo exchange.

The site of what was Saint Peter's Field extends from Central Station to the Free Trade Hall, from the Friends' Meeting House (the only building on the original site) to beyond the BBC's administrative offices, incorporating the YMCA, the Midland Hotel, the Central Library and the whole of Saint Peter's Square. It is appropriate that the Central Library should stand in what was the field, for it is one of the best libraries in England. The Radicals would have appreciated its presence; although such an edifice, with so many thousands of books free to each and every member of the public, was beyond the wildest dreams of the members of the Union Societies who hoped to open libraries in their dingy rooms, funds permitting.

Of the rural miles the Peterloo marchers trod so hopefully on the inward journey, so wearily on the outward one, few glimpses remain. From Manchester to Stockport is a jumble of terraced houses, semi-detached suburbia, mills and warehouses. From Manchester to Oldham is tarmac and cobble, streets of back-to-back Victorian houses, then modern council estates thinning to red-brick semi-detached, then detached, with the sight of trees and fields, and thickening to the Victorian rows again, with the mill chimneys and many windowed factories, many lying desolate. Only in Boggart Hole Clough and up on Tandle Hill is it possible to visualize what the countryside looked like in 1819.

Boggart Hole Clough is now a public park lying half way between Middleton and Manchester. It was one of Bamford's favourite spots. The deserted Boggart House, or Ho, lay in a silent, shaded kloof and Bamford often fancied he heard the spirits or boggarts. The sounds you hear today are the buses and cars changing gear on the hill outside the park's main entrance. But if the flowers are cultivated, if the wild honeysuckle and roses have long since gone, there is grass and there are trees. Tandle Hill, where the weavers and spinners drilled so assiduously and ill-advisedly in the summer hours after work, is a perpetual open space. It was presented to the citizens of Royton after the First World War. On the top of the hill there is a memorial to those who fell in the years between 1914 and 1918, but they probably would not mind sharing it with their Peterloo ancestors. Tandle is only a small hill, and it is surrounded by the smoke and houses of Middleton and Royton, Oldham and Rochdale. But there is one spot on the track up from Slattocks where you can see neither smoke nor mill chimney nor factory nor house, only the grey-green grass, a clump of stumpy, wind-blown trees and the sky. That was how it was in 1819.

In Middleton churchyard, up the hill from the square, lies Bamford's grave. In the churchyard there is also a monument to her most famous citizen, 'Erected by Public Subscription in his native town in 1877', with John Bright's epigraph, 'Bamford was a Reformer when to be so was unsafe, and he suffered for his faith'. But her most famous citizen's house was pulled down only a few years ago in a clearance scheme. All that remains is a neat blue and white plaque which states that 'Samuel Bamford Reformer Resided and was arrested in this house August 26th, 1819, 61 Union Street, Cheapside'. However, it is in Middleton's public library, a snug mock-Tudor building, that the surviving Peterloo relics have come to rest. In the librarian's office are the red plume from a Hussar's helmet; the remains of a flagpole that carried a Cap of Liberty and which bears the faint inscription *Hunt and Liberty*; and a heavy black constable's baton, in excellent condition, with the gold leaf of the royal insignia clearly stamped. In the children's section, Middleton's green Peterloo banner with its gold inscriptions, *Unity and Strength* and *Liberty and Fraternity*, hangs in a glass case, the silk tattered, the colours faded.

Unity and Strength in the sense the Radicals meant have taken large steps forward since 1819, so large that nobody is sure where the unified strength should go next. Some of the Liberty and Fraternity the Radicals wanted has been achieved, but generally they are in as parlous and as delicate a state as they were in 1819. For human nature has not noticeably or radically changed, and the problems confronting the radically minded are as noticeably great as they were 150 years ago.

NOTES AND SOURCES

Contemporary Peterloo material is voluminous. It was an extremely well documented event. In some instances the material could have more than one source, e.g., reported in a newspaper and at a trial and in a deposition. In these notes I give *my* source or sources. The contemporary material also tended towards excessively long titles, so I have used abbreviations, the full titles and dates of publication appearing in the bibliography.

1. AGRICULTURE COULD NOT HAVE MADE SUCH A PLACE AS MANCHESTER

The chapter heading is my misquotation of William Cobbett. His fuller text was, 'Agriculture, *alone,* could not have made such a place as Manchester; but supposing such a place to be a national good (which, however, I deny) it could not have been made unless the people had first *eaten*'. The justification for dropping *alone,* which alters Cobbet's meaning but serves mine, was Cobbett's undying hatred for such places as Manchester, the concrete evidence of the Industrial Revolution that was destroying *his* England. When he visited Frome in Somerset, for example, he dismissed it contemptuously as 'a sort of little Manchester'.

Pages 1–9. My source for information on John Lees's early days was the *Inquest on the Body of John Lees.*

Pages 1–9. One of my main sources for the conditions in Lancashire was the *History of the Cotton Manufacture in Great Britain,* a veritable bible written by Edward Baines Jr who was on the Peterloo hustings as the reporter for the *Leeds Mercury.* His father, also Edward Baines, was the editor of the paper and the more noted contemporary figure. The *Leeds Mercury* supported the Radicals to a degree, though politically the Baines were Whig cum middle-class Radicals.

Page 4. Regarding the earlier high wages Baines Jr quoting contemporary sources, said, 'Every family could be bringing home 40s, 60s, 80s, 100s or

even 120s a week'. The italics are mine for this was an astronomical sum. I
have not used it in the text as I cannot believe many families earned so much.
But these inordinately high wages account partially for the later militancy.
Page 8. For those interested in Manchester's geography Chorlton Row is now
Chorlton-on-Medlock.

2. THE MOST WICKED AND SEDITIOUS PART OF THE COUNTRY

That south-east Lancashire was the most turbulent, seditious, wicked and
troublesome area of the country was the familiar theme of Liverpool's administration. Hence the chapter heading.

Page 12. An interesting fact about the Luddite Riots, this first violent phase
of industrial unrest, was the strength of the Government's counter-action.
12,000 troops were used in the suppression of Luddism, troops urgently
required by the Duke of Wellington (or Wellesley as he then was) in Spain
and Portugal. The number of soldiers tied up on 'home duty' makes it less
surprising that the French wars were so long drawn out, and illustrates the
repressive backcloth against which the Radicals operated, and conversely
explains the fears in the loyalist minds.
Page 15. The description of Cartwright as 'the old heart ...' is Canning's.
Page 27. Bamford's comment on his baby daughter appears in *Passages in the
Life of a Radical.*
Page 19. As regards the reference to the various names 'the people' were called,
Cobbett said that within his lifetime 'the Commons of England had become
"the lower orders", "the peasantry" and when they organised "the mob"'.
Page 20. The weaver's sardonic comment about the watching soldiers is taken
from Bamford's *Passages in the Life of a Radical.*
Page 23. Bamford's reference to the Sunday schools, ibid.
My general sources for the lives of the local Radical leaders were, Bamford's
Passages in the Life of a Radical; Prentice's *Historical Sketches;* Shaw's *Annals of
Oldham* and the *Manchester Observer.*

3. THE CONSTITUTION OF ENGLAND IS THE BUSINESS OF
EVERY ENGLISHMAN

The chapter heading is a statement by Henry St John, Earl of Bolingbroke, often
quoted by Henry Hunt. Bolingbroke may have made the statement nearly a
century earlier, but this was the era in which the people seriously began to regard
the constitution as their business. Hunt's demagogic instincts recognized this fact.

Page 25. Cobbett's comment on the Methodists is quoted in the Hammonds' *Town Labourer 1760–1832.*

Page 26. His comment on his own unaccommodating disposition comes from *Life and Adventures of Peter Porcupine.*

Page 27. Cobbett's assessment of the causes of the rioting appeared in the *Political Register*, November 23th, 1811.

Page 27. His remarks about 'antalluct' and 'feelosofers' appear throughout his writings.

Page 27. The spy's comment on the 'Twopenny Trash' is quoted by Marshall in *Development of Public Opinion in Manchester 1780–1820.*

Page 28. Cobbett's comment on Hunt riding the country with a whore etc. comes from a private letter written April 10th, 1808.

Page 29. Hunt's comment on Cobbett's physical appearance is from his *Memoirs.*

Page 29. Hunt's legs were thus described by Bamford in *Passages in the Life of A Radical*: 'His leg and foot were about the firmest and neatest I ever saw'. The praise was general, the only point about Hunt on which everybody agreed.

Page 29. Bamford's statement that Hunt 'would sell his soul for the cheers of the mob' is from *Passages in the Life of a Radical.*

Page 31. Cobbett's list of what a reformed Parliament would do appeared in the *Political Register*, October 12th, 1816.

Page 34. The remark about the High Tory oligarchy being a 'strange anomalous' system is from Taylor's *Notes and Observations.*

Page 35. The comment on the country not submitting to be led by the Radicals is from the *Manchester Gazette*, June 19th, 1819.

Page 35. The statement about the Radicals lacking in high moral tone is from John Edward Taylor's pamphlet.

For my information on Cobbett I am indebted to Cole's *Life of William Cobbett* as well as Cobbett's own massive writing; for Hunt my sources were his *Memoirs* and the *Dictionary of National Biography*; for the middle-class Radicals I used Prentice's *Historical Sketches*, Read's *Peterloo, the Massacre and its Background* and the Coles' 'Index of Persons' in the Peter Davis edition of *Rural Rides.*

4. BRITAIN'S GUARDIAN GANDERS

Canning called Sidmouth 'Britain's Guardian Gander' in the days of his premiership as Henry Addington. I have borrowed the phrase to embrace the whole Liverpool administration. Sidmouth, incidentally, possessed the unhappy knack of attracting opprobrium from all sides. It was Canning who also penned the lines:

Pitt is to Addington
As London to Paddington

which so succinctly expressed the relationship. Lord Roseberry said he had 'the indefinable air of the village apothecary inspecting the tongue of state'.

Page 37. Lord Grey's question on the Radicals is quoted in Ziegler's *Addington*.

Page 40 (footnote). The story told by Lady Bessborough is also quoted in Ziegler's book.

Page 44. Cobbett's pledge that 'There would be none of this disgraceful spy work' is from the *Political Register*, October 12th, 1816.

My sources for Sidmouth were Pellew's biography, *The Life and Correspondence of H. Addington*, and Ziegler's *Addington*. Pellew was Sidmouth's son-in-law and produced a hagiographical book of infinite boredom; Ziegler's is the reverse.

My sources for Liverpool were Yonge's *The Life and Administration of Robert Banks, 2nd Earl of Liverpool*, K.G. (another piece of hagiography containing the splendid statement that Liverpool was 'not infallible'—though almost one infers); and Brock's *Lord Liverpool and Liberal Toryism*.

5. THAT ANOMALOUS HERMAPHRODITE RACE CALLED PARSON-JUSTICES

The chapter heading is from Hunt's *Memoirs*, one of the few felicitous descriptions in those arid wastes.

For the structure of Manchester's government I am indebted to the *History of Local Government in Manchester* by the late Professor Arthur Redford and to Marshall's *Development of Public Opinion in Manchester*.

Page 47. Pitt the Younger's remark on the Anglican church is quoted in Read's *Peterloo*.

Page 47. The Hay papers are in Rylands English Mss. 1197/1–89.

Page 48. Ethelston's remark about the reformers is quoted by Taylor in his *Notes and Observations*.

Page 49. I obtained the information about Tatton's short-sightedness from the Treasury Solicitor files, T.S.11/4763/1055–56. Their current repository is the Asbridge, Herts, branch of the Public Records Office. I use the Asbridge branch. On arriving to study the Home Office material I was told there were some Treasury Solicitor files of Manchester Disturbances that had lain unexamined and uncatalogued for years, and would I like to examine them in case they were of relevance to Peterloo. They were. And I was delighted to look at them. They do not shed blindingly new light on the day, but they do contain depositions and letters that I have not found elsewhere and provide many human touches of which I have made use throughout the book. Tatton's home, Wythenshawe Hall, still stands within the public park of the vast housing estate.

Page 51. The reference to Nadin as the real ruler of Manchester is made in Prentice's *Historical Sketches*: 'These miserable creatures [i.e., the oligarchy] were in their turn ruled by one of their own servants, the noted Joseph Nadin ... for more than ten years this coarse man was the real ruler of Manchester'.

Page 51. The song is quoted in Shaw's *Annals of Oldham*.

Page 51. The reference to the 7th Hussars appeared in the *Manchester Observer*, February 20th, 1819.

Page 52. I found the character of Major Dyneley among the Treasury Solicitor papers, T.S.11/4763/1055–56. Mention of him does not to my knowledge occur elsewhere.

Page 53. A complete list of the occupations of the MYC members was given in *Wooler's British Gazette and Manchester Observer* (as it by then was called) on August 10th, 1822.

6. ALL THE GAOLS OF THE COUNTY ARE REMARKABLY CROWDED

The chapter heading is from a letter to the Home Office from magistrate Sylvester written the day after the Blanket March: 'All the gaols of the County, and especially the New Bayley prison, are remarkably crowded'. It is quoted in Wearmouth's *Methodism and the Working Class Movement*. I would like to clarify a simplification of the facts which I have made throughout the book. Some of the magistrates' letters were written to the Under Secretary at the Home Office rather than directly to Lord Sidmouth, this post being held by Hiley Addington and, mainly, by Henry Hobhouse during the relevant period. Nearly *all* the replies came from Hobhouse, Sidmouth himself only writing in extreme cases. But the content was dictated by Sidmouth so for simplicity I have used his name throughout.

Page 56. The Prince Regent's statement on the prevailing distresses is quoted by Wearmouth whose book is cited above.

Page 57. Cobbett's famous comment: 'They sigh for a plot ...' is from the *Political Register*, December 14th, 1816.

Page 57. Sidmouth's statements on the suspension of Habeas Corpus are quoted from Ziegler's *Addington*.

Page 60. Johnston's warning to the Blanketeers is quoted from Davis's *Lancashire Reformers*.

Page 60. Bamford's view of the Blanket March is from *Passages in the Life of a Radical*.

Page 62. The spy's report on the Ardwick Conspiracy is quoted from Prentice's *Historical Sketches*.

Page 62. The quotation from the *Leeds Mercury* appeared on April 12th, 1817.

Page 62. Sidmouth's letter is taken from Davis's *Lancashire Reformers*.

Pages 63–4. Bamford's experiences, and descriptions of Sidmouth and Castlereagh, are taken from *Passages in the Life of a Radical*; so is the story about Healey.

Page 65. It was one William Turner who accused Oliver on the scaffold.

Page 65. Oliver was well treated by his masters, however dubiously his over-enthusiasm served them. He obtained sufficient money to leave the country and was last heard of in South America under the name of Jones. His real name, incidentally, was W. J. Richards.

Page 66. Bamford wrote of Oliver in *Passages in the Life of a Radical*, and Prentice mentions him in his *Historical Sketches*.

7. THE LOWER CLASSES ARE RADICALLY CORRUPTED

The chapter heading is from a letter from Ethelston to Sidmouth written in September 1818. The source is Aspinall's *Early English Trade Unions*, that most invaluable assembly of Home Office/magistrate correspondence to which I am much indebted, in particular, for the following seven quotations:

Page 68. Extract from *The Cotton Spinners' Address to the Public*.

Page 69. Hobhouse to Hay, July 1818.

Page 69. Norris to Hobhouse, July 1818.

Page 70. Hobhouse to Norris, August 1818.

Page 70. Ethelston to Sidmouth, September 1818, as chapter heading.

Page 71. Hay to Hobhouse, July 1818.

Page 73. Sir John Byng to Hobhouse, July 1818.

Page 74. The incident about female voting appears in Bamford's *Passages in the Life of a Radical*.

Page 75. Bamford published six verses of the *Lancashire Hymn* in *Passages in the Life of a Radical*. The *Manchester Observer* originally published nine verses, in two parts, the first of four verses on July 17th, 1819, the second of five on August 7th, 1819. The *Observer* also gave the information that it was sung to the tune of *Falmouth*. But as the author himself preferred six verses and gave no tune I have abided by his wishes.

8. DO UNTO OTHERS AS YOU WOULD THEY SHOULD DO UNTO YOU

The chapter heading was the maxim of the Union Societies, and is referred to in the text (p. 77). My sources for the Societies were the aims and rules published in the *Manchester Observer* on May 8th, 1819 and Wearmouth's *Methodism and the Working Class Movement.*

Page 78. Harrison's comment on the costs of the Union Society is quoted in Read's *Peterloo.*

Page 79. An 'established' Methodist's reaction to the reformers' foray into the field of education is taken from Wild's *History of the Stockport Sunday Schools.*

Page 80. The aims of the Blackburn Female Union appeared in the Union's Rules, published in the *Manchester Observer*, June 26th, 1819.

Page 80. Susanna Saxton's formidable pamphlet was issued in July 1819 as *THE MANCHESTER FEMALE REFORMERS ADDRESS to the Wives, Mothers, Sisters and Daughters of the higher and middling Classes of Society.* The non-Radical reaction to the female unions was one of scathing astonishment. On July 10th, 1819, the *British Volunteer* wrote: 'Among the many schemes which now endanger the peace of our society, are some for forming female political associations, to inculcate in the minds of mothers and of the rising generation a disrespect for parliament. One of these, it is alleged, has been formed at Blackburn, in this county!!!'

Page 81. The parody of a speech by the Prince Regent appeared in the *Manchester Observer*, February 6th, 1819.

Page 82. The attack on Sidmouth in ibid, January 16th, 1819.

Page 82. The Radical song, in ibid, April 3rd, 1819.

Page 82. Hugh Oldham's letter from America was written in April 1819 and published on July 17th, 1819.

Page 84. The *Manchester Observer* printed Hunt's testimonial to themselves on August 14th, 1819.

Page 84. Copies of Paley's *Reasons for Contentment*, published in Carlisle in 1819, were widely circulated throughout the North of England. A paraphrase of the *Reasons* appeared in the *British Volunteer* on August 14th. It may well have induced a few more starving weavers and spinners to attend the meeting on August 16th.

Page 86. Sidmouth's statement on Manchester is taken from Prentice's *Historical Sketches.*

9. I ACCEPT WITH PLEASURE THE INVITATION OF THE COMMITTEE

The chapter heading is from Hunt's acceptance letter written from Middleton Cottage, his Hampshire home, on January 11th and published in the *Manchester Observer*, January 16th, 1819.

Page 91. The toast at the January dinner was published in the *Manchester Observer*, January 23rd, 1819.

Page 92. Harriet Martineau quoted Bamford and the 'bloody butchers' phrase in her *History of the Thirty Years' Peace*; Bamford himself recorded it in *Passages in the Life of a Radical*; I am not convinced Hunt necessarily said it.

Page 93. The quote about a Radical being libellous, seditious etc. was contained in a letter to the *Manchester Observer*.

Page 94. The Stockport meeting was reported at great length in the *Manchester Observer*, February 20th, 1819.

Page 95. Bamford's poem was published in the *Manchester Observer*, June 19th, 1819.

Pages 95–6. The letters quoted on these pages are taken from the following sources: Norris to Sidmouth, February 1819 (H.O.42/184); Hobhouse to Norris, February 1819 (H.O.41/4); and Norris to Sidmouth, March 1819 (State Trials, Appendix B).

10. A GENERAL INSURRECTION IS SERIOUSLY MEDITATED

The chapter heading is from the letter from Norris to Sidmouth, March 1819, State Trials, Appendix B.

Page 97. The quote on the purpose of the Blackburn meeting is taken from the *Manchester Observer*, July 3rd, 1819. The meeting was fully reported in the July 10th edition. Incidentally, the female reformers led by Mrs Alice Kitchen played a prominent part, presenting Fitton with a Cap of Liberty.

Page 98. The Stockport meeting and Wolseley's and Harrison's statements are from the *Manchester Observer*, July 3rd, 1819.

Page 98. The Oldham meeting was reported in the *Manchester Observer*, June 12th, 1819.

Page 99. The list of Leeds's delegates appeared in the *Manchester Observer*, June 19th, 1819.

Page 100. Sidmouth's views on emigration are from Ziegler's *Addington*.

Page 101. The quotation from Norris about the working classes being beset by reformers is taken from his letter to Sidmouth, June 1818, State Trials, Appendix B.

Pages 102. Ethelston's statement is taken from the Dossier on Weapons, H.O.41/4.

Page 103. Bamford's remarks on the organization of the meeting appear in *Passages in the Life of a Radical*.

wordery
your online bookshop

Your Details

Order date:	29/11/2018
Order reference:	AUK-42845619
Dispatch note:	20181156227001

Quantity

Your Order

ISBN	Title	
9781785038648	The Peterloo Massacre	1

For returns information visit wordery.com/returns. Please keep this receipt for your records.

Thank you for your Wordery order. We hope you enjoy your book #HappyReading

wordery
your online bookshop

20181156227001

Page 104. Hunt's reply to Johnson's invitation is to be found in State Trials, Appendix B. A selection of the Hunt/Johnson correspondence is also in T.S.11/4763/1055–56.

Page 105. The Radical witness's statement is from *Radford v. Birley, Peterloo Trials.*

Page 106. The Resolutions issued after the July meeting were posted throughout the town and published in the local newspapers.

Page 107. The comment that 'Havock' was being cried etc. is from the *Manchester Observer*, July 24th, 1819.

Page 107. Taylor's accusation is from his *Notes and Observations.*

Page 107. Lord Sidmouth's letter to the commanders of the local yeomanry is in Rylands English Mss. 1197/1–89.

Page 108. The descriptions of the MYC are from Bruton's *The Story of Peterloo.*

11. MANCHESTER KNEW NOUGHT OF MISERY UNTIL NOW

The chapter heading is from the *Manchester Observer*, April 24th, 1819: 'If something be not done, and that speedily too, then may we safely say that Manchester knew nought of misery until now.'

Page 111. The quote about the Birmingham Radicals deciding to elect a 'legis-latorial attorney' etc, is taken from the *Manchester Observer*, July 24th, 1819.

Page 112. The *British Volunteer*'s comment on Sir Charles Wolseley's election appeared on July 17th, 1819.

Page 112. The Smithfield resolutions are to be found in State Trials, and the *Manchester Observer*, July 31st, 1819.

Page 113. The Government's reaction to the Birch shooting is in a letter from Hobhouse to Lloyd (a Stockport magistrate), July 1819 (H.O.41/4).

Page 113. Hunt's letter to Johnson is in State Trials, Appendix B.

Page 113 (footnote). Archibald Prentice's comment is from his *Historical Sketches.*

Page 113. Ethelston's reactions to the Birch conspiracy is from his letter to Sidmouth, July 1819 (H.O.42/190).

Page 114. Johnson's letter to Hunt is in State Trials, Appendix B.

Pages 114. The announcement of the meeting appeared in the *Manchester Observer*, July 31st, 1819.

Page 115. The most crucial letter was that written by Hobhouse to Norris, State Trials, Appendix B.

Page 116. The magistrates' faulty grammar was commented upon in the *Manchester Observer*, August 15th, 1819. Hunt wrote: 'The magistrates having ordered all persons to abstain at their peril, which means in plain English that those who stay away from the Meeting will do it at their peril, of course all those who are under the influence of the said magistrates will certainly attend under pain of their displeasure'.

Page 117. The quotation from Lord Sidmouth is taken from the series of letters from the Home Office to the magistrates. Norris in fact was the recipient of this one (H.O.41/4).

Page 118. The amended text announcing the meeting appeared in the *Manchester Observer*, August 7th, 1819.

12. THE TOWN HAS BEEN DELUGED WITH PLACARDS

The chapter heading is from the *Manchester Observer*. It was part of a lengthy and reasonably temperate editorial of August 14th, 1819.

Page 121. The *Manchester Observer*'s comment on the town being deluged with placards appeared on August 14th, 1819.

Page 121. The original posters and placards from which the extracts are taken are among Rylands English Mss. 1197/1–89. The Manchester Reform Club Library also has examples of the original posters. The reformers 'sinking manufacturers' attack was also published in the *Manchester Observer*, July 26th, 1819.

Page 122. Fitton's indictment was printed in the *Manchester Observer*, August 14th, 1819.

Page 123. Sir John Byng's letter expressing his views on the conference was written to Hobhouse, July 1819 (H.O.42/190).

Page 124. Byng's and Hay's correspondence is among Rylands English Mss. 1197/1–89.

Page 125. The admonishing letter quoted was sent by Hobhouse to Norris, July 1819 (H.O.41/4).

13. THE ALARM IN ALL THE NEIGHBOURING TOWNS BEGINS TO BE EXCESSIVE

The chapter heading is from a letter from Norris to Sidmouth, July 1819, State Trials, Appendix B.

Page 127. Johnson's cancellation letter to Hunt is taken from the same source.

Page 128. Hunt's statement appears in his *Memoirs*.

Page 128. Hunt's respect for the law was noted in a letter from Hobhouse to Norris, August 1819 (H.O.41/4).

Page 128. Hunt's Address appeared in the *Manchester Observer*, August 14th, 1819, and a copy is in Rylands English Mss. 1197/1 89.

Page 131. The Home Office's advice on the subject of Hunt's arrest is contained in a letter from Hobhouse to Norris, August 1819 (H.O.41/4).

Page 131. The comment that Hunt only offered himself up 'in order that his bail might be accepted on Monday ...' is from *The Times*, August 17th, 1819.

Page 131. Hunt's explanation for going to the New Bailey is from his *Memoirs*.

Page 132. The White Moss incident is well documented but I have followed the depositions of the men involved, T.S.11/4763/1055–56.

Page 133. The quotation from a witness's statement on the incident is taken from *Redford v. Birley*, *Peterloo Trials*.

Page 133. Bamford's comment on the incident is taken from *Passages in the Life of a Radical*.

Page 133. Norris's final letter to Sidmouth, August 15th, 1819, is in State Trials, Appendix B.

Page 134. The information about Lord Sidmouth's return is contained in a letter from Hobhouse to Morris, August 13th, 1819 (H.O.41/4).

14. THE MOST NUMEROUS MEETING THAT EVER TOOK PLACE IN GREAT BRITAIN

The chapter heading is based on the *Manchester Observer*'s editorial of August 14th, 1819: 'The meeting will doubtless be the most numerous one, that ever took place, either in London, or any other place in Great Britain'.

Page 135. My information on the heat of the day was gained from Edward Baines, senior, in his *History of the County Palatine of Lancaster* who gives meteorological records for the period. It was one of the hottest and driest spells for years.

Page 135. Robert Lees's testimony is taken from *Inquest on the Body of John Lees*.

Page 136. My sources for the banners were *Inquest on the Body of John Lees*, *Peterloo Trials* and Hunt's Trial, *Peterloo Trials*.

Pages 136–44. All Bamford quotations are from *Passages in the Life of A Radical*.

Page 137. Bamford's statement was supported by witnesses at Hunt's Trial at York.

Page 140. Francis Philip's statement is taken from his *Exposure of the Calumnies*.

Page 140. Prentice's comment is from his *Historical Sketches*.

Page 140. John Benjamin Smith's account of the Massacre was written for his *Reminiscences*. I have relied upon Bruton's *Three Accounts of Peterloo* which includes that of Smith.

Pages 140–2. Murray's testimony throughout is from T.S.11/4763/1055–56.

Page 141. Hunt's comments are from his *Memoirs*.

Page 142. The statement of the witness from the Oldham contingent is from *Birley v. Redford, Peterloo Trials*

Page 142. The statements to the waiting crowd are from T.S.11/4763/1055–56.

15. THEN YOU SHALL HAVE MILITARY FORCE

The chapter heading is from Hulton's words to Nadin, recorded in the magistrates' statement to Lord Sidmouth, October 7th, 1819, of which there is a copy in Rylands English Mss. 1197/1–89.

Pages 145–7. I have based the disposition of the troops mainly on L'Estrange's deposition, T.S. 11/4763/1055–56, and the MYC deposition in Rylands English Mss. 1197/1–89, with assistance from Bruton's *Story of Peterloo*.

Page 147. My source for Moore's and Nadin's depositions was T.S. 11/4763/1055–56.

Page 148. My information on Mr Horrall and the scavengers is from the magistrates' Supplementary Statement, April 1820.

Page 148. Jeremiah Smith's deposition is in T.S. 11/4763/1055–56; it is also quoted by Bruton in *The Story of Peterloo*.

Page 148. Lieutenant Jolliffe's account of Peterloo was written for Pellew's *Life of Sidmouth*. It is also published in Bruton's *Three Accounts of Peterloo*. Jolliffe went on to become an MP and was created Baron Hylton.

Page 148. The Reverend (later Bishop) Stanley's account comes from *Three Accounts of Peterloo*.

Page 151. The incident of Moorhouse trapping his hand is recorded in T.S. 11/4763/1055–56.

Page 151. Hunt's explanation of the realignment is from his *Memoirs*.

Page 151. The Reverend Stanley's comment is taken from Bruton's *Three Accounts of Peterloo*.

Page 151. The Reverend Hay's statement is in Papers Relative to the Internal State of the Country, and Rylands English Mss. 1197/1–89.

Page 152. The terms of the affidavit were published in the *Manchester Observer*, August 28th, 1819.

Page 153. Hunt's comments on the use of the military are from his *Memoirs*.

Page 154. The conversation between the crowd and constables comes from the *Inquest on the Body of John Lees*.

Page 154. I have put into dialogue form, 'Nadin was in the room. Mr Hulton had hold of Nadin by the arm and asked him whether it was not possible for the Police aided by the Special Constables to execute the warrant.' Otherwise the words are as recorded in the magistrates' statement, October 7th, 1819, Rylands English Mss. 1197/1–89.

Page 154. The text of the messages is from Hulton's and other magistrates' testimony, T.S. 11/4763/1055–56 and Rylands English Mss. 1197/1–89.

Pages 155–6. Birley's deposition is in T.S. 11/4763/1055–56; the MYC's deposition is among Rylands English Mss. 1197/1–89.

Page 156. The Radical's description of the MYC advance is from the *Inquest on the Body of John Lees*.

Page 157. A Radical's comment on the MYC's state of intoxication, ibid.

Page 157. A Radical witness's comment on reading two chapters of the Bible, ibid.

Page 157. Hunt's words are from witnesses's depositions, T.S. 11/4763/1055–56

16. AH, BEHOLD THEIR SABRES GLEAMING

The chapter heading is from Bamford's *Song of Slaughter*.

Pages 159–68. All the words of the crowd are from *Inquest on the Body of John Lees*; those of Bamford from *Passages in the Life of a Radical*; Lieutenant Jolliffe's from his own account; Major Dyneley's from his letters, T.S. 11/4763/1055–56.

Page 160. Birley's, Hunt's and Nadin's words while the arrest was being carried out are all quoted in Bruton's *Story of Peterloo*.

Page 160. The incident of Mrs Fildes's dress catching on the hustings is from *The Manchester Man*. As Mrs Linnaeus Banks knew Mrs Fildes presumably she had the story first hand.

Page 161. Hay's description of the reading of the Riot Act is taken from *Redford v. Birley, Peterloo Trials*.

Page 162. Hulton's comment to L'Estrange as the Hussars rode in is taken from the magistrates' Supplementary Statement, October 7th, 1819, Rylands English Mss. 1197/1–89.

Page 167. Burdett's words on the subject of the crowd being armed are from H. of C. debate, May 18th, 1821 (when he tried yet again to obtain an enquiry into Peterloo).

17. THE BATTLE OF MANCHESTER IS OVER

The chapter heading is from Major Dyneley's letter, T.S. 11/4763/1055–56.

Page 169. Meagher's activities are from the *Inquest on the Body of John Lees*.
Page 170. Prentice's description of the scene is from his *Historical Sketches*.

Page 170. The story of the Staleybridge band I found in a clipping from the *Manchester Guardian* in the Reform Club Library, Manchester. It was told by descendents for the 100th anniversary in August 1919.

Page 171. Tyas's comment on Hunt's treatment by the constables appeared in *The Times*, August 19th, 1819.

Page 171. The attack on Saxton is from the *Inquest on the Body of John Lees.*

Page 172. Hunt's comment on the arrest of John Tyas appears in his *Memoirs.*

Page 172. The quotation explaining why John Edward Taylor and Archibald Prentice sat down and wrote accounts of the day's proceedings is from Prentice's *Historical Sketches.*

Page 173. *The Times'* Comment appeared on August 19th, 1819.

Page 174. Major Dyneley's letter is in T.S. 11/4763/1055–56.

Pages 174. A copy of Hay's letter to Sidmouth of August 16th, from which his comment is taken, is to be found in Rylands English Mss. 1197/1–89.

Page 178. The official title of the Metropolitan Relief Committee's report was *The Report of the Metropolitan and Central Committee for the Relief of the Manchester Sufferers.*

Page 178. The MYC's deposition is in Rylands English Mss. 1197/1–89.

18. I NEVER SAW SUCH A CORPSE AS THIS IN ALL MY LIFE

The chapter heading is taken from the words of Betty Ireland, the woman who laid out John Lees's body, and are from the *Inquest on the Body of John Lees.*

Page 181. Major Dyneley's letters are in T.S. 11/4763/1055–56.

Page 182. Bamford's statement comes from *Passages in the Life of a Radical.*

Page 184. The advice to the magistrates on Johnson was contained in letters from Hobhouse to Norris, of August 23rd, 25th and 26th, 1819 (H.O.41/4).

Page 184. Hunt's censure of Johnson is from his *Memoirs.*

Page 185. The middle-class Radicals, Taylor in particular (in his *Notes and Observations* and in editing the *Peterloo Massacre*) seized upon such mistakes as the arrest of the pregnant Mrs Gaunt to build up their case against the magistrates.

Page 185. Hunt's condemnation of Nadin is from his *Memoirs.*

Page 185. Bamford's comment on Hunt's behaviour during the journey to Lancaster is recorded in *Passages in the Life of a Radical.*

Page 186. Hunt's comment on Sir Charles Wolseley is from his *Memoirs.*

Page 186. The *Manchester Observer* ran a pathetic story on the death of Hunt's horse with the words 'Alas! Poor Bob!!!' ringed round with wavy black lines on September 11th, 1819.

Page 187. The list of horses' casualties is in Rylands English Mss. 1197/1–89.

Page 159. Hunt's farewell letter was printed in the *Manchester Observer*, September 11th, 1819.

Pages 189–93. All information is from the *Inquest on the Body of John Lees*. This is the most readable of the many Peterloo documents. From the intimacy of the various public houses in which the Inquest was held, from the acid, angry, quaint and stone-walling interchanges between coroner and witnesses, coroner and Radical solicitors, coroner and press, and respective counsels, the participants spring to life.

Page 193. Prentice's comment is from *Historical Sketches*.

19. SHAME! WIND YOUR BLOOD SPRINKLED SURPLICE AROUND YOU

The chapter heading is from James Neville's letter to the Reverend Hay, as in the text. Hay papers, Rylands English Mss. 1197/1–89.

Page 197. The 'Important Communication' was published in the *Manchester Chronicle* and the *Manchester Observer*, August 21st, 1819.

Page 199. Sidmouth's first response to Peterloo is from a personal letter to Hay, August 18th, 1819 (H.O.4114).

Page 199. The refusal to print the above is contained in a letter from Hobhouse to Hulton, August 23rd, 1819 (H.O.41/4).

Page 200. The replies to the magistrates' complaints are in letters from Hobhouse to Norris, September 2nd and 11th, 1819 (H.O.41/4).

Page 200. The long-suffering letter from Moore and Andrew to Sidmouth of September 16th is in Papers Relative to the Internal State of the Country.

Page 201. The letters to Hay are in Rylands English Mss. 1197/1–89.

Page 202. Copies of the Magistrates' statements of November 1819 and April 1820 are in Rylands English Mss. 1197/1–89.

Page 202. The episode of Horall and the stones is from the magisstates' April 1820 statement.

Page 203. L'Estrange depositions are in T.S. 11/476311055–56, the mvc's in Rylands English Mss. 1197/1–89.

Page 205. The parody is from *The Manchester Man*.

Page 205. The poem appeared in the *Manchester Observer*, November 13th, 1819.

Page 206. Bamford's poem was issued with Hunt's *Letter to Radical Reformers*.

Page 206. Shelley's letter to his publisher and the story of the vicissitudes of *The Masque of Anarchy* is contained in the preface to its early limited edition—of which the Reform Club Library in Manchester has a copy.

Page 208. The poem about Hunt is from *The Manchester Man*.

20. WHAT DO REASONABLE PEOPLE THINK OF THE MANCHESTER BUSINESS?

The chapter heading is from a letter from Mr Ward quoted in Harriet Martineau's *History of the Thirty Years' Peace*.

Page 210. Sidmouth's public comment on the proceedings at Manchester is quoted from Bruton's *Story of Peterloo*.

Page 210. The Duke of Wellington's comment to Lord Sidmouth is quoted from Ziegler's *Addington*.

Page 210. Lord Liverpool's private letter to Canning (who was out of the country) of September 23rd, 1819, is quoted from Yonge's *Life of Lord Liverpool*.

Page 210. Canning's statement is from Brock's *Lord Liverpool and Liberal Toryism*.

Page 210. Lord Chancellor Eldon's comment on the need to support the magistrates is quoted from Bruton's *Story of Peterloo*.

Page 210. Lord Carlisle's statement that the Government's behaviour was 'characterized by downright insanity' is quoted from Bruton's *Story of Peterloo*.

Page 211. The comment by a friend of Canning's on the Governmental behaviour after Peterloo is quoted from Harriet Martineau's *History of the Thirty Years' Peace*.

Page 211. The full text of the *Declaration and Protest* appeared in the *Manchester Observer*, September 4th and 11th, 1819, and in most local papers except for the *British Volunteer*.

Page 215. Eldon's comment was made in a letter to Sir William Scott, September 29th, 1819, and is taken from Read's *Peterloo*.

Page 216. For details of Cobbett's return I am indebted to Cole's *Life of William Cobbett*.

Page 217. Byron's verse on Cobbett bringing home the bones of Tom Paine was sent privately to Tom Moore. It is quoted in Cole's *Life of William Cobbett*.

21. THERE IS AN END TO LIBERTY

The chapter heading is from Sir Francis Burdett's speech in the H. of C., May 1821. Referring to Owen's affidavit he said: 'If arrests are to follow the opinions which may find place in men's heads, there is an end to liberty.'

Page 221. Johnson's view of the Manchester Reformers was contained in a letter to the *Manchester Observer*, October 23rd, 1819.

Page 221. The *Manchester Observer*'s comment on the meeting appeared on December 11th, 1819.

Page 222. Ellenborough's words are from Parliamentary Debates XLI 1819–20.

Page 223. The rectorship of Rochdale was worth £1,730 a year according to Donald Read in *Peterloo*; £2,400 according to Prentice in his *Historical Sketches*. At either sum it was a plum.

Page 223. Hay's earlier applications are in Rylands English Mss. 1197/1–89.

Page 223. Bennet's 'Respectful Petition of the Undersigned Merchants, Manufacturers and Others, of the Town of Manchester, Salford and Neighbourhood ... Respecting the Conduct of the Magistrates ...' was presented to Parliament on November 29th, 1819. Parliamentary Debates XLI 1819–20.

Page 223. The Shuttleworth papers in the Manchester Central Library contain interesting information about the middle-class Radical activities post-Peterloo.

Page 224. Bennet's motion for an inquiry into the state of the manufacturing districts was introduced on December 9th, 1819.

Page 224. Hunt's advice to his followers was contained in a letter to the *Manchester Observer*, December 18th, 1819.

Page 225. Norris's comment on the Radical Reformers is from his letter to Sidmouth, January 10th, 1820 (H.O.42/203).

Page 226. Wellington's comment is from Ziegler's *Addington*.

Page 227. Bamford's record of the walk from Manchester to York is in *Passages in the Life of a Radical*.

Pages 227–9. Bamford's comments on Healey are from *Passages the Life of a Radical*; except the Luther cry which is from Shaw's *Annals of Oldham*.

Page 228. Hunt spoke for nearly five hours in his own defence.

Page 228. Sydney Smith's comment on Hunt is from Read's *Peterloo*.

Page 230. Richard Carlile fought a long and hard battle for the freedom of the printed word. Between 1818 and 1843 he spent over nine years in prison.

22. RISE LIKE LIONS AFTER SLUMBER IN UNVANQUISHABLE NUMBER

The chapter heading is Shelley's rousing cry from the last stanza of *The Masque of Anarchy*. The men of England whom he addressed did not rise like lions but some of them gnawed away like persistent rats.

Page 232. Sidmouth's and Castlereagh's words are quoted from Ziegler's *Addington*.

Page 233. Two further comments on 'The Queen's Scandal' were as follows. Halévy in *The Liberal Awakening* wrote: 'The British people gave another proof of its ingrained devotion to monarchy ... by dropping the cause of manhood suffrage to display its sympathy with a persecuted Queen.' Lord

John Russell said: 'The Queen's cause has done a great deal of good in renewing the old, rational alliance between the Whigs and the people, weakening the influence of the Radicals with the latter.' (This is also quoted by Halévy.)

Page 234. Scarlett's comment is from a letter to Lord Fitzwilliam, the dismissed Lord Lieutenant of Yorkshire. Scarlett though then a Whig later became a Tory and was created Baron Abinger.

Page 234. My information on the Lancaster case is from *Birley v. Redford*, *Peterloo Trials*.

Page 235. Cobden recalled the memory of Peterloo in his pamphlet *Incorporate Your Borough* (1838).

Page 237. The quote from a Liberal election pamphlet is taken from Read's *Peterloo*.

Pages 238–44. My sources for the later middle-class Radical activities were: Prentice's *Historical Sketches*; Shuttleworth's *Scrapbook*; Donald Read's *Peterloo*.

Pages 238–44. My sources for the later lives of the participants were as follows: For Hunt the *Dictionary of National Biography* and Huish's biography; for Bamford, H. Dunckley's introductory notes to *Passages in the Life of a Radical* (1893 edition) and the reminiscences of local people in Middleton; for Healey, Shaw's *Annals of Oldham*; for other local Radicals, Read's *Peterloo*; for Sir Charles Wolseley the D.N.B.; for Cobbett, Cole's *Life of William Cobbett*; for Sidmouth, the D.N.B. and Ziegler's *Addington*; for Lord Liverpool, the D.N.B. and Yonge's biography; for Hay, mainly his own papers in Rylands English Mss 1197/1–89; for Birley and Nadin, several local Manchester history books; for the middle-class Radicals, the same sources as for their activities.

Page 240. *The Times* obituary notice on Cobbett was published in the *Political Register*, June 27th, 1835.

Page 241. Sidmouth's comment on the Reform Bill is quoted from Ziegler's *Addington*.

Page 241. Byron's epitaph for Castlereagh is quoted in the Coles' prolific notes to the Peter Davies edition of *Rural Rides*.

BIBLIOGRAPHY

Manuscript Material
Home Office and Treasury Solicitor Papers, Public Records Office.
Peterloo Relief Committee Account Book, John Rylands Library, Manchester.
Peterloo Papers, John Rylands Library, Manchester.
Reverend W. R. Hay Papers, John Rylands Library, Manchester.
'Vicars of Rochdale', by F. R. Raines, Central Library, Manchester (photocopy
    of original papers).
'Shuttleworth Scrapbook 1809–1839', Central Library, Manchester.

Newspapers
Aston's *Manchester Exchange Herald.*
British Volunteer.
Cobbett's *Political Register.*
Cowdroy's *Manchester Gazette.*
Leeds Mercury.
Manchester Mercury.
Manchester Observer.
The Times.
Wardle's *Manchester Observer.*
Wheeler's *Manchester Chronicle.*

Contemporary Books and Pamphlets
ASTON, J. *Historical Records of Manchester* (London, 1822).
COBBETT, WILLIAM. *Rural Rides* (first published 1830) edited by G. D. H. and
    M. Cole (Peter Davies, 1930).
    Autobiography of . . . The Progress of a Plough-boy to a seat in Parliament (Faber
    and Faber ed., 1947).
HUNT, HENRY. *Letters to Radical Reformers* (London, 1822–23).

Memoirs of Henry Hunt (London, 1820).

An Impartial Narrative of the late Melancholy Occurences in Manchester (Liverpool, 1819).

Inquest on the Body of John Lees, the Whole proceedings before the Coroner's Inquest at Oldham on the body of John Lees, who died of sabre wounds at Manchester. Taken in shorthand with a plan of St Peter's Field. Edited by Joseph A. Dowling (London, 1820).

PALEY, WILLIAM A. M. Archdeacon of Carlisle. *Reasons for Contentment Addressed to the Labouring part of the British Public* (Newcastle, 1819).

Peterloo Trials. Taken from the short hand notes of Mr Farquharson (Manchester, 1822).

PHILIPS, FRANCIS. *Exposure of the Calumnies Circulated by the Enemies of Social Order and reiterated by their abettors Against the Magistrates and Yeomanry Cavalry of Manchester and Salford* (London, 1819).

Report of the Metropolitan and Central Committee appointed for the Relief of the Manchester Sufferers (London, 1820).

TAYLOR, JOHN EDWARD. *Notes and Observations. Critical and Explanatory, on the Papers Relative to the Internal State of the Country recently presented in Parliament; To which is intended a Reply to Mr Francis Philip's Exposure* (London, 1820).

Parliamentary Debates XLI 1819–20. Papers Relative to the Internal State of the Country.

Reports of State Trials. Vol 1. New Series 1820–1823. Appendix B.

Later Nineteenth-century Works

AXON, W. E. A. *Annals of Manchester* (Manchester, 1886).

BAINES, EDWARD. *History of the County Palatine and Duchy of Lancaster* (London, 1836).

BAINES, EDWARD Junior. *History of the Cotton Manufacture of Great Britain* (London, 1835) (new edition Frank Cass & Co. Ltd, 1966).

BAMFORD, SAMUEL. *Early Days* (Manchester, 1859); *Passages in the Life of a Radical* (Heywood, 1842) (new edition MacGibbon and Kee, 1967).

BANKS, MRS LINNAEUS. *The Manchester Man* (Altrincham, 1876).

ELLISON, THOMAS. *The Cotton Trade of Great Britain* (London, 1886).

HUISH, ROBERT. *The History of the Private and Political Life of the late Henry Hunt, Esq.* (London, 1836).

MARTINEAU, HARRIET. *The History of the Thirty Years' Peace* (London, 1846) (revised edition George Bell & Sons, 1877).

PELLEW, HON. GEORGE. *The Life and Correspondence of H. Addington, Viscount Sidmouth* (London, 1847).

PRENTICE, ARCHIBALD. *Historical Sketches and Personal Recollections of Manchester intended to illustrate the Progress of Public Opinion from 1729 to 1832* (London, 1851).

WILD, W. I. *The History of the Stockport Sunday Schools* (London, 1891).

YONGE, CHARLES DUKE. *The Life and Administration of Robert Banks, 2nd Earl of Liverpool, K.G.* (London, 1868).

Twentieth-century works

ASPINALL, ARTHUR. *The Early English Trade Unions* (Batchworth Press, 1949).

BARKER, SIR ERNEST. *Traditions of Civility* (Cambridge University Press, 1948).

BATESON, HARTLEY. *History of Oldham* (Oldham Borough Council, 1949).

BRUTON, F. A. *The Story of Peterloo* (Manchester University Press, 1919); *Three Accounts of Peterloo by Eyewitnesses, Bishop Stanley, Lord Hylton, Mr Benjamin Smith* (Manchester University Press, 1921); *Short History of Manchester and Salford* (Sherratt & Hughes 1924).

BROCK, W. R. *Lord Liverpool and Liberal Toryism* (Cambridge University Press, 1941)

BARTLETT, C. J. *Castlereagh* (Macmillan, 1966).

COLE, G. D. H. *Attempts at General Union* (Macmillan, 1953); *Life of William Cobbett* (Home and Van Thai, 1947).

DARVALL, F. O. *Popular Disturbance and Public Order in Regency England* (Oxford University Press, 1934).

DAVIS, H. W. C. *The Age of Grey and Peel* (Oxford University Press, 1929); *Lancashire Reformers 1816–1817* (Manchester University Press, 1926).

FEILING, K. G. *The Second Tory Party 1714–1832* (Macmillan, 1938).

GEORGE, M. DOROTHY. *England in Transition* (Routledge, 1931).

HAMMOND, J. L. and BARBARA. *Country Labourer 1760–1832* (Longmans Green, 1911); *Town Labourer 1760–1832* (Longmans Green, 1917); *Skilled Labourer 1760–1832* (Longmans Green, 1919).

HALEVY, ELIE. *History of the English People in the 19th Century—England in 1815* (Ernest Benn, 1924); *Liberal Awakening 1815–1830* (Ernest Benn, 1926).

MATBY, S. E. *Manchester and the Movement for National Elementtary Reform 1800–1870* (Manchester University Press, 1918).

MARSHALL, LEON S. *Development of Public Opinion in Manchester 1780–1820* (Syracuse University Press, 1946); *Emergence of the First Industrial City. Manchester 1780–1850* (photostat of an article, in Manchester Central library).

PINCHBECK, IVY. *Women Workers and the Industrial Revolution 1750–1850* (Routledge, 1930).

PETRIE, SIR CHARLES. *Lord Liverpool and his Times* (James Barrie, 1954).

READ, DONALD. *Peterloo, the Massacre and its Background* (Manchester University Press, 1958).

REDFORD, ARTHUR. *History of Local Government in Manchester*, Vol. 1 (Longmans Green, 1939); *Labour Migration in England 1800–1850* (Manchester University Press, 1926).

SELLEY, W. T. *England in the 18th Century* (Adam & Charles Black, 1934).

SHAW, GILES. *Annals of Oldham* (Privately printed, 1909).

WEARMOUTH, ROBERT. *Methodism and the Working Class Movement of England 1800–1850* (Epworth Press, 1937); *Some Working Class Movements of the 19th Century* (Epworth Press, 1948).

WEBLEY, LAURENCE. *Across the Atlantic* (Stevens and Son, 1960).

WHITE, R. J. *Waterloo to Peterloo* (Heinemann, 1957).

ZIEGLER, PHILIP. *Addington* (Macmillan, 1966).

PICTURE CREDITS

INDEX